Also by Marshall Berman

Adventures in Marxism

The Politics of Authenticity: Radical Individualism and the Emergence of Modern Society

All That Is Solid Melts into Air

ON THE TOWN

RANDOM HOUSE New York

THE TIMES BUILDING   N.Y.

MARSHALL BERMAN

ON THE TOWN

*One Hundred Years of
Spectacle in Times Square*

Published in the United States by Random House, an imprint of The Random House
Publishing Group, a division of Random House, Inc., New York.

RANDOM HOUSE and colophon are registered trademarks of Random House, Inc.

LIBRARY OF CONGRESS CATALOGING-IN-PUBLICATION DATA
Berman, Marshall
On the Town: one hundred years of spectacle in Times Square / by Marshall Berman.
— 1st ed.
p. cm.
Includes bibliographical references and index.
ISBN 1-4000-6331-0
1. Times Square (New York, N.Y.) — History.   2. Times Square (New York, N.Y.) —
Intellectual life.   3. Times Square (New York, N.Y.) — In art.   4. Times Square (New
York, N.Y.) — In literature.   5. New York (N.Y.) — History.   6. New York (N.Y.) —
Intellectual life.   7. New York (N.Y.) — In art.   8. New York (N.Y.) — In literature.
9. Arts — New York (State) — New York — History.
10. Performing arts — New York (State) — New York — History.   I. Title.

F128.65.T5B47 2006
974.7'1 — dc22   2005048954

Printed in the United States of America on acid-free paper

www.atrandom.com

1 2 3 4 5 6 7 8 9

FIRST EDITION

Book design by Dana Leigh Blanchette

For Shellie My Love
Dance, Girl, Dance

Contents

Illustrations

It was as if Times Square were a kind of shell, with colors and noises breaking in great waves inside it.
> —George Selden, *The Cricket in Times Square*

Suddenly I found myself on Times Square. I had traveled eight thousand miles around the American continent and I was back on Times Square; and right in the middle of a rush-hour, too, seeing with my innocent road-eyes the absolute madness and fantastic hoorair of New York with its millions and millions hustling forever for a buck among themselves, the mad dream—grabbing, taking, giving, sighing, dying, so they could be buried in those awful cemetery cities beyond Long Island City. The high towers of the land—the other end of the land, where paper America is born.
> —Jack Kerouac, *On the Road*

And any night you can see Times Square
Tremulous with its busloads
Of tourists who are seeing all of this
For the first and last time
Before they are flown
Back to the republic of Azerbaidzhan
On the shore of the Caspian
Where for weeks they will dream of our faces
Drenched with unbelievable light.
> —Thomas Disch, "In Praise of New York"

It doesn't matter what you wear
Just as long as you are there.
> —Martha and the Vandellas,
> "Dancing in the Street"

Author's Note

New Girl in Town

Back in the 1990s, when I was just starting to think about Times Square, I found this girl in the picture collections of the Museum of the City of New York. She came from a souvenir postcard issued in the year 1903.[1] In 1903, the Square was still known as Longacre Square. The grand High Renaissance façade of the Times Tower was in place, at the convergence of 42nd Street, Seventh Avenue, and Broadway, but work was still going on underground, not only on the paper's new high-tech printing presses but on the IRT subway tunnel that ran dangerously close to them. Both the building and the subway had their debuts in the winter of 1904–05, when Times Square got its name and became something like the place it is today.

This postcard is a montage of a photograph of the building and a cartoon of the girl. The girl is dressed in the provocative outfit of a chorus girl in dishabille. She radiates both a grown woman's sexuality and the ordinary sweetness of the girl next door. In the imaginative world of this montage she is almost as big as the tower. She smiles playfully as she sits on it, entwines herself around it, kicks her legs out like a girl on a swing. Notice how both the Tower and the girl are spectacularly out of scale. In fact, they both helped to establish Times Square as a place with a new scale. By the end of the 1900s, both the building and the girl had plenty of company.

THE TIMES BUILDING   N.Y.

Design only copyrighted by Chas. Rose 1903.

Fans of Degas, Manet, and Lautrec will recognize this girl from late-nineteenth-century Paris. But it is hard to find her image in the iconography of America's Gilded Age. I don't mean there weren't girls like her there; I'm sure there were plenty. But they lived and moved in the shadows. They appeared in private clubs and at private parties, behind closed doors. They didn't display themselves on the streets and they didn't send their images through the public mails. Part of this girl's allure is the way she looks so effortlessly at home in public. As the twentieth century dawns, she is just coming over the horizon, a sign of her times. I will call her "Times Girl." The fusion of this youthful girl and this brand-new building marks the first "New Times Square."

Look at this girl! See how her arms, shoulders, and legs are visible under short skirts blowing in the wind. She curves her right hip into the Times Building's phallic tower and caresses it with her right hand while she kicks her left leg out into the expanse of Broadway. I'm surprised that a Comstocked post office let her through the mails. (The P.O. was probably swamped, and never saw her.) Times Girl's sexiness is open and artless, casual and messy, without apparent shame or guilt, but also without pomp or pretension; she looks nice rather than *fatale*. Her style prefigures the formula that Florenz Ziegfeld would create for his Follies, just down the block at the New Amsterdam: full-blown sexuality combines with the artless sweetness of the girl next door. Note that she is half-dressed, ungroomed, she seems to be talking fluently without being in the least dressed up. Her anonymous creator must have believed that her dishabille signified authenticity, and that authenticity was important. It also suggests seriousness, a work ethic, a form of professionalism. Times Girl doesn't look like a woman who would reject admirers; she might even invite them into her dressing room, dressed as she is. But she is telling the world she does not want to be rescued from what she is doing. As much as anybody at the *Times*, she is at home in her work.

I fell in love with this girl the minute I saw her. As soon as I gave her a name, I realized I had to write a book for her. This book will span a hundred years, and Times Girl, brimming over with fresh energy, looking into our eyes and hoping we look back, yearning to connect and to shine, will be with us all the way. She knows she is somewhere special: even when she's behind the scenes, she's *on the town*. In an idiom of my youth, she "makes the scene": her presence in the Square makes it a human scene.

In her youth, Times Girl will sing songs like "Gabey's comin'. . . . He's on the town." After a few years in the Square she won't be a "girl" anymore. Too close to the bright lights, or too far from the lights, she will grow up too fast. She will get herself knocked around, even knocked out. But she will keep coming back. And she will keep on singing songs like Stephen Sondheim's "I'm Still Here."[2] As an homage to all those girls, and not only girls, who are *still here*, I want to explore and explain what it means to be here.

PREFACE

One Hundred Years of Spectacle

. . . take a bath of multitude . . .
—Baudelaire, "Crowds," around 1860

Streets that lead you to an overwhelming question . . .
—T. S. Eliot, "The Love Song of J. Alfred Prufrock," 1917

Let's take a bath of light.
—Betty Berman in Times Square, around 1960

Entertainment and Identity

Ever since the opening of the Times Tower and the IRT subway a century ago, in the winter of 1904–05, Times Square has been a remarkable environment. With its huge crowds, multiple banks of lights, layers of enormous signs, this place has been exceptional, maybe even unique, in its physical density. At the same time, anyone who tries to read the signs, or to understand where all the people are coming from and going to, will see that it is even more special in its cultural density. A century ago, this vibrant city neighborhood made a kind of quantum leap and became a hyper-city neighborhood. In its century of life, it has taken one of the primal urban experiences — being in the midst of a physical and semiotic overflow, feeling the flow all over you — and concentrated it and focused it and sped it up and blown it up. The signature experience of being there is being surrounded by too many in the midst of too much. Rem Koolhaas calls it "Manhattanism," or "The Culture of Congestion."[1] It is loved all over the world. It gives people a thrill, a rush, a power surge from being there. I want to give people even more of a thrill by portraying, along with the Square's excess of density in space, its equally excessive density in *time:* a continuing, even escalating production and reflection and inspiration in every imaginable style and medium and genre high and low. In this book, I want to plunge into the Square's culture of congestion: congestion not only in people, in buildings, in cars, in signs, but, most alluring of all, congestion in meaning. It is a place where we can drown, or fight to stay afloat, in a superabundance of meanings.

Much of modern culture prepares us for this kind of thrill. I will cite just three writers: the Enlightenment philosopher Montesquieu at the start of the eighteenth century; the Romantic poet William Blake in the midst of the French Revolution; and the archetypal modernist poet Charles Baudelaire in the 1860s. *The Persian Letters*, Montesquieu's 1721 novel, may be the greatest-ever celebration of the modern city. (Balzac said this book had taught him everything.) His heroes are expatriate sultans who are thrilled to be on a street where everybody is unveiled. "Here everything speaks out; everything can be seen; everything can be heard; the heart is as open as the face." It is impossible for Paris to collect taxes, one sultan says, because people's main capital is in their heads: It is "their wit and energy. Everyone has his own, and he exploits it as best he can." All these people "live, or try to live, in the city that is the mother of invention." But many of Paris's most striking inventions are hustles and rackets: people who "use the cleverness of their art to repair the damage of time"; women who "make of virginity a flower that flourishes and is born again every day, a flower that is plucked more painfully the hundredth time than the first"; "masters of languages and arts and sciences who teach what they do not know"—it doesn't take much creativity to teach what you know, but it takes plenty to teach what you don't. In Paris, "Liberty and equality reign in the street." Everybody in the street is stuck in an endless traffic jam, but everybody is stuck together.[2]

At the century's end, in the midst of the French Revolution, the radical poet William Blake tries to lift his audience to a plane of vision where they can feel at home with paradox and contradiction. The Blakean poem that does this best is called "The Marriage of Heaven and Hell." It was written and engraved in 1793, at the French Revolution's most radical point. "Enough! or too much," Blake's narrator says. The poem's most shocking section is called "Proverbs of Hell." There the poet's voice says "no virtue can exist without breaking these [Biblical] commandments," that "You never know what is enough until you know what is more than enough," and many more shocking things.[3]

Many of the great nineteenth-century writers develop the Romantic feeling for paradox and contradiction into a vision of the modern city. The most accessible of these writers is Baudelaire, especially in his 1860s "prose poems," which he published as op-ed pieces in Parisian newspapers. In "Crowds" (1861), he compares the joy of life in a crowd to participating in "an orgy of vitality," to writing poetry, to "universal communion," and to being high. The modern city enables an individual "to be both himself and someone else." Not everyone can expand beyond themselves. But if we can, if we have the capacity to *épouser la foule,* to "marry the crowd," and to "take a bath of multitude," this experience can bring us "feverish delights" that people who are "locked up in themselves" can never imagine. "What people call love is small . . . compared with that orgy, that holy prostitution of the soul that gives itself totally, in all its poetry and charity, to the unexpected that appears, to the unknown that passes by."[4]

All these writers are writing both within and about the culture of "individualism." Alexis de Tocqueville coined that word in the 1830s, in his seminal work, *Democracy in America.*[5] Tocqueville saw individualism as one of the primary forces in modern life. He worried that the culture of individualism would lock men and women up in private worlds of their own, and erase or radically shrink the sphere of shared community. These are legitimate and important things to worry about, in our century as much as in Tocqueville's. But his perspective occludes some of the new forms of community that modern democracy creates. Some of these forms emerge only in the twentieth century, when the dreams of immigrants, the technologies of electric light, photography, and mass transportation, public entertainment, advertising and publicity, freedom of the press, and the raw power of thousands of individualisms get thrown together on the street. Then we get neighborhoods like Times Square: grand spectacles that are *individualistic* spectacles, where baths of light and "feverish delight" are also modes of Enlightenment, where orgies of vitality lead us to "overwhelming questions," where simultaneously we can have great fun and learn who we are and explore what we can be; where the perennial great hope, dramatized so well in Michael Bennett and Marvin Hamlisch's *A Chorus Line,* is to get work and make money and win prizes and find soulmates and be "one singular sensation" by being ourselves.[6] Times Square has lived and grown as a place that interweaves entertainment and identity.

Let's Go Downtown: My Family Romance

Entertainment and identity: Times Square and I go back a long way, and my strongest and sweetest memories are also the ones that hurt most. I was a child in the Bronx, but in my high school years, in the mid-1950s, I started taking the subway, leaving the Bronx on my own, learning the geography of downtown and the great art of hanging out. In those days my father worked at 130 West 42nd Street, half a block from the Square. I would meet him at his office or at Lindy's, sometimes with my friends, sometimes with his customers (for the Betmar Tag & Label Co., my parents' doomed mom-and-pop company, where mom and pop were the only assets), and we would hang out or walk around. In the fall of 1955, he had a heart attack, he went to the hospital, in a week he was dead. He was not quite forty-eight, I was not quite fifteen. It knocked me to the floor; I felt at one blow my adolescence was over, just when I was hoping it would start. For the next few years, my friends played variations of *Rebel Without a Cause*, but I stayed close to my family, a sad good boy in mourning. There was a hit song then, sung by Frankie Lymon in his soaring falsetto,

> *Now come on, baby, let's go downtown, . . .*
> *I love you, baby, and I want you to be my girl . . .*[7]

What "Come on, baby, let's go downtown" meant to me was an invitation to live, to share in a life that was at once easy—you could get there on the subway—and overflowing. When I heard it, I was alone with my radio in the Bronx. I remember how I knew "downtown" was there, just a subway ride away, and I knew I'd been there only yesterday, or maybe the day before, yet today, with my father dead, it sounded so hopelessly far away, and the verb "to go" sounded like a cosmically doomed command. I couldn't believe I'd ever have the strength to accept such an invitation, let alone invite anybody else to go down with me.

"Mama told me": My mother, Betty Berman, just like the primal mothers in rock-and-roll songs, told me I'd get back my strength and my desire for life; she knew it would happen "by and by." One way she helped restore me was by telling stories about her and Dad, and some of those stories were about Times Square as a bower for adult love. She told me what I can see now was our family's founding myth. My father and mother were about as old as the Square—he was born in 1907, she in 1908 (she lived till 1994). The neighborhood around the Square was where they both spent most of their working lives, at first by accident, later on purpose. Here, in the depths of the Depression, they met and fell in love. "It was just like in the movies," she said. He was a traveler, she was the bookkeeper, for a hearing-aid company under the Sixth Avenue el. For a year or more they couldn't stand each other and made nasty cracks that made the whole office laugh. But then one night they were forced to work together overtime alone, and they found they couldn't stop looking into each other's eyes and making each other laugh. Finishing their work took longer than they had planned. He bought her a late dinner at Child's, and they walked for hours under the lights. Then he did what no man had ever done for her: He walked her all the way home to Brooklyn. "We walked hand in hand over the Williamsburg Bridge," she said, and they hit Humboldt Street just at dawn. Her parents were hysterical: She was "a good girl" who had never stayed out late before. "But I could handle them," she said. "I'd been waiting for this for years."

I was thrilled, and demanded more stories. By and by, she told me how much it had meant to them to go "out," to get away from their work, to get away from us, my sister Didi and me, to act like lovers. The Square was where they went. My mother was a sober and reserved woman in the Bronx, but she had a special red dress for their nights out. First they would go to a play (her eyes clouded over when she mentioned the plays they'd planned to see, the tickets she gave away), then to a club—she taught him about the theater, he taught her about jazz. They would end the night—she blushed, and said, "you know where we went." What she meant was, they went to a nearby hotel. Hotel rooms in the 1950s didn't give away little bottles of shampoo, as they do today, but they gave plenty of matchbooks. At dinner one night not long before Dad died, I had made a wise-guy remark, something like "Hey, how come we have all these hotel matchbooks? Are you guys doing business in hotels now?" and there had been a long silence. She said how she would miss our Sunday brunches after their nights out. I said, "Mom, we still can have nice Sunday brunches: You'll teach me to cook lox and eggs." And she did, and we did. But I realized later she was missing not only his presence, but that special ambience of sweet contentment. After forty years as an adult, I know where that ambience comes from.

She told me more stories about some of the people my father had introduced me to around the Square, people they had hung out with together "when I spent more time downtown" (i.e., before we were born): the two detectives, the first Jewish cops I'd met; the man who became prop man at the St. James; the man who became the night manager of Lindy's; their old friend Meyer Berger, the great local reporter of the *Times*. My father said, "I want you to know the street like I know it." An impossible dream: Although he never read Balzac, he knew the street the way Balzac did. In his last years, he came to feel the garment center had betrayed him, that was what he said, but he felt he could trust the Square. Just a few minutes' walk, he said, and he would be where he could be himself. They both could trust it. "Come and meet those dancing feet," the *42nd Street* song, meant to them a lot like what "Come on, baby, let's go downtown" meant to me: *People, lots of people, are really alive down there. Let's go be with them and live.*

After he died, it was where my mother insisted we would go, and where our family would get together. "We don't have much money," she said, "but we're going to keep going to Broadway, so we don't become living dead." It was her way of saying "Come on, baby, let's go downtown." (When it began, I still felt too bruised to go anywhere, but I gritted my teeth like Bogart in *Casablanca*, and told myself, If she can take it I can.) For years she organized our routine. First we would go to a play, usually a Sunday matinee— "we," my mother, my sister Didi and I, my mother's sister Idie, her daughter Marilyn, and various people we were "seeing" or being in love with through the years. Then we would go somewhere to eat and talk and argue. Our family loved to talk and argue; I can see now that we were testing our friends and lovers, to see if they could get into the flow of our family talk. As dinner wound down, my mother would say, "Now we're going to take a bath of light." I have never heard anyone besides my mother use that delicious image. (Did she and my father take baths of light together after they had picked up those hotel matchbooks?) We would walk through the Square, bask in the bright light—it gave our faces wild colors—point out people and signs. Then we would get on the subway at 42nd Street and go to our respective homes. Being there together was our family sacrament.

Aunt Idie, my mom's kid sister Ida Gordon (1911–2004), was a major force in our lives. Idie was a flamboyant redhead who for most of her life made everybody's heads turn when she walked down the street. But there was some inner shadow that trapped her in loneliness; she could never transform her overflowing vivacity into the happiness she craved. Anyway, one spring Sunday late in the 1960s, we all met for a matinee. I can't remember the play, but like many plays then it was about people and drugs. Half the people in the theater that day seemed to be family groups like ours, and as we came out you could hear the generations arguing about drugs. I mentioned that I used some drugs sometimes, they didn't make me want to commit either murder or suicide, I could live without them, but they were nice. We walked east on a narrow side street, and soon we came out into the Square's immensity, where the early spring twilight interfused with the fire signs, and the light and the breeze picked us all up and whirled us around, and we all stopped arguing and said, "*Wow!*" In a little while we started again. "I just don't get it," Aunt Idie said. "What are all these people getting out of drugs? We didn't need it; why should you need it? Tell me," she urged as she squeezed my arm, "why do you do it? How does it feel? What does it mean? What's the world like when you're high?" I said, "Maybe something like this," and I made an expansive gesture into the flood of light. "Aha!" she exclaimed triumphantly. "You see, you just proved it. You don't really need drugs at all. All you have to do is come to Times Square."

Ordinary People, Primal Scenes

The Times Square neighborhood has always been a great source of primal scenes, scenes from many cultural genres that focus our minds on overwhelming questions about who people are and how they can live together. Many of these scenes from the first half of the twentieth century helped to create a kind of Times Square cultural tradition; this tradition went through all sorts of developments, travesties, and reversals in the century's second

half. These scenes are all bound up not only with the Square's multiple forms of show business and popular culture, but with show business as a series of complex and clashing metaphors for modern life.

My first primal scene comes from Theodore Dreiser's 1900 novel *Sister Carrie*, the first serious work set in the Square, shortly before the *Times* arrives. The heroine, a farm girl and then a factory girl in her youth, becomes a Broadway star. (More about her rise later on.) But even as she moves up, her middle-aged lover, George Hurstwood, who has brought her here, crashes down. Dreiser plots him on a downward spiral that plunges him into unemployment, alcoholism, depression, despair, and finally suicide.* But Hurstwood gets to be the star in a scene that features his disintegration. We are close to the story's end. He looks like a skeleton, he is dressed in rags, he lives in a Bowery flophouse that lets men flop at night but kicks them out from nine to five and forces them to tramp up and down Manhattan all day. One subzero day, passing through the Square, he is struck by Carrie's name on a marquee. He stops and waits at the stage door for her. We dread the coming explosion. But no, their meeting evokes their old love; they treat each other gently. She bursts into tears, opens her purse, gives him all the

money in it. She keeps saying, "George, what's the matter?" He keeps saying, "I've been sick." Their mutual tenderness and helplessness make this one of the most heartrending scenes in American literature.† But at this point the scene is really just half over. A couple of days later and a couple of steps down the ladder, Hurstwood passes the theater again. At the entrance there is a life-size maquette of the star. The rage and hate he put aside before take hold of

---

*Dreiser calls the theater where Carrie becomes a star "the Casino Players." There actually was such a company, at Broadway and 39th Street. But the point of the name in this story is for readers to see that human success and failure are as random and absurd as turns of the wheel or throws of the dice.

†Readers of *Catch-22* will recognize their call-and-response as a model for the antiphony between the dying Snowden ("I'm cold, I'm cold") and the living Yossarian ("There, there").

him now, and he explodes. He screams at her. "Wasn't good enough for you, was I? Huh . . . She's got it, let her give me some!"[8] Then he realizes what he has done: It wasn't her at all; he has confused the real woman with her sign. He feels more mortified and hopeless than ever, and sees it as one more reason not to live ("I'll quit this"). But in fact his category-mistake, his confusion between a person and her sign, will become a commonplace event in the age of celebrity that the "fire signs" have come to light in the Square even before it's Times Square.

Our second scene comes from *42nd Street*, the great backstage musical of 1933. Here Ruby Keeler is the star pulled miraculously out of the chorus line, "Sister Carrie" with dancing shoes and a smile. Dick Powell, one of the male leads, spots her in the chorus, likes her, and becomes her mentor; he teaches her all the moves and protects her from competitors and predators (there are plenty of both). Does he feel more for her than he shows? We don't know, but it is rare to see so much generosity with no strings attached coming from a man on an American screen. About halfway through, Keeler performs a tap dance on top of a taxi on West 42nd Street. The routine is awkward; it doesn't really work in the play-within-a-play that it's meant to be part of. Yet it works as a set piece in the big show itself, and it works on us: We can see it's going to be one of the all-time classic images of a woman in Times Square. It enlarges both the producers' and our own image of Keeler, so that, when designated star Bebe Daniels gets hurt, both they and we can imagine Keeler in her place. Just before she goes on, director Warner Baxter explains what sort of place this is:

> Now listen to me—listen hard. Two hundred people—two hundred jobs—two hundred thousand dollars . . . depend on you. It's the life of all these people who have worked with you. You've got to go on—and you've got to give and give and give—and they've GOT to like you— GOT to, you understand. (Beads of sweat stand out on his forehead now.) You can't fall down—you can't . . . You're going out a youngster—you've GOT to come back a star![9]

What's special here, in the New Deal year of 1933—FDR was inaugurated the same month the movie opened—is the political economy. *It's the life of all these people who have worked with you*. Stardom means not only glory for the person at the top, but the cooperative labor of hundreds of people. *42nd Street* opens up a space where the ancient morality of "No man is an island" and the modern political economy of job creation converge. Songwriters Al Dubin and Harry Warren portray the street scene:

> *Side by side they're glorified*, . . .
> *Naughty, bawdy, gaudy, sporty Forty-second Street.*[10]

Ruby Keeler does an elated tap dance across the theater street. As we are wondering where all the people have gone, she makes a leap that shows she has been dancing on the roof of a taxicab stuck in a traffic jam. (Remember Montesquieu: "Liberty and equality reign in the street" because everybody is caught in the same traffic jam.) Now the jam abates, the cab moves out, and we see a spectacular diversity of people moving fast in all directions at once, but somehow not pushing each other or tripping each other up. Is this the triumph of what Rousseau called "the art of living together"?

In a moment the art turns lethal. Or is it a *failure* of the art that is lethal? The camera focuses on a room in a poor boardinghouse (in the 1950s and after, an "SRO"). A young woman is lying sadly on her bed. A young man breaks in and attacks her savagely. She tears away from him, screams, and jumps out the window. He shoots at her, but misses. It's only a second-story window, so she is caught by a man in the crowd, and she is all right. But she forgets she is in danger, and the crowd forgets, too. She starts to dance with the man who caught her. But the man who attacked her is still here: he hurtles himself down the stairs, sees her dancing, stabs her in the back, and melts into the crowd. People scream, but then forget. It's the tremendous momentum of this crowd that seems to matter most. A woman's chorus dances toward a spectacular skyscraper horizon. But then it *becomes* that horizon: every woman bears a cardboard model of a building her own size. Then, in another magical transformation, the horizontal band that is the street (42nd Street) becomes a vertical band, a skyscraper towering over the street. And the girl who was stabbed on the sidewalk only a couple of minutes ago is now strutting her stuff with a new man, towering over the sidewalk from the skyscraper's heights.

Just by being on this street, in this crowd, the individual can be a star. The street's closed contours metamorphose into an open sky with space for all.[11] This Square is a capital of social openness and inclusion. It brings multitudes of people together side by side with multitudes of other people; and not only with others, but with people whom the self sees as "the Other"; and not only to coexist, but actually to meet, to encounter the other in an intimate way that will change everybody. These encounters create a new reality where people *can be more than they are*. That's the point of the sacramental word "glorified." Even as they are having fun, they can overcome. This romantic vision is one of the high points of American urbanism.

I said "space for all." But from all I've read and all the photos I've seen, in the reality of Times Square before World War Two, "all" meant pretty much all white. The war changed things. Even as the U.S.A. spread the wings of its imperial power around the world, more and more of that world found its way into the Square. This dialectic is dramatized in our third primal scene, in a wonderful photograph by William Klein of the Square on New Year's Eve 1954–55.[12] Here are some of the new faces in the crowd, and here is the Square evolving to embrace them.

In the Square's past "golden ages," there was no trace of kids like these. But now, on New Year's Eve 1954, Latins are just beginning to be part of the

action. This may be the first time these kids are here without parents. (That guy in the hat looks more like a big brother.) They've taken the subway down from East Harlem or the Bronx, or the Hudson Tubes (now PATH) in from New Jersey, to participate in the spectacle. It's very likely their first time in a crowd of this size. Their clothes are shabby and unglamorous. (Some of it is surely poverty, but age has to matter, too: You can be pretty sure in a couple of years they'll be more dressed up.) They look tired, and sort of seasick, and wearied by the size and noise of the crowd, and bedazzled (photographer Klein has done very well with dazzling light), and probably cold. But don't they also look resolute? They're hanging in there. They'll die before they say "I wanna go home," even if they're dying to go home. These kids aren't in the crowd for themselves alone. They may not know that, but Klein knows it, and we know it: They're Roberto Clemente, Ritchie Valens, Rita Moreno.

Notice what the kids have in their mouths: those candy cigarettes? They were for play, but they really did lengthen you, extend you, make you feel bigger than you were. Klein's photo sets up an equivalence between putting those things in their mouths and being where they are: It's all part of a process of growth. The growth in the story is not only personal (and sexual) but social. Klein envelops the kids in American commercial icons against the Astor Hotel's grand facade, with a background of bright lights, as if to tell us, "They've arrived, they've made themselves at home here, it's theirs." That the place is theirs doesn't in the least mean it isn't ours. Indeed, they've made themselves at home *with* us. Their story of inclusion and growth is our story as well. A few years later, kids like these would be the vanguard of urban democracy. There is a great line from an early sixties hit song, Martha and the Vandellas' "Dancing in the Street":

> *It doesn't matter what you wear*
> *Just as long as you are there.*[13]

These kids aren't dancing yet, but they are *there*. The Square is taking in more people, and letting the world know it's big enough to hold us all.

Our last primal scene highlights the other side of Times Square's night, what we could call its "night terrors." These are realized brilliantly in Stanley Kubrick's first movie, *Killer's Kiss*, a classic *film noir* released in 1955.

His hero, a young boxer down on his luck, needs to get out of town; he hopes his girlfriend will come with him. But this can't happen until both of them collect money that is due them, he from his manager, she from the owner of the dance hall where she works. They arrange to meet around nine P.M. on the west side of Broadway in the mid-forties. It is a time and place that should be jammed with people. But just when the Square should be full, it is uncannily empty. Kubrick sweeps his camera across enormous voids: The only life in this Square is coming from the signs—he highlights "Scripto," a wonderful cheap automatic pencil, too good to be true and finally wiped out in the conglomerate 1980s; "Sheba," the heroine of a Biblical tale and spectacular movie; and the block-long sign for BOND Clothes. (We will see that BOND sign later.) But the main thing he shows us is vast, dark empty spaces. The emptiness of those spaces is terrifying. Kubrick converts Pascal's poetic reflection, "The silence of the infinite spaces terrifies me," into an urban vision.[14]

The only people on Kubrick's street are two weird brothers in Shriner suits: They do a strange dance up and down the block, laugh at jokes only they understand, undulate in a sort of burlesque of the burlesque that lit up the Square only yesterday. As invisible signs flicker on and off above them, their dancing grows more frantic. They close in on the hero, snatch his scarf, and run away, drawing him out of the frame so that he misses his connections, but also, ironically, misses getting killed. His manager is killed in his place, in one of the dark alleys behind an office tower. Every kid who hung around the Square knew those alleys, but nobody had ever put them on the screen. Kubrick feels the urban nightmare that is about to unfold. The Federal Highway System will soon create a world where danger comes not from the great crowd, but from the *absence* of a crowd, from the new "lonely avenue" *without* a crowd.[15] Kubrick imagines the empty downtowns that are on the way, and that will become primary sources of misery all over America for the next fifty years. This man knows the void; he shows how urban emptiness can be an active, malevolent, urbicidal force. *Killer's Kiss* prophesies the metamorphosis that is about to transform America's bright and busy downtowns into black holes.

Times Square will survive this tidal wave better than most. Half a century later, it will be mangled but intact. Its power to embody the terror of infinite spaces will be unimpaired. Cameron Crowe's *Vanilla Sky* (2001) begins with a dreamlike vision of Tom Cruise driving a sports car through a lit-up but spectacularly empty sunrise Square. There aren't even any cars! Has the city been evacuated? Aghast at the emptiness around him—blue sky, red neon signs, no people—the star ditches his car and runs like hell; but, stripped of people, the Square can't show him which way to go. The movie goes on to unfold another two hours of urban angst; but nothing in it equals the intensity of the first two minutes, because after Times Square, none of Cruise's and Crowe's later environments is so intensely *there*.

Where This Book Is Going

I am going to tell stories, stories about people in the midst of "one hundred years of spectacle" in Times Square. Some of my subjects will be real people: Theodore Dreiser, Al Jolson, Busby Berkeley, Ethel Merman, Jerome Robbins; Tama Starr, CEO of the company that makes the Square's biggest signs; Jane Dickson, who painted "the deuce" so evocatively in the 1980s; "the three witches," the group of managerial women who did so much to blow that street away; Tibor Kalman, the brilliant designer who fought to give "the New Times Square" a human face before he died. Some of my subjects are fictional characters: Sister Carrie, the Jazz Singer, Miss Turnstiles in *On the Town*, Martin Scorsese's Taxi Driver, a heroine of "Sex and the City." Some are signs and visual representations of people, from Times Girl to Betty Boop to "Annie Get Your Gun" to Calvin Klein's takeoffs on Mantegna's Christ selling underwear to Tibor's multiracial array of naked teenagers promoting *COLORS* magazine. Many of my subjects are sailors: the real but unknown sailor who embraced a real but unknown nurse at the Square's Great Noon in August 1945; the heroes of *On the Town*, dancing for democracy; the antiheroes of *The Last Detail*, struggling to stay existentially afloat; the crowds of young sailors who flood the Square today, every Fleet Week in May and June, on their way to the Gulf; and the generations of civilian women and men who have been drawn to them.

Each chapter will move forward, from Sister Carrie's time toward our own, but with different rhythms and tempos, imagined from different angles and perspectives. I tell plenty of stories, and I could tell more; in earlier versions, I did tell more. But I ran into a great hazard: The very richness of life in New York creates a spectacular undertow. "You are a New Yorker," Colson Whitehead reflects poetically but sadly, "when what was here before is more real and solid than what is here now."[16] I had to remember and refocus what I was trying to do. I want to write a book that will overflow with characters, but I want my cast to be a chorus line that readers can join, not a police squad that will block and hold them so they can't be here now. I want to show people living for the city in a life that is open, ongoing, still there to be lived.[17]

In the first part of the twentieth century, Americans took their cities for granted. People could love them or hate them, could try to get closer in or try to get away, but no one doubted that they were overwhelmingly *there*. In the last part, most dramatically in the 1970s, it became shockingly clear that they didn't have to be there after all. In just a few years, all over America, rich and complex urban landscapes turned into ruins. No one could miss the change, but people gave it different meanings. Some said cities were dirty, noisy, nasty places that people didn't need at all—this is an old American theme. Others developed tremendous plans for urban renewal that turned out to be more like urban removal. Two themes from those times meant most to me; they have different tones and emotional coloration, but they belong together, and they come together and live together in this book. First is the idea that one of the primary human rights is *the right to the city*; this means that city life is an experience that all human beings are entitled to, whether they know it or not.[18] Alongside it is the idea that *cities are vulnerable*, they need unending love and care. The first theme should enlist our will to militant action; the second should elicit our less dramatic but equally vital capacity for nursing. I have written this book to show what city life can be, why we need it in order to be fully alive ourselves, and how we can get it if—and it's a big "if"—if we learn to bring together contradictory aspects of our being.

Late in the 1980s, the Beastie Boys, a trio of brilliant rap comedians from New York's downtown, proclaimed what sounded like a paradox: They said, "You gotta fight for your right to party."[19] In the profoundly profane city that New York has always been, their paradox makes deep sense. I want to incarnate it here: to ignite both our senses and our minds; to empower people to think critically while we bask in baths of bright light.

ON THE TOWN

CHAPTER 1

Home Fires Burning: Times Square's Signs

"I'll just go down Broadway," he said to himself. When he reached 42nd Street, the fire signs were already blazing bright.

—Hurstwood, near the end of *Sister Carrie*

Great signs—Bigger! Than! Life!—blink off and on. And a great hungry sign groping luridly at the darkness screams: F*A*S*C*I*N*A*T*I*O*N

—John Rechy, *City of Night*

Signs Square

All through the century, whenever people have talked about Times Square, they have talked about its giant signs. Those signs were there at the Square's very start, and for its whole life they have been designed and arranged to overwhelm the people on the ground. "A spectacular" is the word for these signs. Over the years they have run fifty, sixty, seventy feet high, sometimes a whole block long. They have been extravagantly lit with whatever the state of advertising art allows: with thousands of bulbs, with lovely neon calligraphy, with tremendous spotlights, with throbbing and exploding computer graphics; any style, any technology will do if it can knock us out. I don't mean to say that all Times Square signs are giants bent on knockout blows. Most are not; most are likely to be much smaller and more nuanced. But the Square's ecology is such that the smaller signs are experienced in relation to the big ones. The manager of the Arrow Shirts shop said, "We're just below the waterfall." They make limited claims on the universe, but "Side by side, they're glorified" by the unlimited claims being made just above and around them.

In its effusion of signs, New York has never been alone. Early in the

twentieth century, every city had its "Great White Way."[1] Most of these went
dark after World War Two, when the Federal Highway System engineered
the destruction of downtowns all over the country; New York alone survived
to tell the tale. Many American cities, especially in the Sun Belt, developed
prosperity based on highways and cars, and created spaces with signs as big
and bold as Times Square's. But those spaces tend to be strips (Las Vegas,
Los Angeles, Mexico City) where people come in cars and drive straight
through. Their signs are laid out in straight lines, meant to be seen one or at
most two at a time by drivers or passengers on the road. The deployment of
signs in Times Square is far more complex. Here people are on their feet,
enveloped by crowds of walkers in a hundred directions, impeded from
moving straight ahead even if they want to. The signs come at us from many
directions; they color the people next to us in complex blends, and we become colored, too, all of us overlaid with the moving lights and shadows.
We metamorphose as we turn around, and we have to turn around to make
any headway in this crowd. The development of Cubism in the early twentieth century was made for spaces like this, where we occupy many different
points of view while standing nearly still. Times Square is a place where Cubism is realism. Being there is like being inside a 1920s Cubist experimen-
tal film: "The Man with the Movie Camera" as a home movie. Signs are the
essential landmark, yet generally what grips our hearts is less any one sign

than the complex, the totality, the superabundance of signs, *too many* signs, a perfect complement for the Square's too many people. Since the 1890s, being attuned to Times Square's overfullness has been one of the basic ways of being at home in New York. Even the most wretched people can feel at home with the Square's signs. " 'I'll just go down Broadway,' " Hurstwood says. "When he reached 42nd Street, the fire signs were already blazing bright." This man is starving, freezing, dressed in rags, delirious, one foot in the grave. But he can't stay away from the "fire signs." He is drawn to their warmth and light like a moth to a flame.

Times Square's allure springs from the totality, the superabundance of signs, rather than from any one. But it makes sense for a book on the Square to contain at least a brief historical sweep of the Square's memorable signs, which will also be a sweep through modern commercial mass culture. There is another reason. One important way in which people have always experienced Times Square, and still do, has been to adopt a favorite sign, to be alone with it, to make it part of their inner lives. This means uncoupling the sign from whatever commodity it was meant to promote and placing it in a different system of meaning all our own. If the sign is a human figure, we can talk: "What's a sweetheart like you doing in a place like this?" The human capacity to give things new names is a capacity not to be swept away by floods of commodities, not to be reduced to passive acquiescence, keeping ourselves inwardly, imaginatively alive. (Yet often, just when we feel at home with our special signs, we come and they are gone. "All that is solid melts into air.")

One of Times Square's most arresting early spectaculars was the fifty-foot-tall Miss Heatherbloom, promoting "Heatherbloom Petticoats, Silk's Only Rival." The product seems to have been a typical garment-center knockoff of a high-fashion item, marketed to millions of young women of the sort who passed through the Square every day: typists and switchboard operators, schoolteachers and young wives. The sign was built in the 1900s (different sources give different dates) by O. J. Gude, the Square's first great commercial artist, who painted in bursts and undulations of electric power. It had an elaborately programmed sequence where the heroine walked through a driving rain "depicted by slashing diagonal lines of lamps." The wind whipped at her dress, lifted her skirt, and revealed the petticoat cling-ing to her legs and her hips and her thighs. The gale receded, her clothes fell into place, she resumed her high-heeled, mincing walk—only to be swept up in the wind and rain again, and again and again.[2]

This sign attracted big crowds, and the crowds included plenty of women. Not the most affluent women, who would surely have stuck with silk, a warm and voluptuous material that has been a symbol of class since ancient times. But imagine seamstresses and switchboard operators on their way to work, or schoolteachers and stenographers going to plays. What the ad promised is something that the New York garment industry, just a few blocks south, knew how (and still knows how) to deliver: cheap knockoffs of expensive fabrics and designs; aristocratic fantasies that a plebeian mass public can afford. It was structurally similar to the electrified mass culture embodied in its sign. It sought and found a large body of respectable women who would respond to a public, flamboyant sexual display, and would buy a garment that they hoped would help them change.

One thing that petticoat could mean: women's disgust with the multiple layers of clothing that then defined women's wear. In those clothes, nobody would ever see what a woman's body looked like. (In those days, too, from what we can tell, sex happened in the dark: Touch but don't look.) Feminism in the early twentieth century demanded "dress reform" from clothes that treated women like prisoners. But not much changed till World War One, when suddenly there was a lot less cloth around, and then things changed fast. Since then, the visibility of women's bodies has become a primary hallmark of the twentieth century, of the West, of the big city, of modern times. Anyone who doubts this should note the rage against women's visibility in all the aggressively anti-modern movements around the world. The Heatherbloom product, although marketed to youth, stays firmly within the traditional layered wardrobe. But the Heatherbloom *sign* performs a leap into the open. It is a curtain-raiser for the century-long drama of women's exposure and display. This is "legitimate" theater because the girl can't help it. She does not take her clothes off; she is not stripped by a lustful husband or boyfriend; she is undressed by the primal force of nature itself. But in Times Square it is also *comic* theater. Its comic irony is defined by the program of the sign: In Act One the heroine is swept up and stripped by the storm; in Act Two the storm abates and her clothes cover her up; in Act Three she is out in the storm again.

Smoke, Water, and America

The discourse of nostalgia in Times Square often gravitates toward the 1940s, the age of World War Two and its prosperous aftermath. Survivors and memoirists of these years portray a New York that may have been physically distinct from the rest of America, but that culturally blended in with it, and that had the capacity to incarnate it. In Alfred Eisenstaedt's *Life* photograph of the sailor and the nurse embracing in the Square as the Japanese surrender, we see a historical moment free of the tension between "New York" and "America" that marked American culture in the 1960s and 1970s, when I was growing up, and that was nourished by the GOP. (It peaked in President Ford's "Drop Dead" speech of 1976.) People who yearn for the Square of the 1940s are often, in Paul Simon's poignant words, coming to "look for America." They still feel a vast distance between New York and America today, and they yearn for a fusion between them that they think existed yesterday. They often focus on the Square's spectacular signs, which they feel performed feats of spiritual integration.

On the "looking for America" nostalgia trip, the great BOND Clothes waterfall and the Camel smoke ring sign are favorite stops. Both signs made their debuts shortly before the war. They were imagined and planned by one of Times Square's unsung heroes, the artist, engineer, landlord, and promoter Douglas Leigh, and assembled by Artkraft Strauss.[3] The BOND sign opened in 1940, just above the company's main showroom. It proclaimed "The Cathedral of Clothing." This was where my father got his suits, cheap but "smart." The Camel sign, just a block below, opened in 1941. All through my childhood, these two dominated the Square. They didn't look much alike, yet everybody agreed they belonged together. I think I know why people blended the signs into a single whole: Both signs were dramatizations of danger and deliverance from danger.

The waterfall, a city block long, had a tremendous seething flow. At night, everything in the Square seemed to flow toward it. If you stood there and looked at it for a while, it could put you in a kind of trance, you could lose track of everything around you. The falls were high off the ground, but was there a way you could fall in? Could kids fall in? Was there something there that we couldn't see but that could pull us in? On the northern and southern fringes of the waterfall, there were giant bronze statues of a man and a woman. Looking at photos today, I see I was right about them: They were naked! No clothes at all! And yet they were totally unsexy. Not that my cousins and my friends and I knew much about sex, but still we could feel its absence. The compelling thing about these statues was their solemnity. There was a Longfellow poem we read in school, beginning "This is the forest primeval," where the great trees

Stand like Druids of eld, with voices sad and prophetic. . . .

Were the bronze statues so solemn because they were guarding us from the edge, from falling in, from fatal currents and hidden rocks that we couldn't see or even imagine, but that they knew all too well? Did the danger come, in some weird way, from the smart clothes themselves and from the BOND?

The Camel sign just below the waterfall was something else. Here was another giant adult, and a man in uniform,[4] too—which meant, in the 1940s, somebody who was risking his life to protect us all from Hitler. Who was Hitler? Somebody who had magic powers to raise fabulous armies that killed so many Jews (my grandma's whole extended family was trapped in Lithuania; they were all killed), and so many other people. But this Camel smoker was ready to take Hitler on. How did he fight? He blew smoke rings in the dictator's face. I thought, *Wow!* The smoke rings were collected from the building's heating system; they signified not only American bravery, but American cool. I loved standing beneath the sign, where I couldn't see the man at all, but I could see his rings; as long as they kept coming, I felt protected. My parents both were chain-smokers: They brushed each other's lips as they lit each other's cigs. I asked if they could blow rings like the sign did. My mother scoffed at it as a silly guy thing, but my father could do it, and he swore that someday so would I.

How signs change their meanings as time goes by! When I was thirteen, my father's doctor said he was seriously Under Stress, and he'd have to quit smoking right away. He did quit, with what struck me as remarkably little fuss. But before we knew it, he was dead anyway. After he died, I turned bitter and cynical and angry. I never became a smoker, and that Camel sign became gall and wormwood to me. When our family went to Times Square and took our baths of light, I would start to rant when we got near the sign.

I would say it was really an ad for American imperialism. All around the world we promise to protect people, but we're spreading more death than life; as for that kid, the soldier-smoker, he is an addict and he doesn't even know it; we kill our own kids along with all the others for the tobacco companies' sake. My mother's overall political sense was fairly close to mine, but she couldn't translate it into rage against the sign. For her, the sign's basic truth was the playful young man who had won her heart in the Square all those years ago. The act of smoking became a kind of *séance* that could bring that young man back to her. I thought the Surgeon General's Report would give her pause; but she said the fact that the smoker put himself in danger only made him nobler. When I went to Columbia and read *King Lear*, she read along with me. As we read together, it felt like smoke was coming out of her ears. She said, "It's how I defy the foul fiend."

Coppola: The Square or the Library

Let's leap to my Aunt Idie's Times Square, in the 1960s: the place that removed the need for drugs because it was a psychedelic trip in itself. One film from those days shows very vividly how people personalize and internalize Times Square's signs: Francis Ford Coppola's commercial debut, *You're a Big Boy Now* (1966). Coppola's hero, Bernard (Peter Kastner), is the son of an executive at the New York Public Library. While he works at an entry-level job in the NYPL, rushing through the stacks on roller skates, his parents subsidize an apartment for him, enabling him to discover New York City on his own. The movie is framed as a *Bildungsroman*, a story of a boy becoming a man. The library is right down the street from Times Square, and Bernard is happy to explore the scene. The features that engage him most are the great fire signs around the bowtie and the pornographic book shops along the deuce.* Quite early in the movie, he uses his imagination to rewrite the signs. His first rewrite job is simple. From inside a porn shop he contemplates 42nd Street's long-lived arcade, "Playland," and retitles it "Layland." He is putting his stamp on the Square.

---

*The "bowtie" is the great, open, X-shaped expanse where Broadway crosses Seventh Avenue. The "deuce" is West 42nd Street, which runs perpendicular to the bowtie.

When the hero of a *Bildungsroman* is male, his growth is often presented as a conflict between two women, one more flashy, the other more real; his task, both moral and developmental, is to overcome the allure of the glamorous one (Calypso, Veronica) and love the real one (Penelope, Betty). Here, Barbara Darling is an exotic dancer with fashionable Mary Quant clothes and a "Swinging London" walk. Amy Bartlett, the hero's fellow worker at the NYPL, is wholesome and nice, has lots of patience, and is smarter and more original than she looks. Coppola locates Amy on West 42nd Street one fine spring day, taking a walk and looking around: perfectly ordinary, except that she is the only woman on the street. She spots the hero in a porn shop, where he is watching a striptease on a stereopticon. She then does something remarkable: goes into the store, comes up behind him, blindfolds his eyes, draws him away from the parade of images, and says, "I like you, come on, be with *me*." We in the audience will be struck by Amy's nerve and guts. But Bernard, who has lots of growing to do, is obsessed with Barbara's image, blinded by her light.

One of the movie's most poignant scenes is a walk that Bernard and Amy take through the Square. When they part, she throws her arms around him. But even as he embraces one woman, we see him looking over her shoulder and finding a giant sign that features the other. It is on the old Times Tower, the Square's visual focus. We are not meant to read the sign as something real—Barbara Darling has a long way to go before her "Jazz Singer" moment arrives—but rather as a projection of the hero's fantasies. He imagines a flashing silhouette of Barbara dancing, shaking her hips wildly, while the giant news "zipper" flashes BARBARABARBARABARBARABARBARABAR-BARA on an infinite loop. He is giving the Square a paint job in the blatant forms and colors of his imagination.

Bernard eventually meets the real Barbara, only to find a woman who dreads reality. She is at home in situations where she can act like a sign, a distant representation of herself—specifically, where she can play the role of a pornographic diva—but terrified of human encounters in which she would have to respond to other people's feelings or express her own. He keeps getting hurt by her, and doesn't know what has hit him. But finally he wrenches himself away, and walks into the horizon with Amy. It is a happy ending: The hero is growing up at last.

In this movie's world, Amy is obviously the right choice. But there is a peculiar undercurrent of suggestion that Barbara is a mess because she is in "show biz," and Amy is a solid and honest human being because she is not. One of the film's dubious undertows is an "anti-theatrical prejudice."[5] This is the idea that to be a performer, a man or woman "with a sign," is to be phony, split, alienated, unreal; it is only those "without signs," who do *not* perform, who can be honest and authentic human beings. This complex of beliefs has a long history, especially in the history of Christianity. It puts Coppola in Puritan and fundamentalist company where few of his admirers would expect to find him. It makes him an ally of Sister Sarah Brown in *Guys and Dolls*, a Broadway heroine who yearns "to take a pick-ax to Broadway and smash it end to end."

To see the world this way is to cast a cold eye on Times Square. Its perpetually flashing lights and signs, which at first seemed so enchanting, now look like so many empty vanities. It also gives a new meaning to the New York Public Library. At the movie's start, the library is just a marvelous building. By the end, it takes on a lot of new weight as the Square's metaphysical antithesis. Its august stone archways, the unchanging soft light of its main reading room, its magnificent classic vistas, emerge as hallmarks of true being, of authenticity. As a lifelong lover of the library, I was flattered by this dualism the first time I encountered it. On second thought, I reflected that with friends like this, the NYPL might not need enemies. If we remove from the library all the books whose authors strut and fret and somersault across the page, and who strive to seduce and dazzle their readers, and all the building's architectural flourishes that are meant to blow its users away, *just like Times Square signs*, we will create lots of empty space very fast, and we will empty our culture of vitality. If we can't see the unity of thought and spirit between the Square and the Library, we might as well turn out the lights right now.*

---

*John Rechy offers a much more vital dialectic between the Library and the Street: "Escape!—I would read greedily . . . at that library on Fifth Avenue, I would try to shut my ears to the echoes of that [hustler's] world roaring outside, immediately beyond these very walls. . . . I was constantly on a seesaw." *City of Night*, 55. That seesaw is part of a life story that culminates in the writing of his book, a book full of allusions to other books, a book he knows will take a place in that library, and will be read by more people, people like his young man or like you or me. The seesaw will go up and down in the circle game.

The Sixties: The Psychedelic Goddess

In those days, my favorite Times Square sign was a promo for a revival of *Annie Get Your Gun*. It was situated on top of the Palace Theatre. The sign was a great goddess with guns. But the guns were futuristic, shooting brightly colored plastic balls, and the goddess, too, looked on loan from a science-fiction comic. I haven't been able to find an image of this goddess, and wondered if I hadn't imagined her. But then I found her, both in the testimony of sign CEO Tama Starr—"Annie Oakley tall as a four-story building, firing lightbulb bullets across the width of a building"[6]—and in a luminous vision by Isaac Bashevis Singer.

Singer's sign surges up at the climax of a story called "The Third One."[7] It is set in the enormous Horn & Hardart Automat on the west side of Broadway between 47th and 48th streets. Two characters are present, the narrator and an old friend, but the focus is on two who are absent, the friend's wife and "the third one," her lover. All are survivors of the Holocaust; there are no children. The narrator and his friend sit drinking tea and agreeing God is dead. Then the friend unrolls his story-within-a-story, a hot love triangle set on Coney Island. If the characters were American, the only question would be who is going to kill whom. But in this world of survivors, sex and romance swim in a deep sea of passivity and helplessness. The two men wonder what women want, but they are equally mystified about what *they* want. The narrator gradually feels this story is sucking him in like a whirlpool. He has to get out: It will be saner in the street.

> We walked out on Broadway and the heat hit me like a furnace. It was still daylight, but the neon signs were already lit, announcing in fiery language the bliss to be bought by Pepsi-Cola, Bond suits, Camel cigarettes, Wrigley's chewing gum.

Anyone who knew Times Square even a little would remember these signs. But now there is a new sign in town, and she is taking over:

> Over a movie house hung a billboard of a half-naked woman four stories high, lit up by spotlights—her hair disheveled, her eyes wild, her legs spread out, a gun in each hand. Around her waist was a fringed

scarf that covered her private parts. . . . I looked at Zelig. Half his face was green, the other red—like a modern painting. I said to him, "If there is a God, she is our God."

Zelig Fingerbein shook as if he had been awakened from a trance. "What *she* is promising, she can deliver."

"What she is promising." But what *is* she promising? Fingerbein is as clueless about this psychedelic amazon in Times Square as he is about his wife on Coney Island. Singer leaves us plenty of clues, maybe too many. Are her futuristic guns and bullets meant to push people away, or, like Cupid's bow and arrows, to bring them close? Is her loincloth a suggestion of Christ, and a blending of pagan and Christian forms of divinity? Or an enticing secular modern undress, in the mode that Gypsy Rose Lee put on the map at Minsky's and opened up to every respectable wife in Peoria or the Bronx? Is Singer trying to tell us that some values and other values just can't coexist? Or that everything and everything else *can* coexist here, if people can find ways to walk the walk and talk the talk "side by side"?

Singer perfectly captures the spirit of the late-1960s Square, where so much of the recreation seemed to cater to existential desperation. It was a psychedelic trip, just as my Aunt Idie said, but like many such trips it took people to weird places they hadn't planned to go. An image that looked like an exclamation point—hot sex forty feet high and in your face—could turn out to be a question mark. An ordinary man under the lights could look "like a modern painting." Was this a branch of the Museum of Modern Art? Or was it the *real* Museum of Modern Art? Imagine ourselves metamorphosing into works of art! It is a thrill. But we need to remember, as Singer does, that modern art is an art that reduces, magnifies, colorizes, strips down, blows up, twists around, turns inside out, shreds, recombines, dramatizes, and displays all the radical splits in our being. If there are "seven types of ambiguity," this Square had all of them.

The Nineties: Colors and Nakedness

The most striking signs in Times Square in recent times build on some of the ambiguities opened up by the signs of the 1960s. My favorite was cre-

ated by the brilliant designer Tibor Kalman (1949–99), who died at the
height of his powers.

Kalman's fire sign was a spectacular ad for *Colors*, a glossy magazine put
out by the Italian sportswear company United Colors of Benetton. The sign
was on display in 1992 and 1993. It was fifty feet high, maybe twice as long;
it curved around the corner of 47th Street and Broadway, and it showed full
frontal nude photos of six teenagers. Actually, they weren't quite teenagers:
Two of them looked closer to twenty-five, another two seemed more like fifteen. And they weren't quite nude; they were holding small signs over their
genitals, something like the fig leaves in Renaissance paintings of Adam and

Eve. It was hard for a spectator not to enjoy the nakedness of these beautiful kids; but their genital fig leaves forced us also to share their embarrassment.

The color contrasts among the kids were striking: One was clearly Asian, one clearly African (Afro-American? Afro-European?), two clearly Caucasian, and two unclear or mixed; for that matter, it was very likely that all of them were mixed. The contrasts in ideas were striking, too. At the far left, a punklike blond boy with an Axl Rose look held an ATTITUDE placard. Next, a voluptuous Asian girl held RACE. An olive-skinned boy carried a TRUTH sign. A black girl had a POWER sign. A short, compact Asian man signed LIES. At right, the youngest-looking of the six, a girl with a *gamine* aura, covered herself with FIRST DATE. It was impossible (or let's say very hard) for a spectator not to enjoy the near nakedness of these kids, to feast our eyes on them. At the same time, the way the sign was crafted, it was impossible not to feel guilt and embarrassment. The sudden vision of their bodies was revelatory and shocking. There was something about the way they stood, the ambient light and color, the innocence on their faces—even when innocence was mixed with defiance—that made them seem vulnerable and overexposed; they looked more like suspects in a police lineup than participants in an orgy. But what was their crime? There was human depth in this sign, it drew us into the action. Before the picture could mean anything, we spectators had to imagine actively, to "write the book." My wife and I imagined a strip search after a drug raid on a club. We noticed that at least two of these kids were "underage," but we couldn't tell what the age spread was supposed to mean. Was the point that age meant nothing? (But then, I thought, shouldn't there be some older people with wrinkled or sagging bodies in the scene?) We never figured out their genital signs, fig leaves in print. Were we meant to think of those tags as social labels imposed by the powers that took their clothes and lined them up? Was this a generation of kids caught in the crossfire of adult big words? Yet wasn't "victim" another adult big word?

At the end of the last decade, in 1998, I had the privilege of meeting Kalman in person, interviewing him at length, and getting to know him. (Yet until our last phone call I didn't know how sick he was.) He was one of the most delightful people I ever met: brilliant, imaginative, overflowing with life. After we reminisced about our years protesting the Vietnam War, he said Times Square showed the one nice thing about American imperialism: It embraced everybody. Now more then ever, the whole world was there, every race and ethnic group right out on the street. Did I know what made it all happen, he asked, what it was that brought all the colors together? It was sex: Sex gave the Square its allure; sex was the primal force that leaped across all the color lines and all the national borders, and created the family of man. The point of the sign, he said, was that if we were stirred by these kids, we should recognize ourselves along with them as part of that family. I asked him if his erotic vision was really shared by Benetton, which manufactured and sold well-crafted but genteel and very conservative lines of clothes. He agreed there was a great gulf between the commodity and its publicity apparatus, said it was a window of freedom but it was closing—he laughed, said he had already had two nervous breakdowns, and it was only a matter of time before the sign and the signifier split apart forever.

I told him how much his sign thrilled me. But I said he had to know there were other ways, not so nice, to read the sign. This picture could put us in the position of policemen, of Humberts and Quiltys, maybe even of slave marketers, scrutinizing and comparing the kids' colors while we enjoy their curves. It could put the experience of nakedness in a murky light, where it is not a joyous condition that all human beings can share, but a situation that some people (usually young) are subjected to while they are examined by other people (usually older) in clothes.[8] He said he knew. But wasn't this problem inherent in the production of culture? He asked, What about my book? If it should have the success it no doubt deserved, wouldn't it be subject to the same dynamic and the same abuse?

The ambiguities of the COLORS sign put its spectators to a kind of test. Our desires to protect these kids and our desires to *have* them, our identities as parents and as lovers, will surge up together if the sign works on us the way it should. Once again, the Square rewards us for being there by favoring us with its terrible special gift of *too much*. Do we have the inner strength to control our conflicting desires, do the right thing, and stay sane? This predicament is a sign of Times Square's spiritual power. Ever since the birth of mass culture, its enemies here and everywhere have claimed that it reduces its audiences to passivity, that it closes down our minds. That may be true somewhere, but not here. The unrelenting pressure of *this* environment forces the people in it to put ourselves in the picture, to sort our feelings out, to struggle to overcome. If we can, we can affirm what I believe is

Times Square's dialectical faith: Side by side, they're glorified. If we reach out and stretch and grasp it, it will give us the power not only to live through it, but to be more alive.

In 1992, we felt we'd seen that sign before, but we couldn't say where. It was like a hidden cell phone ringing somewhere in an endless pile of clothes. Once I started serious work on this book, the source was easy to see: It was *A Chorus Line*, the longest-running show in Broadway's history. Alas, by that time Tibor was dead; too late to talk to him! *A Chorus Line*'s canonical image is a bunch of young people lined up in a row, wearing very few clothes, all holding up their chosen headshots covering their faces: It is an image of affirmation and freedom. Broadway has always supplied America with happy images like this. But in the years since World War Two, the American theater's civic virtue has wrestled with darker visions. Stephen Sondheim's *Follies*, the source of "I'm Still Here," and the great musical of the Nixon era, was "a Broadway musical . . . about the death of the Broadway musical," and about the larger death of American innocence.[9] In *A Chorus Line*, only a couple of years later, innocence was triumphantly reborn: Individuals brought all their powers into action in their struggle to get a part, to get on the line; even if they failed, they still could do a dance that had human value in itself. Here Broadway affirmed its power to overcome destructive nihilism, to give people reasons to live. The COLORS chorus line gives Broadway affirmation a Bronx cheer. The naked kids on this line are detainees. Their sign propels us toward primal scenes of horror, chain gangs and military prisons and concentration camps around the world. And yet, whatever may be happening to them, their faces are naked and open and radiant. Nobody can take their beauty, their COLORS, away from them. Their Times Square sign is an affirmation of life in spite of itself.

CHAPTER 2

Broadway, Love, and Theft:
Al Jolson's Jazz Singer

—my name in electric lights—everything . . .
—the hero to his mother in *The Jazz Singer*

Mutual forgiveness of each vice,
Such are the gates of Paradise.
—William Blake, "For the Sexes:
The Gates of Paradise"

We used to hear about the Broadway white lights,
The very serious dazzling White-Way white lights . . .
It's getting very dark on old Broadway . . .
Real dark-town entertainers hold the stage.
You must black up to be the latest rage.
—"It's Getting Very Dark on Old Broadway,"
sung by Gilda Gray in Ziegfeld Follies, 1922

I wanna be black.
—Lou Reed, "I Wanna Be Black," 1980

One of the most stunning visions of Times Square comes at the climax of *The Jazz Singer* (1927), the first-ever sound movie, the first music video, and one of the great American *Bildungsromans*. The hero, played by Al Jolson, wants to sing to the whole world, and Times Square symbolizes that world. Here is where he breaks on through, becomes who he is, fulfills his crossover dreams, sings his heart out, and gets to have it all. His story began in the Lower East Side's gray day; it ends in Times Square's gaudy night, in brilliant contrasts of black and white. A long shot unrolls a three-part structure of space stretching to the horizon: at ground level, a parade of *people*; above them, pulsating neon and electric signs, a flood of *light*; over all, a great expanse of open *sky* that frames and embraces the people and the signs and fuses them into a whole. This is the great Times Square spectacle. These few frames—they last less than a minute—can help us see Times Square fresh, as if for the first time. This is America's gift to the modern world, the most dynamic and intense urban space of the twentieth century, the commercial sublime.

We see the spectacular Times Square, with the hero's name in electric lights, only at the movie's end. When we see it, it's the place where Jakie has *arrived*. How did he get here? What did he give of himself? What did he give

up? The trajectory that leads to "my name in electric light" is the primal arc of the twentieth-century American life story. *The Jazz Singer* traces that arc and sings that story.

The Jazz Singer has long been recognized as a great *Bildungsroman*. But it's also a synthesis of the *Bildungsroman* with what seems like a completely different genre: the minstrel show.[1] Most literate Americans know how important the *Bildungsroman*, the super-serious story of growing up, has always been in our national self-awareness. Not many people are aware of the importance of our minstrel tradition, in which the highest seriousness masks and mocks itself. Times Square is a place where these traditions converge like subway lines, where inwardness and emotional depth get saturated by neon and displayed as entertainment. It's the place where Jolson appeared not only as "the world's first cinematic voice," but maybe as "the world's first superstar."[2] When he appeared so big, he appeared in black: He was in blackface when he rocked the house with "Mammy."

Since American minstrel shows made their debut in the 1830s, all their actors have been in blackface, yet many have been white. Working in blackface doesn't entail being black, just *acting* black. A century ago, many of the most talented blackface comedians were immigrant Jews: Jolson, Sophie

Tucker, Eddie Cantor. The Ziegfeld Follies cultivated a blackface partner-
ship between Cantor and the great black comedian Bert Williams. Williams
insisted blackface didn't "come naturally" to him:

> I do not believe there is such a thing as innate humor. It has to be de-
> veloped by hard work and study. . . . It was not until *I was able to see
> myself as another person* that my sense of humor developed.[3]

Eric Lott, one of blackface's most perceptive historians, sees it this way:

> *Acting black:* a whole social world of irony, violence, negotiation and
> learning is contained in that phrase. . . . an unstable or indeed contra-
> dictory power, linked to social and political conflicts, that issues from
> the weak, the uncanny, the outside. Above all, slipperiness.*

The most remarkable moment of *The Jazz Singer* comes about two
thirds of the way through, when the hero "blacks up."

Before we can understand why this hero is blacking up, we have to ask,
Who is this hero, anyway? We need to form some idea of his identity. But it
may not be easy. The fact that he is working in blackface in the first place
suggests a sense of identity that is, in Lott's word, "slippery," and a capacity,
as Bert Williams said, to see himself as another person. His name, at this
point in the movie, is "Jack Robin," but that is not the name he was born
with. The name his parents gave him is "Jakie Rabinowitz." He grew up on
the Lower East Side, a cantor's son. From his earliest years, he was in serious conflict with his father. His father taught him the *nigunim*, the holy
melodies; he learned them well and made his father proud. But he felt that
the songs and the world of the *shul* were not enough. He roamed the streets
of the Lower East Side, listened to the secular music he heard there, and got
a job singing in a cabaret. Before he goes on, the announcer says, "It's *Ragtime Jackie*, folks; give him a break." So we see he has taken a new name,
what my parents called a "stage name"; in his life history, it is Name #2. His
father is tipped off, horrible things happen, and the sequence ends with the

---

*Love and Theft: Black Minstrelsy and the American Working Class cited above. As a lover of this book,
I was delighted to see it become the object of a theft by Bob Dylan, in his powerful 2002 album, *Love
and Theft.* More on Dylan later.

hero leaving home. He is born again into show business, anoints himself with a new name, "Jack Robin," and dedicates himself to a life on the road. In his life history, this is *another* New Name, Name #3, other-name #2. (I'm not going to go into this any further here, except to say the great book on Jews and names—maybe "from Jacob to Bob Dylan"—is waiting to be written.) The name change does show us something important, what Bert Williams called the capacity to "see himself as another person." But that person won't come together until many years later, when he returns to Broadway at last, blacks up, and encounters his mother backstage.

Jakie's songs from the street were the first sounds, not quite in the history of film, but in the history of *commercial* film, film made to be shown on those same city streets where the sounds were made. As a matter of fact, "the street" is one of *The Jazz Singer*'s uncredited stars. Jolson was one of the masses of Jews who grew up in America's immigrant ghettos, but felt out of tune with the patriarchial "world of our fathers."* After World War One, in the 1920s, they helped to create a culture in which they and their most intimate audiences could feel more at home. This was the culture of "Broadway," of "show biz," of "the Jazz Age," of what Ann Douglas, in her wonderful book on the Harlem Renaissance, calls "Mongrel Manhattan." Douglas has a fine sentence fragment that suggests the breadth and depth of this culture: she alludes to "the moderns' finest achievements in popular culture, from Al Jolson's vaudeville act to the new skyscrapers of Manhattan."† She wants us to see how buildings of stone and glass and performances by live people can grow out of the same modern desires and drives.

One of *The Jazz Singer*'s primary axes is the polarity of "The Street" versus "The House." The polarization was even sharper in the shooting script. One sequence apparently shot but cut featured the sounds of a "street piano." This instrument, also known as a "hurdy-gurdy," was supposed to be playing that

---

World of Our Fathers, by Irving Howe and Kenneth Libo (Harcourt Brace Jovanovich, 1976), the classic study of the culture of the Lower East Side. The book aches with nostalgia for that lost world; but its most spirited portraits are of people who spent their lives as transgressors against it. In the sections on entertainment and popular culture, Howe's heroes—Jolson, Irving Berlin, Sophie Tucker, Eddie Cantor—turn out to be people who not only worked in blackface but felt personally close to black people, black music, and black culture. Howe and Libo note this in passing but don't explore it in depth.

†*Terrible Honesty: Mongrel Manhattan in the 1920s* (Farrar, Straus & Giroux, 1995). Douglas's "mongrel" title is a variation on a metaphor used by Dorothy Parker to describe herself, 5. For Jolson and skyscrapers, 8. This fine book, also a classic study, is also very interested in people who practiced "crossovers" between Jewish and black worlds. The Gershwin brothers play leading roles in both.

perennially popular song, "The Sidewalks of New York." The camera showed a *cheder*, an after-school "Hebrew School." The script says, "The sound of a street piano comes through an open window, And the kids rush to the window." The cantor enters, he hears the street music, "a look of disgust comes over him, and he closes the door"(51).[4]* Soon he is tipped off that his own son is singing in a cabaret, as "Ragtime Jackie"; he pulls the kid off the stage, drags him through the streets, beats him with a strap at home for embracing "your lowlife music from the streets." When Jakie's mother suggests he might not want to follow his father (and four generations before him) and become a cantor, the father rears up and roars, "*What he wants means nothing!*" (titles 21–23, pages 62–65). Soon he throws Jakie out of the house and tells people his son is dead. Here, as in many other works about immigrants in many genres, there is a convergence of conflicts: conflict between immigrant fathers and American sons, and conflict between the rigid pietism of the house and the open wildness of the streets. Al Jolson was one of the creators of the culture of "Broadway," and Broadway was a street culture created by sons.

Jakie leaves home and anoints himself with his third name, "Jack Robin." Like so many great American performers, he grows up on the road; the road is his school, his college, his university. For years he doesn't look back. We are supposed to feel he does all right for himself. (A lot better than Mama Rose and her enslaved kids in *Gypsy*.) But he never reaches the big time—he's in the Omaha-Denver-Seattle orbit, something like class AA in minor league baseball—and his singing is pretty good, but nothing that would change anybody's life. When we first meet Jack Robin, "he is shabbily dressed and, although neat of person, it is obvious that he is down on his luck"(68). But then one day he hears a cantor sing (59, 84ff.),† and what he hears brings back all that's missing in the self and the life he has made. He realizes he needs more of something. But what? Is it Jewish religion? Not exactly. It's Jewish, all right, but in the sense of, first, Jewish "roots," connection to his past, and, second, Jewish soulfulness and gravity, qualities missing in the world of show biz.

---

*Numbers in parentheses designate title and page numbers in Wisconsin edition. See also endnote no. 4, page 234.

†That cantor was a real person, Josef/Yossele Rosenblatt, one of the first Jewish religious figures to not only record his voice but market it. His capacity to incarnate both religious and market values prefigures *The Jazz Singer*'s happy ending.

Soon the jazz singer lands a job in a Broadway revue called "The April Follies." Now, at last, he has a chance to break through and get recognition as a star in his hometown. We the audience know he has immense talent. But we also know his morbid undertows. His act evokes many of the sad clowns who haunt the Western theatrical tradition: Harlequin, Pagliacci, "He Who Gets Slapped," and a whole line of great minstrels.* Jolson had in fact played with Lew Dockstader's minstrels as a kid. But the adult Jack Robin does not seem at home in his sadness; the planes in his face drift off in different directions and don't connect. *The Jazz Singer's* narrative, pacing, and tonalities are all carefully constructed to show us that the hero's story is not mainly about performance, or about success, but about the process that Keats called "soul-making" and Erik Erikson called "ego-identity."[5] Can this man pull his life together? The movie forces us to feel that nothing less than identity is at stake; and, like it or not, we all have a stake in that.

Everything is set up to prepare us for the dress rehearsal, the solemn moment when we see the hero actually construct the self he is trying to become. Jolson blacks up, and behold! For the first time in the movie, he looks like a serious and integrated person. He faces himself in the mirror. The encounter between him and his newly constructed image is staged very carefully. Will he recognize himself? How will he deal with the man he sees? As he gazes, his vision fragments kaleidoscopically into a montage—in the 1920s, that technique was still new and fresh—and propels him back into his father's synagogue, into "Jakie Rabinowitz," the kid whose spontaneity and joy he has repressed for twenty years. But at the same time, framing that youthful being is the face of a thoughtful, serious, mature man—not exactly a black man, but a man who has made blackness a *project*. There's something amazing about the black face he has constructed. It's as if this singer has transformed the minstrel "Swanee River" into an inner River Jordan

---

*Jolson developed blackface routines in the 1900s, in his teens, while he was working as a solo performer and traveling from carnivals to burlesque houses around the country. He attracted the attention of Lew Dockstader, the head of a widely admired minstrel traveling show, worked in blackface with the company for the next five years, became increasingly prominent, and was written up in *Variety*. In 1909 he went to work for the Shubert Brothers. Within a few months, in a Shubert musical called *La Belle Paree*, he became "the first performer to perform minstrel comedy in what was then called the legitimate theatre." The best account I have found of Jolson's early career is Michael Alexander, *Jazz Age Jews* (Princeton University Press, 2001), especially chapters 14–17, on "Jewish Minstrelsy" and "Jewish versions of blackness."

that he needs to cross in order to grow up. Look into those eyes: For the first time he looks like a *mensch*. Putting on someone else's face is enabling him to recognize his own. By being someone else, he can become himself. There's some sort of magic working here. In fact, it's a very old and venerable magic, going back to the origins of the theater thousands of years ago. But it's also a very up-to-date and contemporary magic, the "Magic Realism" that is thriving on jazz-age Broadway and that defines the 1920s Times Square.

But why does he need to be black? What is the power of blackness for Jakie, for Jack? Right after this revelatory moment, another clown breaks onstage with another revelation. He is the shambling, sleazy "Yudelson, the Kibitzer from the Ghetto" (Otto Lederer) who has come to tell Jack his father is dying, and to urge him to return to the family, the ghetto, the synagogue, and God (141–50, 119–23). He can recognize the hero by his voice: "Yes, that's Jakie—with the cry in his voice, just like in the temple." But he is disoriented when he meets him face to face in blackface: "Jakie, this ain't you." Then he turns to his audience to comment on the metamorphosis he has just seen and the action he is part of, and he changes his mind. He recognizes that this is Jakie, after all, but a Jakie who has put himself through big changes: "It talks like Jakie," he says, "but it *looks like his shadow.*"

What does a shadow look like? In fact, the shadow is a prime image in the history of reflection on the self and the other. For many modern psychologists, the shadow metaphor is about mental processes they call "projection" and "identification." These processes work within the self in radically different ways. In projection, we ascribe to other people feelings we cannot accept in ourselves. When we do this, we constrict the scope of our being, and enlist in an unending state of war, not only with the people next door, but with ourselves, prime suspects in a hopeless quest for purity. (Jews and blacks have both been longtime casualties in these psychic wars.) In identification we yearn for others, want to reach out and touch them, talk to them, be close to them, merge with them. Identification helps people grow up, become more than they were, enlarge who they are, and learn to live in peace. But none of us is capable of identifying with other people until we can identify with the dark side of ourselves, until we can bring our shadows into the light and find ways to live with them.

We still haven't figured out what psychic undertows might be lurking in the Jazz Singer's shadows. There must be some emotional strength that he feels deprived of when he walks around with his Jewish face, but that he gains when he puts on a black one. In 1927, when *The Jazz Singer* was made, American Jews were believed to have "arrived," to be "at home" at last; they were supposed to feel comfortable and grateful. (In those years, Hitler was still a face in the crowd.) Black people, on the other hand, although freed from slavery, were being lynched and humiliated by laws that could have been made by slaveholders. Some black people were making a mark in Northern cities, most strikingly in the development of jazz and in the cultural explosion known as the "Harlem Renaissance." But the great majority of black Americans were still, like Faulkner's characters, locked into the police states of the underdeveloped rural South. Barred from social striving, living under something close to house arrest, they were forced to preserve "the cry in their voice," the sound of unmediated human emotion. If we listen to some classic Delta Blues today—to Leadbelly, to Robert Johnson, to Bessie Smith—the idea that social imprisonment could evoke primal emotion doesn't sound farfetched. And of course it's a great tradition, in fact a great *Jewish* tradition, born in the world of the Psalms: "How can we sing the Lord's song in a strange land."

You could say the Kibitzer's "shadow" line gives away the whole story: a twentieth-century epic where immigrant Jews identify with blacks in ways that help to develop both mass culture and multicultural liberalism. All this is true, but this isn't all. When I looked up this scene in Alfred Cohn's script, it said something startlingly different from what's on the screen. What Yudelson says in the printed version is, "It talks like Jakie, but it looks like *a nigger*" (143, 120). So the original version was a crude racist insult. Amazing! What happened? No one seems to know. But somehow, in the process of cultural production, some obscure, unnoticed, maybe even unconscious revolution took place. Did that word call up the horrors of *Birth of a Nation*? Did the guys behind the scenes recoil and think, "Never Again"? In an instant, a spit in the black face turned into something close to an embrace, and the movie grew up.

Let's come back to Jack in his dressing room. There are many ways a black face can help a Jew. Michael Alexander says it well at the very start of his fine historical study, *Jazz Age Jews*. Even as Jolson's generation moved up from the ghetto into the American middle class, he says,

> Some of its members displayed a peculiar behavior that did not corre-
> spond to their social position. They acted as though they were increas-
> ingly marginalized. What is more, they identified with less fortunate
> individuals and groups . . . by imitating, defending, and actually partic-
> ipating in the group life of marginalized Americans. Outsider identifi-
> cation . . . is a paradox in the psychology of American Jews. *As Jews
> moved up, they identified down.*[6]

From the standpoint of *Bildung*, identification with blacks could open up fruitful paths. For Jewish kids who did not want to be comfortable "allright-niks," blackface enabled them to feel firmly, even righteously American without having to feel white. Over the generations, it could help them become Jerome Kern and the Gershwins, Artie Shaw and Benny Goodman, the Schiffmans and the Chesses, Phil Spector and all the brave knights of the Brill Building, Bob Dylan and Laura Nyro, Doc Pomus and Dr. John, Richard Price and Rick Rubin. Jews attuned to black music have opened up the gold mine of black experience to the whole world. They have confronted America with a *J'accuse*: Its betrayal of its black people proves its betrayal of itself. Michael Alexander has a nice term for this attitude: "romantic marginality."[7]

All this is fine, and yet any Jew who is hip enough to imagine he or she "wants to be black" will be smart enough to know there's something un-kosher about the deal. This guilty unease shapes *The Jazz Singer*'s climax. When Yudelson asks Jack/Jakie to come back and help his father die, the sacrament he wants him to perform is called *Kol Nidre*. For many Jews, this is the most dramatic and spiritually intense moment of the year. It happens on the night that begins Yom Kippur, the Day of Atonement. Many secular Jews who wouldn't dream of going to synagogue all through the year feel they have to be there for this. The *Kol Nidre* prayer is special in that it isn't addressed to God, but to other people. We are supposed to recognize all the ways we have hurt each other all year, not just openly but in the shadows; we are supposed to seek and to offer forgiveness. There is a catalogue of sins and crimes. The idea is for all of us to confess, plead guilty to them all, and cover for each other:

> *We abuse, we betray, we are cruel . . .*
> *We destroy, we embitter, we falsify . . .*
> *We mock, we neglect, we oppress . . .*
> *We steal, we transgress, we are unkind . . .*
> *We yield to evil, we are zealots for bad causes.* *

Few of us have done all these things, but all of us have done some. Our leap of faith is that if we can face each other and admit what we have done, or even what we have imagined doing, then we will have the right to ask each other to forgive. And

> *Mutual forgiveness of each vice,*
> *Such are the gates of Paradise.*[8]

More than any other Jewish ritual, *Kol Nidre* is driven by music. The cantor's solo is the most passionate, heartrending music of the whole year. Jews believe nothing else can break down people's resistance or open up their emotional floodgates. Many people complain about spending money on a cantor's salary—but then, if the cantor is singing as he should (or, more and more, as *she* should), they leave *shul* in tears and hope to be forgiven for doubts. At *The Jazz Singer*'s climax, Jolson sings the *Kol Nidre* prayer. He leads the congregation with an amazing emotional fervor and intensity that have eluded him till now: Now, at last, he's *there*. His heroic act—returning to the ghetto, sacrificing for a father who didn't sacrifice for him, renewing his thrilling but dangerous bond with his mother—unites his adulthood with his childhood, frees unconscious energy, and taps emotional depths

---

**MAHZOR for Rosh Hashanah and Yom Kippur: A Prayer Book for the Days of Awe*, ed. Rabbi Jules Harlow (Rabbinical Assembly, 1972), 376–79. This is a Conservative prayer book, and Jack/Jakie's of course would have been Orthodox (and untranslated). The idea of a collective confessional and the basic items in it go back to Rabbinic times and are shared by Jews all over the world. But some congregations since the 1960s have added to the catalogue of sins. (Rabbi Jeremy Kalmanovsky, note, October 14, 2004).

Fans of Walt Whitman will notice that "Crossing Brooklyn Ferry," Part 6, contains a collective confessional very like this one: "I am he who knew what it was to be evil," then a Yom Kippur–esque catalogue, then a collectivization of guilt where the speaker sees his evil self as "one with the rest."

that he has had to repress in order to work and live for twenty years under his father's curse. Now, as his father dies, chains lift from his heart. He learns from his life what his father's religion couldn't teach him because it was too narrow, and what secular show biz couldn't teach him because it was too shallow: the universal lesson that *"music is the voice of God"* (86, 99; italics mine). In *The Jazz Singer*, mass culture stakes a claim to universal value, not only for its global reach but for its emotional power and depth.

After Jolson blacks up, when he faces himself in the mirror, he is affirming his act of theft, and recognizing that he has something to answer for. He wants to be forgiven, and believes he should be, on the grounds that his grand theft springs from love. This encounter with himself liberates waves of unconscious energy, and sets him free to become somebody new, somebody bigger and deeper and more grown up than he has ever been.[9]

There is one more big thing that needs to be on the Jazz Singer's *Kol Nidre* list, something else that springs from love, and that is his incestuous love for his mother. The color of this love comes across most vividly in a scene called "Jack Robin Comes Home and Sings for Mother" (77–87, 96–100).* Here Jack sits at the piano and plays her some of what he is going to sing on Broadway. This is the one scene where Vitaphone Sound records lots of talk along with music, and where the distinction between speech and song gets blurred. He plays and sings an up-tempo, jazzed-up arrangement of Irving Berlin's "Blue Skies," a cascade of pure joy. As he sings, he jokes and flirts with her, vows to move her to the Bronx, "a lot of nice green grass there and a lot of people you know . . ." His patter grows both more frantic and more intimate, and now that they are alone together, we see that the incestuous love that has been only a subtext till now has become a text. He grows ever more outrageous, and pulls her close:

> And I'm gonna buy you a nice black silk dress, Mama. You see Mrs. Friedman, the butcher's wife, she'll be jealous of you. . . . And I'm gonna get you a nice pink dress that'll go with your brown eyes. . . . What? Who is telling you? Whatta you mean, no? Yes, you'll wear pink

---

*The screenplay, 144–45, gives intricate dialogue beyond what is in the script, and something like what is actually on the screen. Samson Raphaelson, author of the story and the play on which the movie was based, felt let down by the movie. But this mother-son encounter was the one scene he really liked.

or else. Or else you'll wear pink. And I'm gonna take you to Coney Island. . . . An' you know in the Dark Mill? Ever been in the Dark Mill?
Well, with me it's all right. I'll kiss you and hug you. You see if I
don't. . . .

To our surprise, she responds as if quoting some primal flirtation textbook.
Her body language abruptly changes, she speeds up and bounces with the
beat. She says "Oh, no!" in a way that suggests "Of course," and "and what
else?" As he talks and plays on, the directness and ardor are amazing—and
visibly mutual. The expression "Oedipus complex" hardly seems the word,
the waves of love between them look so *simple*. This is a scene that takes us
into emotional spaces that are thrilling but also scary, and neither American
culture nor any other can tell us convincingly how to react. When the old
man returns and shrieks "*Stop!*" it is a disappointment, but also a relief.

Jakie's mother (Eugenie Besserer) is a fascinating character, far more
complex and original than she seems. She looks like the sentimental
Mamas in a thousand novels, plays, and songs, including the 1930s jazz hit,
"My Yiddishe Mama," and Gertrude Berg's mama-diva figure, Molly Goldberg. But she is more special. Although she herself is a devout person, she
adamantly supports the right of her son *not* to be devout. Her husband the
cantor says Jakie "has all the songs and prayers in his head." She responds
with two different but related ideas: "*But it's not in his heart. He is of America*" (title 16, page 59). In other words, first, Jakie has a right to a life of his
own based on what is "in his heart"; second, this is the meaning of America.
Later on, she visits her son in the theater, sees him in his new element, talks
with his *goyishe* girlfriend May, the show's female lead, and she says, "Here
he belongs" (149, 123). This woman has slow, solemn, old-fashioned body
language, but an ultramodern sensibility.

Jakie's mother draws on a reserve of collective feeling about mothers.
When the conflict of generations boils over, the father often erupts and
throws the child violently out of the house. But the mother opens up a back
channel of communication with the excommunicated child and sustains a
bond deeper than bad behavior. (This happens in Sholem Aleichem's story
cycle, "Tevye and His Daughters," and in its descendant, *Fiddler on the
Roof*, after the hero has denounced his daughter for marrying a goy.) Jakie's
mother leans on what Hegel called "the law of the heart," and on a feeling

all her audience will know: "a mama's heart." But she is also inspired by something that in her world is far more unusual: a mother's *mind*. She is the most supportive parent in the history of the *Bildungsroman*. Fighting for her child's right to a life project radically different from her own, she could be the Existentialist Mother of the Year. Virginia Woolf, in *A Room of One's Own*, written just a year after *The Jazz Singer*, had a word to say about her: "When, however, one reads of a very remarkable man who had a mother, we are on the track of a lost novelist, a suppressed poet, of some mute and inglorious Jane Austen, some Emily Brontë." She has plenty of sisters.* She is a very important modern type of person, split between her conventional life and her sympathy for unconventional ideas—and for unconventional choices by her children. She is a patron saint, not only of the liberal Broadway audience that I grew up with—and, indeed, grew up *in*—but of every twentieth- and now twenty-first-century avant-garde.

The hero's *Kol Nidre* solo lasts only a couple of minutes, but it is dynamite. It features a counterpoint between Jack/Jakie and the choir. He pulls against them, they resist him, he and they seem to fight each other, the emotional momentum gets frantic, then finally the choir gives way and they blend marvelously together. I was amazed how well these two minutes prefigure the sounds, a generation later, of the great flowering of rhythm and blues: Ray Charles, Sam Cooke, Stevie Wonder, Aretha Franklin, Curtis Mayfield, Al Green, Marvin Gaye, Mavis Staples, Patti LaBelle. But why not? After all, R & B was made largely by Blacks who were participants in what historians call "The Great Migration," and who, just like the Rabinowitz family, were going through a traumatic first-generation encounter with modern life in the northern cities of the USA. Their music was driven by religious fervor, yet they were also staking out a claim to a secular good life. Some of the greatest R & B songs, like "Higher and Higher," "For Your Precious Love," "A Place in the Sun," "Many Rivers to Cross," "I'll Take You

---

*A Room of One's Own (1928; Harvest, 1981, foreword by Mary Gordon), 49. One of those sisters was the mother of the great liberal philosopher Isaiah Berlin. Berlin was my supervisor at Oxford forty years ago, and I met his mother at his stepson's Bar Mitzvah in early 1963. She asked me and my friend Jerry Cohen what we thought of the Bar Mitzvah boy's *Haftarah*. I said I thought he had read very well. When Jerry didn't seem to know what to say, I explained, "My friend had a very strict Communist upbringing." This didn't faze her at all. She said, with a warm smile, Yes, God had made human beings different so they could talk and argue, and so teaching and learning could go on. She spent the next few minutes developing this theme, a remarkable fusion of Molly Goldberg and John Stuart Mill.

There," get their depth and power from a vision of sacred love and profane love as metaphors for each other. Martin Luther King defined the politics of their project, their quest for religious ways to affirm secular modern city life.

Part of *The Jazz Singer*'s mythic power comes from its conquest of many media. Its first incarnation was a story by Samson Raphaelson, published in 1921 under the title "The Day of Atonement" in *Everybody's Magazine*. Its second, also written by Raphaelson, was a Broadway adaptation starring George Jessel, whose early biography and inner conflicts were a lot like Jolson's. The play ran from 1925 to 1927, and closed just before the movie opened across Broadway. In "The Day of Atonement," the cynical Broadway producer is angry at Jack/Jakie for leaving the show. But he follows him down into the depths of the Lower East Side, and hears his solo. (The *tallis*, the traditional Jewish prayer shawl, is his disguise.) He is thrilled, and phones his partner uptown:

> "Harry," said Lee, "do you want to hear the greatest ragtime singer in America in the making? A wonder, Harry, a wonder! Come down right away, it's a dirty little hole on the East Side called the Hester Street Synagogue, I'll meet you at the corner of Hester and Norfolk."[10]

In the sound era, Raphaelson became a great comic screenwriter, and worked closely with Ernst Lubitsch (*The Shop Around the Corner, Trouble in Paradise*, etc.). He always used the English language with precision and finesse; the way he says things can tell us a lot. In his story, the producer is on the Lower East Side on what later generations would call a scouting trip. He calls his partner uptown and says something great is happening down here. The singer, the synagogue he sings in, the neighborhood itself, are all something much bigger than themselves *"in the making"*; they are phases in a historical dialectic they don't understand. Forty-second Street and Broadway, terminal for the IRT subway, is also the terminal for Raphaelson's dialectic, the place where cultural history comes out.

The story and the play both end with the prodigal son's return: Jakie gives up a career on Broadway and sings for his people and God alone. In the shooting script, as in the play, that's the end. The screen fades to black. But then, an instant later, things change: In fact, we go through an instant 180-degree change, from renunciation to jubilation, and we see a jubilant ending on the screen, the ending with which this chapter began. Was this ending always part of the deal? If so, why isn't it in the script? Here is how the change is registered in "Appendix I: The Synchronized Sound Sequences": "The season passes—time heals—the show goes on" (146). Those dashes wouldn't get over in any respectable grammar book or English class. But fans of Keats's letters, and of Emily Dickinson's poems, will remember them: They push the narrative forward; they ensure that life will go on in spite of many formidable objections. As the dashes flash, the soundtrack turns jazzy. Then there is a quick cut to a spectacular panorama of Times Square and Broadway's blinding lights. This thrilling perspective is Times Square's special contribution to modernism. It defines the Square's spectacular trinity—people, lights, sky—as the new totality of being. The dashes are like the subway, an underground way to get there fast.

The grand finale brings us inside a jammed Broadway theater. (In fact, it's the Winter Garden.) The flood of light means "Broadway forgives all." The hero sings in blackface again, but it doesn't seem to carry the tragic weight it had only a few minutes ago. "Mammy," the song he sings, is addressed to a woman supposedly near death, yet he sings in a state of pure exuberance. He leaves the stage and focuses on his mother in the audience; they share an up-close ecstatic smile. With the wicked witch of an old man dead, the third leg of the Oedipal triangle collapsed, and the hero a star with his name in electric lights, they don't need a Dark Mill anymore. Now they can enjoy a communion that needs no *Kol Nidre*. Or so we're told. *The Jazz Singer* takes us for a ride, but it is a ride that most of us will be glad to take. This is the magic realism that is the heart of modern mass culture, where tragedy can morph instantly into comedy, incest can symbolize innocence, and the project of giving up everything can turn out to be just a chapter in the dialectics of having it all.

If my phrase "having it all" sounds disrespectful, that isn't what I meant at all. In fact, at *The Jazz Singer*'s moment in history, the word "all" marked a bitter controversy. For a whole century, the USA had had a policy of amazingly open immigration. But in the 1920s, in the aftermath of World War One, Congress passed a series of laws that pretty much closed the gates for the next forty years. America was hoping to stop its slide into being a nation of "all," and to stand fast instead as "fortress America" open only to "some."[11] Griffith's *Birth of a Nation* showed how America's ultramodern mass culture could be bent in the service of a pastoral vision of a lost Anglo-

Saxon purity before it was polluted by a great stream of dark and dirty "others." Chaplin's cinema gave a spectacular new visual life to the drives and dreams of these others. His comedy came from neighborhoods like our "dirty little hole on the East Side." These places were the birthplace of movies and jazz and comics and the whole culture of "vulgar modernism" that made twentieth-century America a truly "new world." *The Jazz Singer*, more than any other work, defined that world's look and its sound.

In the middle of World War One, Randolph Bourne, a young disciple of John Dewey, wrote an essay, "Trans-National America" (1915), that may be the first theory of this world. Bourne argued that immigrants to America don't "assimilate" into a preexisting Anglo world: They mix their old cultures with new conditions to create a blended, hybrid American culture that has never existed anywhere till now. "Only the American," he said, "has a chance to become a citizen of the world." This meant "not a nationality but a trans-nationality, a weaving back and forth, with the other lands, of many threads of all sizes and colors."[12] A year later, many of the Jewish and other

immigrant songwriters of Tin Pan Alley resisted the wartime pressure for "100 per cent Americanism," and argued instead on behalf of "a counter-sentiment for a nation of nations."[13]

In America's "nation of nations," from Jolson's time to our own, Times Square has always been the capital. You can see it on the street or in the subway, any hour of the day or night. You can hear it everywhere, inside and outside. (In my youth you could hear it underground, at the great Times Square Records in the IRT subway arcade.) Today's ingredients are different from those of the Jazz Age—for one thing there are a lot more ingredients, come from a far greater range of places—but now as then it's a *mix*. A mix means more than just different people "side by side." It means integration, but also intercourse, blending and fusion that change everybody. In the Square the mix is insistently *there*, it's on the street, it's in your face. When you are in the mix, under the Square's spectacular light, ego-boundaries liquefy, identities get slippery. You won't be able to avoid the question, "Who are these people?" And brushing against them will raise the collateral question, "Who are you?" You will be changing them just as they will be changing you; you know everybody will change, even if you don't know how. How Americans feel about Times Square, and about New York as a whole, often depends on how ready they are for a liquefaction of their being. For Al Jolson, liquidity of being was his life. When Jolson paints himself black, he performs multicultural America's first sacrament: He metamorphoses into both the mixer and the mix.

P.S. At the end of 2004, the classic *Jazz Singer* cityscape—Times Square at night, in black and white, with its trinity of people, signs, and sky—was reincarnated on the cover of Bob Dylan's *Chronicles, Volume One*, his memoir of his early 1960s arrival and his debut in New York.[14] Some reviewers and many readers were puzzled why his cover featured Times Square rather than Greenwich Village, where Dylan first performed in public and became a star. If we use *The Jazz Singer* as our prism, it is easy to see. Dylan is presenting himself as Jack Robin's descendant, as the true Jazz Singer of our time. Bob Dylan, Jack Robin: Isn't the connection obvious just from the names?* Now look at Dylan's cover. This expansive vision of the Square by

---

*When I brought home my first Bob Dylan album forty years ago, my mother enjoyed the music, but got stuck on the name: "Hmm, Dylan, what was it before?" I got so mad! But of course she was right. For my parents' generation, this question was an ongoing joke with a critical edge. (See the Marx Brothers' "Hurrah for Captain Spalding, the African explorer.") My mother understood why Jewish boys had had to go in disguise in her time (and Jack Robin's), but not in mine. Soon Dylan was outed as "Zimmerman." He seemed to resent it at first, but, like Jack Robin, gradually learned to affirm his real Jewishness along with his wannabe universality in the course of growing up.

night suggests a world that is all before him, a vast horizon, not just musical but imaginative, far beyond the range of the Village folk world where he began; a capacity for metamorphosis—what I called the power to be "at once the mixer and the mix"; an intimacy with electricity (see his battle of Newport, 1965)—as a medium for magnifying both the music and the self; an identification with show biz and a deep need to be an entertainer. There's one more Dylan-Jolson connection we can't leave out: "the cry in his voice, like in the temple." Both jazz singers are driven by a need to infuse profane entertainment with religious fervor and a desire for transcendence. Dylan's religious experience is far more various than Jolson's, more elusive and full of contradictions. Still, the Jewish Bible is right there in his title.

Chronicles has a great first scene. It is set amid the red-leather booths of Jack Dempsey's Restaurant, where Dylan's first producer, Lou Levy, has taken him out, to show him around and also to show him off. His encounter with Dempsey is sweet. First, the champ tells the scrawny kid to put on weight, learn to dress sharp, not be afraid to hit people hard. When Levy explains that Dylan is a songwriter, not a boxer, Dempsey doesn't skip a beat; he tells the kid he can't wait to hear his songs. Anybody old enough to remember Dempsey's place can imagine this scene. The old man loved schmoozing with people, he was patient and gracious with all kinds, terrific with kids. He synthesized in himself two vital parts of American popular culture, "the fights" and show biz. The fact that we know this anorexic kid is about to write one of the all-time great American songs, "Blowin' in the Wind," makes this story a little masterpiece of dramatic irony. Dylan blends modern realism—a real street we know, a great figure who lived long, and whom some of us might even have met—with very old, mythical and folkloric forms of narration: "prophecy of the hero's success," "the old champion anoints the new."

There's just one weird thing about this lovely story. Somehow, he gets the address wrong. Dempsey's restaurant was on Broadway and 49th Street, in the Brill Building, aka "Tin Pan Alley." This is one of the great sites in the history of American culture. For decades it was full of musicians, songwriters, accompanists, record producers, music publishers, agents, publicists. I spoke earlier about the brilliant men and women working here. It was the place where so many songs that defined America after World War Two—"Lonely Avenue," "Chapel of Love," "Be My Baby," "Hound Dog," "Don't Be Cruel," "Stand by Me," "Walk On By," "We Gotta Get Out of This Place," "Society's Child"—were made. (And Dylan knew every note and every line.) Dempsey's was a perfect Times Square location, close to the old Garden,* center of the city's boxing scene, and right at the epicenter of its popular music industry. Dylan was there because some very important music people, like producer John Hammond, spotted his genius right away. But his book removes the scene from its central location and relocates it half a mile away to 58th Street, in the 1960s a dingy, anonymous periphery. What's going on? Wouldn't Jack Dempsey have knocked out anyone who tried to relocate him to that Desolation Row? Dylan's cover picture places him out in the open, at Times Square's center; his stage direction pulls him into the shadows. Even as he unfolds himself, he moves to hide to keep from being seen. He starts his book with an engaging story of his youth in Times Square, then breaks the engagement with a quick change of address that makes the Square disappear.† It seems he still can't bear to admit he is in show biz and always has been, still can't affirm his own life. Like so many modern men and women, Dylan/Zimmerman is still searching for a name that he can feel at home with.

*The old Madison Square Garden—which also figures in Kubrick's *Killer's Kiss*, discussed earlier—was between 49th and 50th Streets, and between Eighth and Ninth Avenues. Dempsey's began at 50th and Eighth, right across the street. For a while he had two restaurants, the original and a "Broadway Restaurant and Bar" in the Brill Building. Then for a generation the Brill Building place reigned alone. The "Jack Dempsey's Broadway Restaurant" website displays a matchbook ad: LOVE MATCHES ARE MADE IN HEAVEN, FIGHT MATCHES ARE MADE AT JACK DEMPSEY'S.

†Even if we can imagine this author's unconscious ambivalence, what's the publisher's excuse? Is there nobody old at Simon and Schuster who remembers, or nobody young who has read, about all the years when Jack Dempsey was king of Times Square? (And what about *The New York Times*? Its Sunday "City" section reprinted this scene, false address and all, on March 26, 2005.)

CHAPTER 3

A Human Eye: Sailors in the Square

Close! stand close to me, Starbuck, and let me look into a human eye . . .

—Captain Ahab in *Moby-Dick*

For me, these carefree young Americans were freedom incarnate: our own, and also the freedom that was about to spread—we had no doubts on this score—throughout the world.

—Simone de Beauvoir, on Americans in Paris, 1944

I guess he learned that sense of balance on board a ship.

—In *The Way We Were* (1973), Barbra Streisand in 1945 discovers Robert Redford, in full dress whites, standing straight in his sleep

August 1945: The Great Noon

The two most famous people in the history of Times Square are anonymous. They are a man and a woman locked in each other's arms. They were
part of the enormous crowd that gathered in the Square on August 15, 1945,
V-J Day, the day and night of Japan's surrender and the end of World War
Two. The *PBS History of New York*, produced by Ric Burns, shows marvelous newsreel footage of that moment. When I first saw this footage in
2001, drawn from the National Archives, I was amazed I'd never seen it before, yet in another sense I felt I'd been seeing it all my life. It was a moment
well choreographed. Around twilight, Mayor LaGuardia announced the
surrender, and then, at a prearranged signal, after four years of blackout, all
the lights in the Square went on. An earthshaking roar went up. A big band
on a bandstand nearby (I have read it was Artie Shaw's) began to swing, and
thousands of men and women instantly started to dance, holding each
other, jitterbugging, men throwing women into the air. The dancing is said
to have gone on all through the night and past sunrise. Even when there was
no music playing, couples moved to their own. As the camera pans the
crowd, it is a thrill to see so many men and women who clearly are strangers

embrace, hug and kiss, dance, squeeze the hell out of one another. Two of them, a sailor and a nurse, locked in a rapt embrace at the very center of the Square, became the subjects of a great photograph. It was taken by the German Jewish refugee photographer Alfred Eisenstaedt, and it ran on the cover of *Life* magazine. They were also photographed at just about the same moment, from a slightly different (and less exciting) angle, by U.S. Navy photographer Victor Jorgensen; Jorgensen's photo was reprinted in the next day's *New York Times*.[1] The sailor and the nurse and the crowd and the Square form one of the classic images of America and Americans in the twentieth century. It is a luminous moment of spontaneous, collective free love.

Some of the fascination of this picture springs from its mystery: Who are this man and this woman? Together they form a sort of counter-monument to all our monuments to the Unknown Soldier: Instead of reminding us of the universality of death, they summon up an equally universal erotic life. Over the years, like claimants to a vacant throne, many men and women have put themselves forward as the real incarnations of this primal couple. In October 1980, *Life* ran a spread entitled "Who Is the Kissing Sailor?"[2] The magazine compiled a kind of short list, ten men and three women. It reprinted their portraits from youth and from middle age, along with brief life stories and sound bites about what they did on the great day. *Life* tried, not very effectively, to assess their rival claims. Every one of the men (and one dead man's brother) was certain he was the sailor, and wanted recognition from the world. The women tended to be more tentative and ironic: They said yes, they had embraced sailors in the Square, but so had many other young women who looked just like them. Eisenstaedt himself, who took hundreds of pictures that day, was of no help in sorting out the lineup. The men's geographical and occupational spread—fish-seller, Rhode Island; school custodian, Illinois; history teacher, New Jersey; psychologist, California—made a fine Popular Front microcosm, reminiscent of so many real and imagined platoons and bomber crews of the Good War, and so many photo spreads in the prime of *Life*. In the 1990s, the Internet brought forth more candidates, and left reality as elusive as ever. *Time* magazine in 1996 ran an editorial on the controversy. The mystery could never be solved, they said, and it didn't matter: "The real kisser remains Everyman."

Eisenstaedt's photo is a perfect Renaissance perspective, with the foreground directly on the lower part of the bowtie, with big buildings converging diagonally toward the vanishing point, and a giant sign with a paternal figure promoting Ruppert Beer right on the point. This sailor and this nurse are surrounded by big buildings, by silver trolley tracks, by neon signs, and by the sky, but also by an assortment of other people. About twenty feet away there is a second sailor (and, in some croppings, a third), smiling on the couple. Another comment is suggested by the huge neon sign just to their right, which advertises BOND, then America's biggest ready-made clothing store. Americans in 1945 all knew Bond Clothes, whether or not they wore them. It was one of those brand names like "5 & 10," like "Life," like "Times Square" itself, whose direct simplicity expressed America's democratic and universal longings, the desire to bring us all together, like the Popular Front,

"The House I Live In," the Good War itself. The sign that proclaims the bond between this primal couple also highlights the more complex bonds that hold together the city, the country, maybe even the world. The other people in the picture are participants in the crowd's festivities, but also, like ourselves, spectators of the couple's embrace. They are both wearing uniforms, which mark them as "public servants" and separate them from the multitude of civilians (like ourselves) who surround them and whom they serve. His uniform is black, hers white. The contrast between them, sharpened by black-and-white film, heightens the clinch that binds them together. It also vests their unity with all sorts of symbolic resonance: man and woman, black and white, land and sea, war and peace, aggression and nurturing, yin and yang. All the great elements that define the picture—the couple, the crowd, the buildings, the signs, the sky—are composed so as to create a very satisfying whole.

Actually, if we look closely, we can see it is a somewhat unstable whole. The two bodies are wound together at a precarious angle, tilting and twisting sharply downward. (In the Jorgensen photo, shot from about thirty degrees to the right, the tilt is even sharper.) If the sailor doesn't get a stronger foothold soon, their momentum is going to throw them to the ground. Do they know they could crash? Are they worried? Not that we can tell. But if we think about this sailor, we will remember he has to be attuned to decks far shakier than any embrace on Broadway. The nurse herself does not look worried; she seems to be giving herself very freely to this embrace. She seems sure, and we can be pretty sure, that in a minute or so he will make some deft move that will stabilize them both. ("I guess he learned that sense of balance on board a ship.") Even though, from what we can see of his face, he is just a kid, we can probably count on him to protect both of them—and so to protect the civilians, to protect us.* One thing that makes this picture so perfect is that, subliminally, it works so well as a parable of World War Two itself: "The Good War," waged to protect both America and the world from real and powerful evil.

---

*Why can't she be the one to make the move? She probably can, in the sense that she physically knows how. But in a year like 1945, she will assume that the man holding her knows how to lead, and she will let him, for their mutual comfort; however, if he can't lead, she will know what to do. Her assumptions will be shared by any woman on the dance floor at the Astor Ballroom a hundred or so yards away, and by any modern single mother.

Eisenstaedt's image shows us how, in the 1940s, the technology of street photography and the social structures of photojournalism gave photographers a power surge: They can open up all the ruptures and polarizations in our being, only to reconcile them and bring them together for all of us to see. It is hard to look on this tableau without nostalgic envy. At the same time, it is hard not to wonder, *What planet was this?* Can the gulf between this couple and ourselves ever be crossed? We'll talk about it.

The civilian and military people looking on are spectators to the embrace—as we ourselves are, so many years after—but also to the act by which the photographer is turning it into art. They may look like they aren't doing much, but in fact their presence in the picture means a lot. They are like the chorus in old Greek comedies and tragedies (this picture looks more like comedy); they function not only as spectators of the action, but as commentators on it, and sometimes as participants in it. The Greek chorus was understood to represent the body of citizens, in a polis that was turning itself into the world's first democracy. In an important sense, the comic and tragic actions were performed for these citizens; they couldn't have been performed without them. They were the first rituals of democracy. The years 1944 and 1945 make up one of the great moments in the history of democracy, the moment of victory against the most murderous regime in history. (For once, thanks to Adolf Hitler, this language of hyperbole and propaganda told the truth.) It was a moment when, as victory unfolded, new rituals were born and made on the streets. Eisenstaedt's photo is an active part of this creative process: It gives us the power to see how an act of totally "free love," an embrace between strangers in the midst of a crowd of strangers, can be a communion of citizens. When Eisenstaedt took these pictures in the midst of Times Square, he was working for *Life* magazine, published only a few blocks away. *Life* in 1945 was both the biggest mass-circulation magazine and the biggest patron of photography in the world. Our photographer and his employers may or may not have known that they were anointing street photography as a distinctively democratic form of art; anointing Times Square as a modern *agora*, a democratic public space; and anointing "free love," the embrace between strangers, as a democratic sacrament.

Two of New York's recent mayors, Koch and Giuliani, have both portrayed this moment and this image as Times Square's all-time pinnacle of

perfection. All their policies toward the Square, they have said, were designed to bring it back: to protect Times Square against time. This was an
ironic joke, but I don't know if they got it.

Sailors on the Street

Where did this sailor come from? How did he find his way to Times Square?
In the course of World War Two, more than five million GIs passed through
the Port of New York on the way to or coming back from Europe and Africa;
about two million were under Navy jurisdiction. Most ships were berthed in
the Brooklyn Navy Yard, which was the USA's biggest repair and salvage
center. But many were docked at the Busch Terminal and Fort Hamilton in
Brooklyn, and many others at the North River Docks in the West 40s. (The
retired aircraft carrier USS *Intrepid* marks this spot today.)[3] Times Square in
the 1940s had an amazing array of hangouts: bars, dance halls, cheap cafeterias (automats were in their prime), gyms, vaudeville and movie houses,
burlesque shows, every class of nightspots, brothels—though in fact all these
public places were routinely denounced as brothels.

Two points in the neighborhood were particular magnets for sailors: the
USO facility, aka the "Stage Door Canteen," on 47th Street just east of
Broadway, and "the deuce," the block of West 42nd Street between Seventh
and Eighth. The deuce was infamous in the 1970s for its ambience of hostility to women, which furnished a pretext for those who wanted to tear the
whole neighborhood down. But if we look back into urban history, we see
that West 42nd Street was infamous even in the 1930s for pretty much the
same reasons.[4] In its heyday as a theater street, this block had been welcom-
ing to women. But in the course of the Depression, changes in its modes of
entertainment seem to have triggered a radical shift in its sexual balance.
George Chauncey, in *Gay New York*, portrays the change this way:

> The transformation of 42nd Street in the 1920s and early 1930s has
> enormous repercussions for the area's gay scene. 42nd Street was the
> site of the oldest theaters in the Times Square district, and the city's
> elite had regarded it as a distinguished address early in the century. By

1931, however, it had effectively become a working-class male domain. The conversion of two prominent 42nd Street theaters, the Republic (later Victory) and the Eltinge (later Empire) into burlesque
houses both signified and contributed to the masculinization of the
street. Not only the strippers inside but the large, quasi-pornographic
billboards and the barkers announcing the shows outside intensified
the image of the street as a male domain, threatening to women.[5]

"A male domain, threatening to women"; "the masculinization of the street."
We have to try to imagine 42nd Street as going through a sort of sex change,
an evolution from a street where women feel completely at home in public
to a street virtually without women. This is unusual in the history of cities,
where the arc of development has gone the other way. In medieval cities,
women were locked out of much urban public space—except for prostitutes, who for centuries, in many legal traditions, were known as "public
women." But in most of the world, sometimes by plan and sometimes by
surprise, sometimes through peaceful economic changes and sometimes
through revolutions, women have come to permeate urban public space
and feel at home there. In the theater and entertainment world of a century
ago, "the Sarah Bernhardt era," women emerged as not only star performers
and fashionable spectators, but even as producers. The mass media and the
entertainment industry have long been among the engines of New York's
prosperity and world renown. For a little more than a century, these industries have been concentrated around Times Square. On the facade of "Maxine Elliot's Theatre," on 39th and Broadway right by the Met, Elliot became
the first American to literally have her name in lights. For decades, West
42nd Street, home of the woman-friendly Ziegfeld Follies, was Times
Square's vortex of theatrical energy; its ongoing life was both a medium and
a symbol of women's ascendancy. In one of the great scenes in *42nd Street*,
Ruby Keeler dances down this block on a taxi's roof. That woman mounted
on the cab, like the goddess on the prow of a ship, became an instant modern icon: The street was telling the world that women had arrived. It is one
of the sad ironies in New York's history that a block that had so grandly signified women's advance so soon became a scene of women's retreat. I think
similar things took place in cities all over America after World War Two;

masculinization was a classic symptom of what sociologists called "urban blight."[6] But in an environment already defined by its abundance of spectacles, the masculinization of the street took a weirdly spectacular form.

One way we can trace this sex change is by looking at pictures. Among the most revealing pictures are photographs of theaters. Starting in the 1940s, one of the classic visions of Times Square was a panoramic view of the line of theaters (eight or nine) on the north side of 42nd, between Seventh and Eighth. This row had always been very grand, and the theaters continued to look splendid even as the people in and around them turned increasingly sleazy. By the late 1960s, the ironic contrast between high lights and low life had become the typical way of seeing the Square. This polarity is a central theme in two of the great Times Square films, John Schlesinger's *Midnight Cowboy* (1969) and Martin Scorsese's *Taxi Driver* (1976); I discuss it in my chapter on Women. But for years before, you can see *Taxi Driver* coming, just by reading the movie titles along the street. Take this double feature from the late 1940s: *This Gun for Hire* and *Northwest Mounted Police* (photographer Rebecca Lepkoff).[7] Or this one: *Home of the Brave* and *Wild Bill Hickock* (Ted Croner).[8] From the early 1950s, *The Man Behind the Gun* and *Wings of the Hawk; The Racers* and *The Green Scarf* (William Klein).[9] Various 1950s and 1960s black-and-whites: *Bachelor Party* and *Bailout at 43000; The Shores of Tripoli* and *The Silent Raiders.*[10] As time goes by, the double features mutate into triple, and the titles grow more sexually explicit: *Golden Girls, Girls on Fire, Panty Raid; Lusty Princess, Secret Dreams, My Sex Rated Wife.*[11] When marquee photos are shot from street level, as they usually are, it is hard to get a perspective that displays more than one or two. Hence photos juxtapose titles that are complete and intelligible with others that are faded or fragmentary, to create totalities that are farcical or surreal. (My favorite fragment, drawn from Geoffrey O'Brien's *Times Square Story*, is the series of first words in an otherwise invisible triple feature: in descending order, "*Beast, Final, Sweet.*") These war, sex, thriller, and horror movies are not all, but overwhelmingly, "guy" films, addressed to men and boys who will see them with other men and boys. Uncounted thousands of films with titles like these, linked together in cheap double features and spread over a generation, add up to a campaign of "niche marketing" for a street where women will have no niche. Liz Phair, author of "Hello Sailor," had a word for a place like this: Her first album (1993), which we will talk about later, is called *Exile in Guyville.*[12]

What did 42nd Street's sex change do to its beat of life? One form of intercourse that became prominent on the street was "rough trade," that is, encounters between "queers," men who considered themselves homosexual, and "trade," men who did not. Sailors were leading candidates for "trade," along with taxi drivers and longshoremen. For queers, "rough trade" was a kind of life on the edge; not only could it end in danger, it seemed to seek it out. (This is one case where the metaphor "courting danger" is just right.) This style was nasty to women, menacing them on the street and gradually pushing them off. But it was at least as menacing to homosexuals of a different style, "fairies,"[13] who had been at home on the street in its theater and fashion heyday but who found themselves increasingly disrespected as the street decayed. They moved east, to the vicinity of Bryant Park, where they became characters in John Rechy's *City of Night,** and north, where they colonized sections of Broadway's great public restaurants. Saturdays in the early 1950s, my father put in half a day at his office on West 42nd Street. I would go downtown with him and read a book or look dreamily out the window while he sorted through label orders. Then he would take me to Lindy's, Toffinetti's, the Astor Bar. There I first saw fairies, many of whom he knew from the garment industry, where they were male models or low-level designers. He was happy to share their patter, which was mostly too fast and too encoded for me; but I was thrilled by their red and purple jackets, which prefigured the great flood of color in men's clothes that finally arrived in the late 1960s, the age of "flower power."

What I have called the Square's sex change subjected it to radical segmentation for the first time in its life. All this happened some years before the war. When the war came, and sailors poured off their ships *en masse*, it is very likely they went different ways. But I don't think the axis they split along was heterosexual versus homosexual. I think it was women that split them: A majority of men wanted to be with women, or to be near them; a minority of men adamantly did not. Think of the "New York, New York" song the sailors sing at the start of *On the Town*. If we focus on the line, "Manhattan women

---

*There, with varying degrees of irony, they referred to themselves as "graduates" of Times Square. John Rechy, *City of Night* (Grove Press, 1963), 34.

are dressed in silk and satin," and think of those sailors who wanted to drink those women in, we could imagine them heading for the bowtie, the USO, the "legitimate" theaters (whose "legitimacy" had a new meaning now), and the great open display spaces of Broadway. But there were other sailors who craved an all-male environment as ironclad as their ships—only darker and more dangerous, because it lacked a clear structure of authority—and we can be pretty sure they would have stuck close to 42nd Street. The sailors who are captured by Eisenstaedt, enjoying women on the open spaces of the Square's bowtie, were inhabiting a very different human space from the sailors just around the corner on the deuce.*[14]

Sailors and Democracy: The Tradition

When Eisenstaedt encountered his sailor and nurse, it was probably accidental, a thing of the moment—or in any case, because "August 15, 1945" was such a special day, a thing of the day. But Western culture inherits the idea that there is some special connection between sailors and democracy. This idea goes a long way back, back to ancient Athens and the first democratic *agora* in history. Sailors first come up sometime in the middle of the fifth century B.C., in a pamphlet about democratic Athens by a writer whom historians know only as "the Old Oligarch."[15] This Old Oligarch belongs to a class that he describes as "men of birth and quality," "the cream of society"; he is frank in his disdain for "the common people and the poorer classes." And yet, against the grain of his class identity, he finds himself apologizing for a polis where these lower classes have substantial power. What entitles them to dominate the city, it turns out, is their virtue as sailors:

> It is only just that the poorer classes and the common people of Athens
> should be better off than the men of birth and wealth, seeing that it is

---

*Jack Kerouac, in *On the Road* (1955; Penguin, 1976), 130ff., explores the phenomenology of sexual segregation on the fringes of the Square: "Ritzy's Bar is the hoodlum bar of the streets around Times Square; it changes names every year. You walk in there and *you don't see a single girl* [my emphasis], not even in the booths, just a great mob of young men dressed in all varieties of hoodlum cloth, from red shirts to zoot suits. It is also the hustlers' bar—the boys who make a living among the sad old homos of the Eighth Avenue night. . . . All kinds of evil plans are hatched in Ritzy's Bar—you can sense it in the air—and all kinds of mad sexual routines are initiated to go with them."

the people who man the fleet, and who have brought the city her power. The steersman, the boatswain, the lieutenant, the lookout man at the prow, the shipwright—these are the people who supply the city with power, rather than her heavy infantry [led by] men of birth and quality.

According to the pamphlet, the fifth-century navy is organized more democratically than the army; it gives ordinary people far more of a chance to display their talent and energy, to take initiative, and to work together. The valor of the *demos* in wartime proves that it is competent to run the city in peacetime. These lower-class sailors have limited aspirations: they want to be something, not to be everything. They want "offices of the state . . . thrown open to everyone"; they say "that the right of speech should belong to anyone who likes, without exception." In other words, they want to run for offices, not to seize them; what they want most of all is the right to *talk*.

People who have lived their lives in modern democracies take talking for granted, and have a hard time imagining that it should be a problem; but if we look around the world, or back in world history, we can see how much of a problem it is. There is one nodal point in early Greek culture, which any fifth-century Athenian would have known, where the warlords crush the people's desire to talk. In Book Two of the *Iliad* (229–320),[16] Thersites and other unnamed "common soldiers" assert the futility of the Greek army's decade-long siege of Troy and clamor for the Greeks to go home. Now, many of the lords have been saying this themselves—that is one of the *Iliad*'s basic ironies—but they've been saying it privately to each other. When a "common soldier" says what they have been saying, Odysseus (here as elsewhere) acts as their enforcer and crushes him: Odysseus knocks him off his feet, and cracks his scepter across his back till he bleeds. As he bleeds the crowd laughs, "good hearty laughter breaking over Thersites' head . . ."(317). And that is the last we hear from the people for the next few centuries. But when Greek democracy develops several centuries later, a democracy of sailors, the people's right to talk is at its core. In a democratic assembly, all citizens enjoy the right to speak, and all have the duty to listen. In Athens' *agora*, talk never stops, you don't have to be a citizen, and, as Socrates says again and again, talk is free.

The sailor is a perfect "new man" for democracy. Like classic or modern heroes, he is physically strong and brave under fire. But unlike them, he presents himself in a group—most often with his male "buddies"—and he is at home there. At the same time, he is delighted to be on land—which, after all, is where we see and meet him—and to be here with us. Part of the romance of sailors, in both ancient and modern times, is a sense of their openness: They are at home with the openness of the sea, which may be thrilling but is also frightening to ordinary civilians; but they are also seen as being open, in the sense of receptive, to an enormous range of places where their ships have landed, or may land next year, a far wider range of places than most civilians will ever see, and (it is assumed by civilians) a far greater diversity of human experiences. On land they are happiest in open spaces like the *agora* (which Athens' old aristocrats and traditionalists sought in vain to close down). All this means that they are open to being here now, and open to being with *us*. The sailor's aura is a primal openness of being.

We don't know very much about that Old Oligarch; historians still argue about who he was. However, if we keep our larger theme in focus—"Sailors in the Square"—we can see plenty that he shares with Alfred Eisenstaedt, and with Herman Melville, and with Jane Austen, and with Sergei Eisenstein, and with Jerome Robbins, and with Paul Cadmus, and with Gene Kelly, and with Paul Goodman, and with Betty Comden and Adolph Green, and with Liz Phair, and with the creators of *The Simpsons* and the creators of *Sex and the City* and with many more people we will be discussing here, and many others I've forgotten or never known. The big thing they share is the romance of sailors. Working in many different media and genres, they have elaborated this romance in fascinating ways.

In modern times, sailors were among the first to assert themselves as democratic men and citizens. In England in 1797, there were great naval mutinies, and for a month the North Sea Fleet blockaded the Thames. The sailors' uprising was crushed by the British Army, but as "The Great Mutiny" it achieved an afterlife in popular imagination and agitation for democracy*—and equally in the ruling classes' anti-democratic fears. In Herman Melville's *Billy Budd*, set in 1797, just after the Great Mutiny, the

---

*It also survived in a nineteenth-century British sea chantey that is a small masterpiece of irony: "King Louis was the King of France before the Revolution / Way, haul away, haul away Joe. / And then he had his head chopped off, which spoiled his constitution. / Way, haul away, haul away Joe . . ."

hero, "the handsome sailor," is kidnapped by the Royal Navy from the merchant ship *Rights-of-Man*. He waves good-bye to his shipmates, "And good-bye to you too, old *Rights-of-Man*." After much plot, his captors kill him; the captain claims that the ambience of the Great Mutiny makes his execution necessary. Sailors stand for human rights and against slavery in Melville's *Benito Cereno* (1856), written just before our Civil War.

In nations like czarist Russia, where there are no traditions of citizenship, no rights to say good-bye to, the only way to be democratic is to be revolutionary. And so Russian sailors were, in 1905, in the mutiny of the crew of the battleship *Potemkin*, and in 1917, when the crew of the cruiser *Aurora* on the Neva seized the Winter Palace. The sailors were heroic in establishing the USSR, but in 1921, from their naval base at Kronstadt on the Gulf of Finland, they revolted against the new Soviet order that they had created, in the name of the radical democratic values that they had always believed in: freedom of speech, press, and assembly, free elections, due process of law. Thousands of them got massacred by the Red Army, and the words "Kronstadt" and "sailors" took on new meanings, as symbols of the tragedy of the Russian Revolution.*

"Close! stand close to me, Starbuck," implores Captain Ahab, "and let me look into a human eye."† The sailor Starbuck signifies "a human eye," a symbol of normal human life; this kind of life is infinitely beyond the

---

*The tragic story of the sailors of 1921 is told best by the great Victor Serge in his *Memoirs of a Revolutionary*, translated and edited by Peter Sedgwick (Oxford, 1963, 1975), 122ff. Serge, the one man in the revolutionary generation who was venerated by everybody, encountered Lenin on the street in Petrograd even as the sailors were being killed by the Red Army, and denounced him for bringing "Thermidor" on the revolution—which means, in Marxist jargon, destroying it. Lenin's tragic response actually conceded his point: "This is Thermidor. But we won't let ourselves be guillotined. We'll make our own Thermidor." (131) Post-Stalin American leftists were very good on the tragic meaning of Kronstadt for the USSR: Robert Daniels, *The Conscience of the Revolution: Communist Opposition in Soviet Russia* (Harvard, 1960), 143ff., and Paul Avrich, *The Russian Anarchists* (Princeton, 1967), 228ff. Gary Shteyngart's novel *The Russian Debutante's Handbook* (Riverhead, 2002) contains a poignant portrait of post-Soviet youth fighting these foundational battles again among themselves.

In Germany, too, sailors were a democratic vanguard. The mutiny of the People's Naval Division in October 1918 led directly to the Kaiser's abdication and the Weimar Republic's birth. But there, too, sailors were massacred by the army. See the novelistic account by Alfred Doeblin, *Karl and Rosa*, and recent discussion by Henry Pachter, *Modern Germany: A Social, Cultural and Political History* (Westview, 1978), 88ff., and by Otto Friedrich, *Before the Deluge: A Portrait of Berlin in the 1920s* (Avon, 1972).

†*Moby-Dick*, chapter 132. This is close to the end, when Starbuck implores Ahab to turn around and go back to land, wives, and children. Starbuck appears as an incarnation of "normal" human life. Ahab admires his humanity but cannot share it, and drags them all to their death.

reach of the charismatic but fatally twisted Captain Ahab, who drags down a whole shipful of sailors to death with him.* Wherever he is, the sailor knows how to cooperate and work with others, how to be *nice*.[17] In Times Square, an aura of "niceness" is something he shares with the nurse he embraces. (Soldiers don't have this aura.) He wants power sometimes, but he wants to share it, to talk, to hang out and interact with people. As he laughs, sings in the city streets, dances all night, he fills romantic observers (like Simone de Beauvoir) with a vision of freedom, freedom that he seems to embody in himself, but also that we hope he will spread throughout the world.[18] He is inherently ambiguous and vulnerable in his relation to authority; he is generally, and unthinkingly, an agent of authority, but sometimes, as on the Thames in 1797, a subverter of authority, and sometimes, in *Billy Budd*, or at Kronstadt in 1921–22, a victim of those who "would murder sailors to defend authority." Those Russian sailors, in a remarkably short time, went through a whole political spectrum, from agents of an old authority to destroyers of that authority to creators of a new authority to victims of the new political world they had made.[19]

Cadmus and Goodman: The Twentieth-Century Sailor Romance

Even when he is being killed, a sailor never stops being the object of civilians' romance. I will explore some of the romantic encounters between sailors and the civilians of both sexes who yearn for them and seek them out. "Many men and women ashore," Paul Goodman says, "cannot keep away from the relieving presence of sailors."[20] In fact, there are strong imaginative works in many genres—in painting, in photography, in literature, in modern dance, musical theater, cinema, popular music, television—that focus on the romance of sailors and their brief encounters with civilians around Times Square. If we look at these works and look into them, it should help us to flesh out a context for Eisenstaedt's primal couple, and to grasp the sources of their aura. The context I want to excavate existed for that sailor

---

*I have been unable either to verify or to refute the story that Melville's sane and sensitive first mate is the primal ancestor of the Starbuck's Coffee chain, chosen by longtime CEO David Schultz as a utopian symbol. I hope this story is true, as it is the basis of much of my affection for Starbuck's stores.

and that nurse and that photographer and that crowd and that space and that city half a century ago. So many things have changed, yet the context and the aura are still there for us. The same American culture has formed us all.

A crucial force in that culture, which I want just to note here, but which will come up later on, is the Popular Front. This was a political and cultural idea proclaimed by the Comintern in 1935. The idea was that all "democratic forces" would come together to keep Fascism and Nazism from taking over the world, and that it was an urgent duty of Communists to support these democratic forces, whether they were Communistic or not. This idea defined Communist cultural policy till the start of the Cold War. In the USA, it liberated Communists to be inclusive and creative, far more than they ever had been or would be again. We can thank the Popular Front for the CIO, the TVA, municipal rent control, *The Grapes of Wrath, Let Us Now Praise Famous Men, Call It Sleep,* "Strange Fruit," *Appalachian Spring, Naked City.* The Front animated American culture throughout World War Two. Although conceived by servants of Stalin, it has probably done far more for the USA than it ever did for the USSR. And it gave our sailor in the Square a sense of who he was.

The first work I want to talk about is Paul Cadmus's 1934 oil painting, "The Fleet's In!" This large not-quite-mural-size painting portrays a crowd of sailors, probably on shore leave. The painting's genre is the *fin-de-siècle* Paris "Sunday in the Park" celebrations of public leisure by Seurat, Renoir, *et al.,* as adapted by various Americans in the twentieth century. The details of landscape and stonework here suggest lower Riverside Park in early spring, but Cadmus gives his picture a density and sexual heat that are more like a rush-hour subway car in high August. His title, with its exclamation point, sounds like a phone call from one sailor groupie (an anachronistic word, snatched from the 1960s rock world) to another: It's like "They won't be in for long, we've got to get down and hang with them *now!*" Cadmus's sailor groupies of both sexes are preening and displaying themselves for the sailors; the sailors are doing the same for them. Except for the lady with the dog at the far left, everybody appears to be looking for a pickup. Cadmus pumps up the heat by creating a sort of sexual equator of multicolored, sculpturally molded, tightly wrapped buttocks and crotches, naval and civilian, male and female, arrayed across the picture plane. The women's dresses cling to their bodies and highlight their curves like silk lingerie. But the sailors' uniforms, too, tight and clinging in some places, loose and flowing in others, are just right for sexual display. The model of masculinity displayed by these uniforms is light, unencumbered, androgynous, alluring to both sexes.* All the civilians here are women, except for the blond man on the left, who displays all the marks of a "fairy": tweezed eyebrows, wavy hair (hair to die for if it were real), red tie, ironical smile.

Cadmus deploys his men and women to convey some of the comedy of shore-leave courtship. The sailor in the cap has just accepted the fairy's cigarette, but the half-passed-out sailor lying between them is not so much hugging his thighs as fending them off, as if to say, "Stay away, this man is mine." At the center, the girl in yellow splits herself in two, making a deft movement that at once pushes her man away and leans in toward him. The two sailors in contrasting uniforms at the right seem to be performing a sort of vaudeville shtick for the three women (prefiguring *Fancy Free* and *On the Town*), who are looking away from them, but, if we look closely, are about to crash into them. At the far right, we see two women who seem to have passed beyond comedy and courtship; or rather we don't see them, we only see their legs and buttocks, as they bend over, apparently to pleasure another sailor who is totally invisible, except (if we look through the other sailors' legs) for a streak of white. What's special about this picture is the throb and flow of sexual energy that envelops the whole crowd. The old lady with the dog seems to look back on it nostalgically, like Picasso in his last paintings, even as, like a Renaissance or Baroque memento mori, she knows where it all will end. The aura of Cadmus's sailors is that, although (or is it because?) they are simple kids, they have an uncanny capacity to ignite-free-floating sexual feeling in everybody.

---

*The "middy blouse," based on a midshipman's uniform, became a staple of fashion for boys shortly after the Civil War, and for girls in the 1880s. *Fairchild Dictionary of Fashion*, 2nd edition (Fairchild, 1988), 475. For girls, the middy both required and proclaimed *chutzpah*: "The wearer of this garment can do anything boys can do." After the Great War, in the Jazz Age, the middy was adapted by grown-up women whose assertiveness took on a sexual force (Anne Hollander, phone conversation, October 9, 2003). "The Fleet's In!," made a decade later, affirmed this sexuality and restored it to its primal, nautical source. At this historical moment Hollywood, too, was discovering the eroticism of sailors: the Astaire-Rogers *Follow the Fleet* (1936) is the first great "sailor musical." *On the Town* (1944, 1949) marks the pinnacle of this adult genre. Kay Thompson fights to reclaim the romance for golden childhood in her *Eloise* books (1955ff.), whose six-year-old middy-clad heroine glides and hurtles through the Plaza Hotel on roller skates.

"The Fleet's In!" has a fascinating, scandalous history. It was made in 1934, at a time when America was at peace but in the midst of the world-wide Great Depression. Cadmus, like most of America's great artists in the years of the New Deal, was working for the federal government, "on the projects," under a commission from the PWPA, the Public Works Progress Administration, one of the great New Deal Federal agencies. His painting was meant to be shown at the Corcoran Art Gallery in Washington as part of an exhibit of WPA art. But Admiral Hugh Rodman saw it at a preview and made an angry call to Henry Latrobe Roosevelt, Secretary of the Navy (and cousin of the President), denouncing it as a portrait of "a disgraceful, drunken, sordid, disreputable brawl." The Secretary may have been as puzzled by this description of the painting as we are likely to be. Nevertheless, he personally removed it from the show—and took it home with him, where he shared it with his invited guests. Art historian Richard Meyer describes what happened next:

> The censorship of "The Fleet's In!" provoked a media sensation, with scores of newspapers and national news magazines running articles and editorials on the episode, many accompanied by reproductions of the work. While the Navy had successfully removed "The Fleet's In!" from the exhibition, it had unwittingly insinuated the picture into the far more powerful flow of mass culture.[21]

Because Cadmus painted his picture in what Walter Benjamin would call "The Age of Mechanical Reproduction," it could be and it was transmitted everywhere.[22] Meyer quotes the July 1937 *Esquire:* "For every individual who might have seen the original at the Corcoran, at least one thousand saw it in black and white reproduction." Overnight Cadmus became the most famous painter in America. His sailors and the crowd around them soon found a place in every port; though many people, like that admiral, couldn't deal with the heat, and put him in their psychic brig.

After "The Fleet's In!" was lifted from public view, it became one of Washington's buried treasures. First, after Navy Secretary Roosevelt confiscated it, he kept it secretly in his house. Then, as he lay dying in 1936, he transferred it to the Alibi Club, a highly exclusive WASP gentleman's club, membership limited to fifty. The name sounds like a storyboard from *The*

Big Sleep or *Some Like It Hot*, but it really did exist, and apparently still does. (George Bush, Sr., was a member throughout his presidency.) The Alibi Club held on to "The Fleet's In!" for the next forty-four years, and gave it up only after the Navy claimed possession and began legal proceedings. This rich subplot gives that classic metaphor "the closet" new resonance. When will some enterprising historian of culture open the closet on the Alibi Club? Today the painting sits in the Navy Museum in the Washington Navy Yard, out of the way but still open to the public. I saw it in the 1980s, on loan to the Whitney; it was still hot.

Paul Goodman's story "Sailors" was written shortly before Pearl Harbor but not published for another four decades. "At the great *Royal Palms*," he writes,

> How vivid are . . . the blue and white uniforms of the boys around the bar! On the walls are painted the huge orange Polynesians in the manner of Gauguin.[23]

Goodman places the romance of sailors in the context of Western romances of "the other." Some of these, like Gauguin's, have inspired luminous art. "Sailors" lays out the basic structure of sailor romance: a quest by a group of three buddies, two older (George, Bat) and one younger (Kenny), who are on shore leave for a day and a night in New York, but who must get back to their ship by dawn. It is written from the perspective of a sailor groupie: a middle-aged man who is clearly "out" but who can see the pathos of his craving. He points out the dissonance between the needs of middle age and those of youth; between men who are "queer," who bond only with other males, and boys who are "trade," and who may pragmatically "ask for money because they have a date tomorrow night"; between the sailors' desire for individual adventure and the intense, claustrophobic solidarity of the buddy system. In the nicest part of the story, the older guys arrange for the younger one to get laid for the first time. When somebody asks why they don't go off and have fun on their own, the answer is that "they're sittin' there because they're froze together, see?"

The last scene, set on the night bus to the Navy Yard, isn't so nice. Harry, a middle-aged predator, tries to hustle George. He offers "Anything you say, sailor! Anything you say!" George's response is short and poignant: He says, "Don't call me sailor!" He is saying that anyone who wants to get close to him will have to recognize him as an individual and call him by his name. Harry moves away: he'd rather forget the whole thing. But he's back for the finale, like Eminem's Slim Shady or Humbert Humbert's "Grim McFate." You can see him smile:

"Cigarettes, sailors?" says Harry.

And that's all, folks: a short turn into a long night. Goodman keeps the sailor romance alive by upbraiding civilians who "can't keep away from sailors" but can't seem to treat them as human beings.

Primal Street Moves: Robbins's Fancy Free

In real time, the moment of "Sailors," like the moment of *From Here to Eternity*, is two minutes before Pearl Harbor. When Jerome Robbins picked up the same matrix two years later, the Navy had been through dreadful massacres, comeback victories, tremendous upheavals. In World War Two jargon, it had been "to hell and back." Robbins's dance, *Fancy Free*, opened in April 1944, with his choreography and his performance as a sailor, and a buoyant, jazzy score by Leonard Bernstein. It reproduced Goodman's plot: a trio of sailors on shore leave in New York, looking for pleasure and adventure, forced to get back to their ship by dawn. What is special about this ballet, what made its first-night audience leap to its feet and shout, is its vision of sailors *on the street*. Robbins may be the first choreographer to capture the incandescence of "street moves." The metropolitan street is one of the basic modern environments, and one of the central scenes in all media of modern culture. Robbins can stand in the company of Baudelaire and Dostoevsky, of Henri Cartier-Bresson and Jane Jacobs, people who have *engaged* the modern street, explored it with an absolute seriousness, and taught us most about what it means to be there.[24] And the street that engaged him most intensely then, he told Tobi Tobias in 1980, was Times Square:

I did it during the war years, when the kinds of people I described in the ballet were all around us. At the time we were dancing at the old

Metropolitan Opera House, situated at 39th-40th Street and Broadway. Times Square was there, and that was all bubbling out over us. We saw it everywhere we looked—the kind of incident, the kind of people, the kind of kids who were dancing then.[25]

You could even say that Times Square is one of the characters in his dance. He is fascinated by what I called "the Eisenstaedt moment": the sailor and the civilian, a man and a woman—or is it a boy and a girl?—strangers to each other but at home in each other's arms, cheered on by the Square's big signs and neon lights. His dance explores the BOND: the sexual and emotional bonds that ordinary people can form with each other, or at least can dream of forming, in a spectacular space like Times Square, and the personal and social forces that can break their bonds down.

When I started looking into *Fancy Free*, I found it was hard to see. There does not seem to be any complete version on film or tape available to the public today. I have seen revivals, in New York and London, but although they contained some terrific dancing, the spirit seemed missing. However, the Lincoln Center Library for the Performing Arts has various rehearsal prints of the original, and in the summer of 2003 I watched as many as I could. Some of the prints in the catalogue were missing, others damaged. The available prints are fragmentary (none seemed to contain the entire ballet), grainy and shadowy, usually silent, shot from different and often oblique angles, and projected in strange light and weird perspectives that suggest German Expressionist silent cinema in its prime.* They have the rough texture but also the raw thrill of great artists' sketches, bootleg record albums, unreleased director's cuts. Their greatest thrill is a sense of absolute seriousness: If you look closely, you can see how the most apparently casual moves are expressions of complex ideas.

Robbins's version of the Eisenstaedt moment is what I have been calling a "primal scene": a magic moment of fusion, prefaced and followed by complexity, conflict, and confusion. He thought the Square had a unique capacity to incubate such scenes. So many ordinary people came here, partly to watch professionals in many genres perform, but also to strut their own stuff and perform for each other and watch each other under the lights. Robbins is intensely responsive to this place and what it does to people. He grasps the fluid energy and dynamics of ordinary people's performances, above all the way they move. I first saw this in 1959, in *West Side Story*, where Robbins puts his moves on two warring gangs, the Jets and the Sharks, and he plunges and hurtles them through Hell's Kitchen's disintegrating streets. But he was there years before: He made the street move in his vision of sailors and girls in the blacked-out but bebopping Times Square in the middle of the war.

One central theme of the Popular Front was that ordinary people, in their vernacular everyday lives, display fabulous unnoticed resources. Three sailors enter a bar, and suddenly explode with exuberant physical energy: First they do stretches and cartwheels together, as if in formation; then, one after the other, each separately pirouettes and unrolls an elaborate series of

---

*Lincoln Center Library also possesses 1944 tapes that are "Not for Public Viewing" and accessible only to people who are granted clearance from the Robbins Trust. In his 1980 interview with Tobi Tobias, Robbins alludes to "the film we have of the original cast," but this film, if still extant, is "Not for Public Viewing" and not even in the catalogue. If Robbins's friends want to celebrate his memory rather than tarnish it, they should end their "clearance" policy, with its echoes of McCarthyism and of the most shameful moment in Robbins's life, his 1953 appearance as a "friendly witness" before HUAC.

ballet moves. It's all so fast, I wondered if the tape I was watching in the Lincoln Center library was running right. The librarians assured me that was Robbins's tempo: fast. John Martin, reviewing the original in *The New York Times*, said "the kids who dance in it dance like mad."[26] These sailors look so thrilled with their bodies and themselves, it's as if they've just got out of Plato's Cave. Tocqueville, in the early nineteenth century, didn't think democracy could engender any great art.[27] He was spectacularly wrong, but much great American art, from Central Park to Mark Twain to jazz to Abstract Expressionism to the Broadway musical to rock and roll, has developed in a cultural tradition that "takes care to hide the care [it] has taken,"* and works to make the most complex, intricate, disciplined, profound work look casual, spontaneous, growing wild, no big deal. (Americans are often fooled; foreigners appreciate what's there.)

After a while the sailors' fabulous exuberance runs down. They can barely stand up, but still they need to compete. In what? They get the idea of a contest in spitting chewing gum: Who can spit his gum farthest? It is as if they have all been magically reduced to age ten. But they can't sustain themselves as ten-year-olds for long. Soon they don't have to. The First Girl, Muriel Bentley, slinks and struts onstage. She fuses an Edith Piaf *gamine* with a bohemian New York Jewish homegirl dressed up like Betty Boop. First she slips and slides and undulates and wraps herself around the sailors; then she sharpens her moves and thrusts her pelvis into one guy, then another. She is so incandescent, even on a silent tape you feel you can hear the bodies banging together. I know what I saw was rehearsal tapes; did they really perform it so "raw" in public in 1944? Think of the Living Theatre in the 1960s, or the Judson in the 1970s, and then project their raucous performance styles back into the old Metropolitan Opera House. Hard to imagine, isn't it? But remember Robbins's vision of "the kids" around Times Square in the midst of the war: *Fancy Free* was meant not only to describe that experience, but to be part of it. Those old tapes transmit an aura of collective discovery and invention, kids walking the edge, seeing how far they can go, feeling the thrill of going too far.

*Coined by Jean-Jacques Rousseau in his romantic novel *La Nouvelle Héloïse* (1761), quoted and discussed in my book *The Politics of Authenticity*, 252 and throughout Part IV. The idea develops first in Enlightenment and Romantic Europe, but it takes on more weight in America, a democratic country with not much of an artistic past.

In the scenario Robbins wrote before the dance began, he vividly described the woman and the human encounter he wanted:

The music breaks out into loud, rhythmic boogie-woogie, and a terrific-looking girl walks by. She wears a tight-fitting blouse and skirt, high patent leather shoes, and carries a red handbag. The girl knows she is being watched; she smiles, and by her walk suggests all the things the sailors are imagining. The sailors are struck numb; standing close together they move as one body—bending so far forward to watch the girl, they almost fall on their faces.

The girl pretends that she hasn't seen them, which sends the boys into action. Suddenly they are three different individuals, each trying to interest the girl in his own special way.[28]

It happened again a few minutes later when the Second Girl appears. She has lighter skin and hair that is red or strawberry blond; she is the "light woman" contrasted with the First Girl's "dark woman." The light woman is softer, gentler, more modest in her body language—at first. But she gets hotter as she dances (and dances with Robbins). After a few minutes they're all excited, they all like one another; but there are five of them, one too many or one too few. What now? Another contest, this time a dance contest, with the women as judges. The good news is, the men will get to perform all their most dazzling moves. The bad news is, the point of their great performance will be to knock one of them out of the box.

I have seen many revivals of *Fancy Free* through the years, and I find there is a tendency to play it "lite." "The boys" don't break out of their street-corner narcissism. Their dancing, while physically splendid, and sometimes also funny, doesn't transcend the emotional level of their spitting gum. They don't bond with the girls, and they don't approach any emotion that even remotely resembles adult love. But I have seen those first rehearsal films, and seen many old photos, and I want to testify that Robbins, from the very first, knew how to bring boys and girls together. Here is Janet Reed, his main partner in the original, in a nostalgic retrospect thirty-six years later:

It was World War Two. The whole attitude of young people was very disoriented. And we were living right in the middle of it. On tour, the

Ballet Theatre cars would be hooked up to the troop cars. . . . All these soldiers and sailors and ballet dancers, in strange places and different towns. We were uprooted, and although we had a very carefree attitude, we were also very tentative about relationships. . . . We were all so very young . . . innocent and rather lonely . . . wanting so much to be close to one another but knowing it couldn't last. So there was this constant reaching out, but knowing it was only temporary. Can you see that is the choreography, in the *pas de deux*?

Yes, we can. Robbins always had this knack for creating instant harmony. Anyone who has seen *West Side Story* or *Fiddler on the Roof* can recall it. I'm sure it was one reason why his first-night audience stood up and screamed. And why, in all his dances, it's so sad when love falls apart.

Many spectators and critics, both then and now, have thought the girls were prostitutes, marketing themselves as alluring commodities. This is a big mistake: Bentley and Reed are playing girls who are "fast" but respectable—that great lost word "fast"—and that is the source of their allure and their pathos. Robbins's girls are characterized with a special tenderness. Maybe he imagined them as products of big, warm, enveloping families like his own, families that would have strokes and heart attacks if they knew where their children were. These girls are dressed respectably as they leave their parents' apartments, but they carry their fast clothes along with them, and change once they are out of range. The aura of the sailors and the aura of the Square, in Robbins's special mix, drives respectable girls to take a walk on the wild side and act like sluts—"act" not only in the sense of behave, but in the sense of perform, put on bravura performances, attune their bodies to a responsive audience, rejoice in being seen and being watched.

Fancy Free is at once a celebration of freedom and a reflection on its human costs. For his sailors, the primary threat is individuation, a form of self-development that carries you away from your buddies, from your ship, from the Navy, from all the institutional anchors of your life, and leaves you in a void where some golden girl may wrap herself around you (as Reed wraps herself around Robbins), or may dump you on a dark street alone. The peril for Robbins's girls is a free-floating sexual frenzy that carries you away, erases your sense of self, transcends any object, overrides your memories of your family and friends, wipes out your defenses, leaves you prey to being played with—for who knows what, by who knows who?—and crumpled up and thrown away. Robbins makes us feel the thrill of defining your own space in the world, the ecstasy of discovering and merging with a soul mate who was a stranger a minute ago, the way the self can soar and then, suddenly, crash.

There are two bad moments when suddenly everything seems about to crash. The first comes early, when Muriel Bentley is the only woman around. The sailors imitate her walk and laugh at her, but she laughs with them, too, and everybody seems comfortable. But then suddenly the tone changes, the boys grab her red purse and throw it around, then they pick *her* up and throw her; they fight over her, she escapes, but "the battle has left one sailor lying in the street" (139). In an instant, playful homage to a woman can turn into violence against her; then their violence recoils against them. It's easy to imagine lawyers and judges zeroing in on that red purse: "She was asking for it."

The second moment comes after the second dance contest: The three men have done their turns, but the two women judges, who are supposed to eliminate one man and make the sexes symmetrical, are unable to deliver a judgment. Suddenly the three buddies start "to tear each other apart. The girls cringe against the bar, thinking this can't be serious. . . . As the battle goes on in earnest, they decide to get out of there fast. The sailors don't notice that the girls have walked out on them." When they notice after a while, they rush out in the street together, but find nobody. "They look at each other with amused disgust, straighten out their uniforms, nurse their aches and pains, and relax again" (141). Just another night in Times Square! Robbins is preparing us for a comic ending, but he has brought us an ominous middle. First, the Navy's beloved buddy system collapses into a state of war. Then, the sailors get so absorbed in their fight that they don't even notice when the women for whom they are fighting disappear. Robbins's script makes a rare editorial comment—and also a theoretical one: "The cycle goes on." After a night in the state of being "fancy free," it looks as though everybody, sailors and civilians, men and women, will be relieved when "the fleet's out" again. The women are right to run.

Why can't the women make a decision, eliminate one man, and resolve the situation? I think there is a conflict in Robbins's own vision that he can't resolve. He believes in democracy, for which our sailors in 1944 are fighting. He also believes in human rights and the primacy of the individual. His strength as a choreographer lies in his feeling for everyday people and his power to show the lyrical beauty and grace in their lives. Don't all these people have the right to love? Is there sufficient reason to take anybody out of the ball game? But if we leave everybody in, is there enough free love to go around?

Fancy Free explores many of the cracks and flaws in our ways of seeking pleasure and love and each other. The narrative is tawdry and unpromising in many of the same ways as in "Sailors." More than once Robbins brings us close to a crash. And yet this dance doesn't *feel* bad. If you sit there and let it wash over you, you are likely to remember the moments when people dance as if they were flying, strangers in the night click with each other, pleasure and energy and love light up the stage like Times Square signs.

In Janet Reed's 1980 recollection, one surprising note is her way of identifying with GIs: "All these soldiers and sailors and ballet dancers, in strange places and different towns." The power of empathy was a key to this ensemble's triumph. It was also a key to America's success in "the Good War" that raged while they danced. These dancers' memories of their young and unformed selves have the poignancy of the most soulful memoirs of that war. The company feels like a sort of lost platoon in the wilderness. Its members remember how they were kids ("We were all so very young"),[29] how they felt lonely ("uprooted," "disoriented"), and how they hurt each other, but also how they reached out and came close and danced like mad together and made things happen that hadn't happened before. Somehow this happy few, this band of brothers and sisters, in freezing halls and narrow beds, rebuilt Times Square. Where did all their solidarity and brilliance come from? Thirty-six years later, Robbins and the dancers, like a general and his old soldiers looking back on a great campaign of their youth, share a sense of the uncanny. It seems even more uncanny to us, another generation later, as we squint our eyes to make out their fever pitch and intimate harmony on old, cracked, disintegrating tape.

One person who deserves recognition in Robbins's story, especially because of our focus on the street, is Madeleine Lee Gilford. Gilford, then Lee, was a young actress and a Communist Party organizer during World War Two. She took pride (and still does) in her ability "to tear up any dance floor." Robbins saw her do this at a Party benefit in 1943, and introduced himself. He said he was doing "a ballet with three sailors," and asked her if she would teach him some "street dances" that he could use. She did; he used the Lindy and other street dances brilliantly in *Fancy Free*. They then had what she called "a very serious flirtation." She helped initiate him into the Party, which he formally joined just after *Fancy Free*'s opening in April 1944.[30] Her reward, she said was to be "named" by him, along with seven strangers, a decade later. By the 1950s she was married to the actor Jack Gilford (*d.* 1990). After Robbins's testimony, both were blacklisted. But they survived, played Off-Broadway theaters (a medium that developed during the blacklist years), tent shows, and Catskill resorts, and lived through it.[31] Half a century later, she is philosophical about it: "*Look, I got named by a genius.* My husband [Gilford] never found out who named him."[32]

Fancy Free is short, but rich in "Eisenstaedt moments," spectacles of sailor boys and girls finding each other, banging their bodies together under the BOND sign. For Robbins in 1944, as for Eisenstaedt a year later, Times Square symbolizes New York, and New York symbolizes America: In the war's last year, the spectacular public space proclaims the meaning of the city, and the city discloses the truth of the country. Both artists, children of the Popular Front, identify with America's power, which in 1944–45 is helping to destroy a power far more evil. (Since both are Jews, and one a Jewish refugee, American power is literally saving their lives.) They rejoice in America's overflowing sexual energy, democratically open to all, a fusion of many ethnicities, light and dark alike; both see it as a crucial force in America's victory. But with Jerome Robbins running the lights and signs, the human bond is more complex and weirder; the play of light over bodies and souls affords plenty of time in the dark. Robbins and his dancers show how much of the thrill of sex lies in its openness, its public and performative character, its capacity to open people up and propel them into new space. But all these new sensations open new channels of conflict and danger, private and public, between people and inside them. Robbins floods his Times Square with the spectacular light of new experience, but also makes us see how perilously volatile that light is bound to be. Those of us who have seen his new light can never feel free from fear of blackout.

Ironically, Robbins's most ardent tribute to the Popular Front comes in the midst of his own blackout. In May 1953 he "caved" to HUAC, named several names (including Gilford's)—they were all far less prominent than he, and he wrecked their lives—and testified that he now rejected Communism in favor of "Americanism." It is grueling to read this testimony, to see him fighting to erase his own inner contradictions, to be anchored in the love of an inquisitorial Big Brother; those of us who love his work can thank God he failed. We are lucky he never figured out how to delete his love for the Popular Front. He said it had made him proud to be a Communist, and he praised Earl Browder, who had been the leader of the CPUSA during the Front and during the war, but was denounced by Stalin and expelled from the Party once the Cold War began. The Committee, of course, hadn't the least idea what he was talking about and didn't care.

Robbins never tried to justify himself *à la* Elia Kazan, and he seems to have carried plenty of regret, torment, and guilt to the grave.* While his grave is still fresh, and while we are soaked in historical irony, I would like to nominate him as the great Communist choreographer. He uses moving human bodies to create great narratives of world-historical change. In his dances, class and ethnic tensions are always clearly marked. His work bears the structural irony that people move in relation to their ideas, to their

---

*See *Dance with Demons*, 198–210, 497–505, etc.; Deborah Jowitt, *Jerome Robbins: His Life, His Theatre, His Dance* (Simon & Schuster, 2004), 228–31, etc. (Alas, Jowitt's monumental book came out too late for me to use it properly.) Victor Navasky discusses Robbins persistently in his classic *Naming Names* (1980; Penguin, 1981). For the testimony, see Eric Bentley, ed., *Thirty Years of Treason: Excerpts from Hearings Before HUAC* (1971; New Press, 2001), 625–34. For a shorter, slightly different version, see Bentley, ed., *Are You Now or Have You Ever Been* (Harper Colophon, 1972), 102–5. Both Lawrence and Jowitt interview many people whom Robbins's testimony directly or indirectly harmed. It is striking to note his victims' compassion for him and the complex irony of their perspectives. Navasky shows how many victims of McCarthyism thought and talked this way.

   Speaking of irony, Robbins's vicious behavior toward his dancers earned him the title "the Stalin of dance." Both biographies are full of horror stories from every stage of his career. When Muriel Bentley, First Girl in *Fancy Free*, talks to Tobias about Robbins and herself, she sounds amazingly like a Stalin-era Communist, using the Party formula (which actually goes back to Napoleon) that "you can't make an omelette without breaking eggs." She offers herself up as a broken egg, but celebrates the glory of the omelette, and even insists that in breaking her he made her whole. (These metaphors and emotions have always been part of dance, but Robbins may have taken them to new depths.)

   Robbins's Stalinesque behavior reached a thaw only in the 1990s, the first post-Soviet decade and the last years of his life. In workshops he gave then, he met a generation of young dancers who had no memories of the Cold War, and who could not only venerate his genius but give him something like unconditional love. (Emily Coates, phone conversation, August 22, 2003.)

   It is fascinating to see Arthur Miller, testifying before HUAC in 1956, offer an analysis of Communism and its deterioration from the Popular Front to the Cold War, that is quite similar to Robbins's. But Miller uses this narrative as a basis for rejecting HUAC's claim to judge art by political standards. (*Thirty Years of Treason*, 789–825.)

music, to each other, but they are all moved by world-historical forces that envelop them and they don't even dream of. But Robbins dreams them, his narrative genius shows us how they look and feel. This is clearest in *West Side Story* and *Fiddler on the Roof,* but really it is everywhere. After I wrote this, I asked myself: Should we carry the irony even farther and elevate Elia Kazan along with him? I think not. Kazan draws inspiration from a much inferior form of Communist imagination: social melodrama. Kazan's stories at their best (*On the Waterfront, Viva Zapata*) are clashes of good guys and bad guys. Robbins's stories are tragic: We are all afloat in long waves that support or sink us all.

The Two On the Towns

I have focused on Robbins's primal trinity of sailors, from *Fancy Free,* rather than on the far better known ones from *On the Town.* In fact, though, *On the Town* grows pretty directly out of *Fancy Free,* and it originally opened in the same calendar year, 1944 (though at the very end of the year, December 31), at a time when World War Two was in its last (but, alas, most lethal) months. The 1944 *On the Town* is harder to reconstruct than the 1944 *Fancy Free* because no filmed or taped versions of any sort seem to have survived.[33] I am working from *The New York Musicals of Comden and Green,* published in 1997 by Applause, which includes scripts and gorgeous photographs. From my perspective, the most striking dance in *On the Town,* about halfway through, is called "The Times Square Ballet."[34] The play includes plenty of Robbins dancing, additional music by Leonard Bernstein with a fresh array of songs, and a rich, delicious book by Betty Comden and Adolph Green.

This story is still propelled by the sailors' yearning for glamorous "New York women" whom they can be with for a day and a night before they get back to their ship at "the Yard," the Brooklyn Navy Yard, at dawn. But the book by Comden and Green makes striking changes from *Fancy Free.* The first new thing is that, instead of competing against each other, these sailors know how to cooperate. At the Times Square subway stop, Gabe sees a girl whom he not only wants but is smitten in love with, before she disappears on the train. He says he will embark on a romantic quest through the city to find her, and his buddies Ozzie (played by Green) and Chip put his happiness ahead of their own. Ozzie tells Chip, "If Gabe hadn't pulled us out of the drink, we wouldn't *be* here in New York! . . . Haven't you got any gratitude?" They agree to "break up and follow all the clues on the poster," and to meet at the Nedick's Orange Drink stand in Times Square at eleven that night.[35] As if to reward them for their nobility, Comden and Green work the plot to present each man with a woman of his own with whom he can dance and feel at home. This plot change dispels the tragic imbalance that drives *Fancy Free*, and supplants it with an essentially comic harmony. It creates a utopia of "free love," though one that can't last long. The question now is no longer who belongs with whom, or whether anybody can "belong with" anybody, but how far these three couples who we can see *do* belong together will be free to go as they go together "on the town."

The second big change is the opening up of the horizon. The sailors are still there, of course, searching for happiness in a day and a night before they sail off to war. But *On the Town* elaborately explores both the New York environments they move through, designed by Oliver Smith (who had also designed *Fancy Free*), and the "New York women" they link up with. Times Square is the cityscape that gets most attention. Robbins's first choreographed crowd scene, about halfway through the play, was called "the Times Square Ballet." Viewers and reviewers singled it out for special praise.[36] Its star, the ballerina Sono Osato, called this great lost dance "a carousel of racing, meandering, meeting and parting, of the throbbing, never-ending crowds of a New York that never sleeps."[37] Her striking image of the carousel makes clear the connection of *On the Town* with Busby Berkeley's *42nd Street* and *Lullaby of Broadway*. All these dances are stories about their location: an immense, spectacular environment that makes people want to dance, but also makes ordinary walking feel like dancing and ordinary people feel like dancers, and that both inspires and drives them to make dance moves that are ever more frantic, audacious, and risky.

Comden and Green's book elaborates the women's parts in rich detail and depth, to the point that the women around the sailors become the play's dramatic and emotional center. They are a sexually brazen taxi driver (Nancy Walker) who is embedded firmly in the working class, a zany anthropologist (played by Comden) who comes from a leisured and cultured ruling class, and the "star," "Miss Turnstiles" (Sono Osato), whose class identity is uncertain and mysterious. Robbins lavishes special attention on the suavely lovely Osato. In the subway scene where the sailors meet her, Comden and Green borrow one of the basic tropes in Times Square literature—we saw it first in *Sister Carrie*—the opposition between the celebrity and her sign. Here the boys meet the sign first, as a man from the Transit Authority puts it in place in their car. Gabe grabs the poster at once and says he's got to have this girl, and then, a couple of minutes later, by power of the magic realism that defines popular culture, the girl appears. In this comic Times Square, there is no ambiguity or confusion between the woman and her sign; we are told, and we believe, that the Transit Authority promo will tell us exactly who the real person is going to be.

So who is she? Comden and Green use her role to satirize America's mass media and its culture of celebrity at the height of the war. They derive "Miss Turnstiles" from the actually existing "Miss Subways," a popular promotion in New York, run by the city's Transit Authority and by Macy's, playing from the 1940s through the 1960s. (She has recently been revived, but without the blaze of publicity she had in her prime.) She was meant to be, and generally was, an ordinary girl from the *demos* who would become a celebrity for a month—something like what Andy Warhol in the 1960s called "famous for fifteen minutes"—and then fade back into the *demos* again. (Sometimes she would be flooded with proposals and marry a rich man, though never as rich as the men who had married the Florodora girls forty years before.) Occasionally she would open a restaurant, like "Ellen's Stardust Diner," for decades across from City Hall, now just north of Times Square, featuring talented young singing waiters and waitresses. There are ongoing arguments, all through the play, about whether Miss Turnstiles is "somebody important" or "nobody at all"; no consensus is ever reached. Much of this discourse goes back to the Age of Jackson (and of Tocqueville), when the drive to bring ordinary people into American political life generated intense debate about what ordinary people were worth. In the 1940s as much as in the 1840s, those who believe the masses are worthless "hollow men" speak with dogmatic total certainty. The democratic masses, as we see them here, are unsure about themselves. But this uncertainty not only gives them an innocent charm, but reveals an inwardness and a depth that their enemies don't know they have, and a capacity for self-scrutiny that their enemies may not have themselves.

Early in the play, a pompous Announcer presides over the "Presentation of Miss Turnstiles"[38] and anoints her with a series of contradictory attributes. In a choreographed charade, Osato acts them out: ordinary and beautiful, plebeian and classy, highbrow and lowbrow, literary and illiterate. As she unrolls her contradictory identities, our heroine, at first ethereal, grows increasingly klunky as she is swamped by her accumulated paraphernalia. (This would have been a perfect scene for Lucille Ball.)

Every month [the Announcer says] some lucky little New York miss is chosen Miss Turnstiles for the month. She's got to be beautiful, she's got to be just an average girl . . .

She adores the Army, the Navy as well, *
And at poetry and polo she's swell.

This ridiculous human menu is a travesty of late Popular Front language as it was incarnated in the propaganda of World War Two. The hyperinflated language was invented to deal with a form of trouble that Americans probably understood better in 1944 than they do today: a clash between the populist and democratic values that America was supposed to be fighting for and the acutely, often viciously class-bound condition of real American life. Robbins and the other creators of *On the Town*—Comden and Green, Leonard Bernstein, producer George Abbott, designer Oliver Smith, Osato—all tried to face the clash and live with it by turning it into a joke. But part of the joke is that the heroine, "Ivy Smith, Miss Turnstiles," doesn't get it. She takes America's clashing values at face value and tries to embody them all, and the ambition turns her into a nervous wreck.

Ivy is a nervous wreck in another way. Like some of the protagonists of Dorothy Arzner's *Dance, Girl, Dance* (1940), and like the hundreds of real women their characters were based on, she sings and dances in a burlesque show by night in order to pay for lessons in "serious" singing and "serious" dancing, i.e., opera and classical ballet, every day. She is as pious about

---

*The 1949 MGM film tips Miss Turnstiles's language farther toward the Navy, to fit the unfolding plot in which homefront girls both adore and identify with sailors.

"High Culture" as she is about "America," and she beats herself up for being unworthy of both. Ivy goes to Carnegie Hall for opera and ballet lessons under the supervision of Madame Dilly, a dragon-lady Russian émigrée. In a hilarious sequence that turns Ivy literally upside down, Madame Dilly insists that, for art's sake, a girl must deprive herself of both sex and love. She believes in people of culture as a sort of priesthood, and Carnegie Hall as a sort of secular convent. But Ivy looks as if she may be open to other gospels. The sailor Gabe has read her sign carefully, and although it is only his first day in New York, he is impressively resourceful in tracking her to Carnegie Hall. This common man's entrance into the Hall is framed as "The Barbarian Invades the Temple." Ironically, in American civil society of the 1940s, even in the midst of the war, nobody worries about "security," no doors are locked, all a barbarian has to do to go anywhere is to just walk in. Gabe walks in while the teacher is out (out drinking?), calls Ivy by her name, and declares his love.

> SHE: But how did you know who I am?
> HE: I saw your picture in the subway.

In comically enhanced New York, signs in the subway reveal the truth. She offers him another sign, her autographed picture. But now that he has found the real woman, signs are not enough. "I found *you* [my italics]. I found Ivy Smith. Miss Smith, do you think you could make it tonight?" The place he wants her to "make it" with him, and with his fellow sailors and their girls, is of course Times Square. She hesitates, but then rushes out after him and says, "I'd love to go out with you."[39] This is the play's emotional climax.

When Gabe asks Ivy for a date, just what is he asking for, and what values are at stake? On a map, Times Square is only a few blocks away from Carnegie Hall, but in Comden and Green's cosmos the trip is an existential leap. Their romantic hero offers her a kind of love that is an existential challenge. He doesn't want her to give up either her identity as "Miss Turnstiles" or her quest for culture. (In a postwar "women's picture," the romantic hero would insist that the heroine give up both, resign her claims to public recognition, and be there for him and him alone.)[40] Gabe wants her, but he doesn't want her to give up anything; to be herself with him means to bring

along all she has, all she is; the more she is, the more he will be through loving her. He sings a love song that ends,

> *There's no other guy I'd rather be . . .*
> *I'm so lucky to be me.*[41]

This pattern of identification is far more typical for women identifying with
their men. In the 1970s, it will become part of the identity of "the new, sensitive male" supportive to the new wave of feminism. Madame Dilly and the
ladies of Carnegie Hall say a woman can't have both love and art. But *On
the Town,* if it says anything, says Yes, she can. Carnegie Hall meant high
culture in the 1940s, and it was meant to exclude and repel the mass culture
that thrived in Times Square. The genius of *On the Town* is to imagine a
Times Square that stretches to include, and embrace, Carnegie Hall.

One crucial fact about Osato's performance is rarely discussed: the way
she looks. This "All-American girl" looks glamorous, soulful, and extremely
Japanese. She shares with us her struggles over cultural identity and class
identity, but she keeps silent about her equally fluid and volatile ethnic identity and national identity. This is a problem, at the height of the most murderous racist war in all history. *On the Town*'s Broadway run coincides with
the last year of this war. Few people on either side now doubt the USA—and
its allies, Great Britain and the USSR—will win; the questions are how long
it will take, how many people on both sides will get killed before the end (as
it turned out, many millions), and how Japan and Germany will be treated
after the end. In the context of 1945, even a half-Japanese star has to be
"the other" for her American sailor, who in the same symbolic but real way
is "the other" for her. (And of course she is "other" for an American audience, even if she is legally American.) In world-war propaganda jargon, she
is his Pearl Harbor, he is her Hiroshima. Osato's *pas de deux* with John Battles and with Ray Harrison enact the theme of "the triumph of love," but
also—really a darker version of the same theme—the theme of "sleeping
with the enemy."

Is American democracy ready to make this kind of leap, to reach out and
do it? Has America any right to call itself a democracy if it won't do it? The
creators of *On the Town* are all, we could say, children of *The Jazz Singer:*
Jews from poor immigrant families who have won far more acceptance and

recognition than their parents would have thought possible, thanks to the flourishing of America's entertainment industry.* They are also leftists and believers in the Popular Front. The Front's basic idea, powerful through the war years, was to fight Fascism with a vision of democracy that highlighted its capacity to *include*: democracy as infinite space, room for everybody to breathe. New York, and especially Times Square, where hundreds of ethnic, religious, class, racial, and national groups bump into one another every day, must have seemed like just the place. The way Robbins and Bernstein, Comden and Green conceived and cast this show, they were betting the house on the American people's readiness for more people in the cast. They see our cosmopolitan sailors as a kind of vanguard of ripeness; they think sailors have the iconic power to pull the rest of the country along with them.

On the Town portrays union with "the other" in many alluring ways. Osato's Ivy oozes both sex and class; she is presented as just the kind of Japanese girl that any American boy would be thrilled to bring home. All the ancient and modern theater arts are deployed to bring Ivy and Gabey to-gether as a multicultural primal couple. But the hero and the heroine are not the only ones to cross the lines. Another "other" is the demon taxi driver Hildy (Nancy Walker), who reveals her real name to the sailors—"Brunn-hilde," like the Valkyrie in Wagner's *Ring* whose job is to ferry dead warriors to Valhalla—and who resembles these sailors, not only in her open and grabby sexuality, but in her caustic wit that disparages yet accepts both the man she wants, the sailor Chip, and herself. Here is her satirical riff on the sailor's traditional virtue of openness:

> You stick to me, kid. I've been waiting for you all my life. Knew you the minute I saw you. You're for me. I like your face. It's open, ya know what I mean? Nothing in it. The kind of face I can fall into. Kiss me![42]

This memorable woman is a modern Mistress Quickly. (It is a pity that the show's creators neglected to provide her with a Falstaff.) But as crucial as

---

*Many Jews in show business dropped their Jewish names, as Robbins dropped the name he was born with, Rabinowitz, "son of a rabbi," ironically the very same name as *The Jazz Singer*'s hero, who morphed into "Jack Robin." But some Jews don't get the joke. It is often said that Harry Rabinowitz never got it at all, and always felt his son's name change was a betrayal. In Robbins's last years, he tried to put together a psychoanalytic dance theater piece called "The Poppa Piece," intended to reach a climax in his encounter with HUAC. His earliest draft begins, "I am Rabinowitz, I did this . . ." (Lawrence, 495; Jowitt, 495).

these stars were in unfolding the romance of the other, the chorus line mattered just as much. *On the Town* soon became famous—in some places, infamous—as "the first integrated show" on Broadway. And it wasn't just that the chorus included both blacks and whites. Robbins and Leonard Bernstein evidently put all their power and prestige on the line to ensure that blacks and whites would partner, and would be seen dancing together, just as they would dance together and be seen in any Times Square dance hall.*

Since the 1890s, the continuous carnival of Times Square has offered a seductive ambience enticing people to "cross the lines"—to make moves across whatever ethnic, racial, class, or sexual barriers mark their lives—and be together; and it has offered a profusion of signs that magnify and sanctify their being. The chance to cross the lines is a crucial aspect of Times Square's "free love." *On the Town* not only celebrates this freedom, but brings out its political weight and depth. As World War Two ends, momentous political changes are brewing just a few blocks away. At the other end of 42nd Street, along the East River, the United Nations is coming into being, based on the destruction of Fascism and the Universal Declaration of Human Rights. Times Square fleshes this vision out when it stands up as "the crossroads of the world," a spectacular panorama of a postwar life that will be open to all. This Square is a place with space for everybody to fit in, and "everybody" means not only the USA's most marginal ethnic groups but even its national enemies. Sono Osato comes to signify a Japan that America is about to subdue, but then to peacefully re-create in its image. The Rising Sun will be accepted and welcomed here, but welcomed as just one in a great array of Times Square lights and signs.† *On the Town* and Eisenstaedt's canonical photo together define the great hopes that mark the end

---

Dance with Demons, 84ff. Lawrence quotes Osato's amazement about her role decades later. He insists on the connection between the Japanese ballerina doing solos and the blacks dancing in the chorus, and he praises Robbins's vision and guts in fighting for both. He also quotes the reminiscences of black dancer Dorothy McNichols: "We left New York and went to Baltimore, Maryland, and they wouldn't let me in backstage to work. They said we weren't in the show, and my picture was out front! . . . Jerry gave them a few choice words. He said, 'If you keep any of my people out of this theatre, you're gonna lose your jobs.'" Stories like this evoke the early years of Jackie Robinson and the people who fought for him. They may also serve as a counterforce to waves of nostalgia for the days of "the Good War."

†But thirty years later, during New York's fiscal crisis, when the great American corporations had abandoned Times Square, Japan bailed it out. Sony, Panasonic, Canon, Samsung, Suntory, Toshiba, Mitsubishi, in a kind of Pearl-Harbor-in-reverse, established a beachhead on the Square's north side, created a whole new generation of spectacular "fire signs," and kept the great space from going dark.

of the Good War. They share a vision of Times Square as a democratic space, a kind of human greenhouse where everybody can grow. The sailors in the Square fill New York, and in 1945 fill America, with a fresh breeze of global openness. The dream of *On the Town*, that nice American boys can dance in the city streets and get driven around the town and find free love with women who are not only total strangers but "others," is a luminous vision of what New York and America after the war might be. Jerome Robbins deserves more credit than anybody for thinking this vision through and fleshing it out. Taken together, *Fancy Free* and *On the Town* may be the deepest and most original art of the Popular Front.

When *On the Town* finally hit the screen, in 1949, it wasn't just that the war was over, it seemed to have left no trace. It appears that some powerful movie person made a decision that in one breath dispelled much of the play's poignancy and depth. With no trace of a war with Germany, there's no reason to worry about our heroes' lives, Hildy is no Brunnhilde, and her vehicle is just another cab. (Frank Sinatra says derisively, "What's a girl doing driving a cab? The war's over." Little does he dream she will drive him right into her bed; he fights her off, but not for long.) With no trace of a war with Japan, there is no meaning in an American sailor's love for a classically Japanese "all-American girl," or in the coronation of an "other" as goddess of the subways of New York. MGM gives the "all-American girl" role to the blond, pert Vera-Ellen, who looks the way all-Americans used to look when "American" meant white. There are no blacks in this chorus; indeed, there is no chorus. The only trace of ambiguity in this cast's identities is that Ivy tries to act like a sophisticated "native New Yorker" when all the while, like Gabey, she is "just a kid from Meadowville, Indiana" who looks as corny as Kansas in August, as does virtually everyone else in this cast. In moving from one medium to another, and from Robbins and Bernstein to Gene Kelly and Stanley Donen, *On the Town* dumbs itself down.

And yet, in spite of all this, the *On the Town* movie is one of the most thrilling musicals ever made. I can see three reasons for this: terrific ensemble playing, imaginative cinematography, and Gene Kelly. The primal ensemble consists of Kelly and "Miss Turnstiles" Vera-Ellen, Frank Sinatra and cabdriver Betty Garrett, Jules Munshin and anthropologist Ann Miller. When the sailors interact, it isn't just that they do intensely strenuous singing and dancing, but the dance star can sing, the singing star can dance,

the guy who's neither can keep up with both, nobody tries to upstage anybody, and they click like a basketball team on a continuous fast break.[43]
When the men and the women interact, they click in a slightly different
way: They address their singing and dancing to each other, and the more intensely each can focus and give themselves to their other—or, as often happens here, throw themselves at their other—the more the other can
concentrate all his or her energy on them, so that, as in our primal dreams
of sex, the more they give, the more they get, and moreover *everybody* gives,
and everybody gets, and everyone comes home happy. When I first saw this
film, at age ten, I saw it as a preview of adult sexual life, and I could hardly
wait to grow up. When I saw it again at thirty, in the midst of the Vietnam
War, I felt more like Liz Phair—"Free love is a whole lot of bullshit"; I wondered what drug they all were on to make them click so well. Seeing it at
sixty, I feel all the different tonalities that *On the Town* blends so perfectly:
sailors' whites, women's luscious colors, human flesh, city stone and grass
and sky; the Brooklyn Bridge as collective lingerie that makes New York's
harbor and people more radiant than ever when you see them through the
bands of wire. This movie shows a harmony between people and each other
and the city and the world that I as a leftist have been working for all my life:
Just look, there it is. It's a hymn to democracy: It shows spectacular beauty
growing from the normal unfolding of ordinary people's desires and needs.

What is special in *On the Town*'s cinematography comes across at its very
start. In a remarkable outdoor montage, accompanied by the "New York,
New York" song and a jazzed-up Bernstein soundtrack, the camera propels
the three sailors across the Brooklyn Bridge, onto Wall Street facing Trinity
Church, through Chinatown, the Lower East Side, the Fulton Fish Market,
in and out and in and out of the subways, sometimes on double-decker
buses (one of New York's great lost treats), into and through Times Square,
up the West Side to Grant's Tomb and Riverside Church, into Central
Park—where we see the three in hansom cabs, on horseback, riding bikes,
sprinting across the grass—to the Empire State Building, where the movie
will return and reach its climax in an hour, and to Rockefeller Center. This
montage clocks in under five minutes, but it contains luminous images that
merge the sailors with so many of the city's most spectacular sites.[44]

The attitude of the three sailors toward all they see is openness, receptivity, fascination, endless delight in new places, tireless yearning for more.

They don't collapse, as I feel I could collapse just from reading out the inventory of all the places they go (I am sure I missed a few). Indeed, the more they see and experience, the more it refreshes their appetites for life: the primeval sailor's romance. Eighty or ninety minutes later, they and their girlfriends are in Hildy's taxi, plunging toward Coney Island, pursued by the police, the camera looking back at them from just in front of the cab. As they pass through a gorgeous red-hot-and-blue Times Square, police sirens start to blare, hot on their tail. Kelly or Sinatra says, "Where's the fire?" Munshin looks back through the opening in the roof and says, "*We're* the fire!" This line is always one of the picture's big laughs. What makes the moment such a delight is the way the movie has drawn us into the sailors' shared faith that they may get burned, but they won't be consumed.

At Coney Island, to evade the police, they engage in a sex-change vaudeville routine. It is a fine comic gesture in its own right, prefiguring Billy Wilder's 1959 masterpiece, *Some Like It Hot*. Alas, their maleness is unmasked, and Shore Patrol locks them up. But Hildy gets them sprung with a stirring oration. Her peroration is, "Where's our civic pride? We should've hugged them to our bosoms, and said *Boys, the town is yours!*" She is proposing a test for urbanity that ancient Athenians would have understood: You can tell a city's belief and confidence in itself from its capacity to identify itself with sailors and make them feel at home.

Gene Kelly's glory here comes from his power as a choreographer as well as a dancer. As a dancer, for most of the movie he is surprisingly modest. He makes no move to dance rings around everybody, though we know he could. His modesty has a political as much as an artistic force: The sailor is trying to be a democratic citizen, staying close to his buddies. But Kelly's brilliant choreography creates a remarkable flow between the people and among them and all through the urban environment around them, and it is this Heraclitean fire that is the movie's brightest sign of life.

About two thirds of the way through, Kelly finally takes an extended solo. In the movie's first few minutes, he has stolen Ivy Smith's "Miss Turnstiles" poster from the subway. Through the plot's twists and turns, he clasps it to his bosom like an amulet. Now he lets his yearning break forth; he makes love to her sign, embraces it, glides across the floor brilliantly, clutching the sign, on an empty stage, with the sky a predawn electric blue (remember, "When a Broadway baby says Goodnight, it's early in the morning") and a horizon of skyscrapers in silhouette. His moves are thrilling, yet also ridiculous; after a while the solo seems to be going on too long; we wish his buddies would break in and bail him out, as they have done before. At last, as if to reward the hero's absurd faith, the material girl Vera-Ellen bursts on the scene and merges with her sign. She comes in gorgeous colors that harmonize with his sailor's whites; as they embrace, the orchestra plays the triumphal chords, "New York, New York!" We are meant to understand the embrace as a triumph not only for the sailor but for the city, a place where total strangers can find free love.

There is one more item that I haven't seen in discussions of Kelly or of *On the Town*, but that I think plays an important part in the history of both: the police. There is just one cop in the play, in the most peripheral of parts. But in the movie the police keep coming back, and occupy important space. Early in the story, they come to suspect the three sailors of destroying a dinosaur. This seems delightfully ridiculous (and an offhand parable about what forces in American society the police are protecting). But the movie just won't let go of them, and they won't settle into the familiar Hollywood mold of Keystone Kops. They keep coming back, place themselves at the center of the action, pursue our heroes from one end of the city to the other, and finally lock them up, so that they won't get to enjoy the romantic night they dreamed of. They are a cloud that won't go away. Their persistent presence throughout Manhattan may tell us something about a specter that comes to haunting the postwar entertainment industry: the Cold War. That great kiss of August 1945 took place in an atmosphere of perfect openness and transparency, something like what Nietzsche called "the great noon."[45] Eisenstaedt's photo helped to define that atmosphere, and its canonical status for more than half a century has helped to keep its memory alive. But by 1949, when the movie *On the Town* opened on Broadway, the light and air had changed, and Times Square's wide open spaces were deep in shadows.

In 1949, Gene Kelly seemed to be on top of the world; but he was a leftist, a union activist, and he knew that in the Cold War even the stars were shaky. His radicalism, rooted in the Popular Front, featured belief in the "ordinary guy" he so often personified in his dances, especially those that featured dancing sailors. Within a couple of years Kelly's first wife, movie actress Betsy Blair, would become a victim of the Hollywood blacklist. In the early 1950s he enjoyed two spectacular movie triumphs, *An American in*

Paris and *Singin' in the Rain*. But he knew, better than most people who celebrated him, that he was vulnerable. At the climax of his great solo in *Singin' in the Rain*, at a moment of supreme triumph, a cop appears. We see only his back, which briefly fills the screen; he orders the hero off the street and takes away his umbrella. A short while after this movie came out, and won many prizes, Kelly and his wife were forced to leave the USA. They returned in 1955, when she found work as the heroine of *Marty*. Kelly went back to work, too, without having caved—compare Robbins—but many people say his career never reached the heights again. (Of course, their belief may stem from movie people's chronic blindness to television, where Kelly did splendid live original work.) I don't want to get heavy, but paying a little attention to the Cold War can help us imagine what those cops were doing in those plots,[46] and what it might have been like to sing in the rain with no umbrella.

The Last Detail: *Tangential to Everywhere*

That is the fate of the heroes of our last "sailor" movie, one of the great films of the Vietnam War years, Hal Ashby's and Robert Towne's *The Last Detail* (1973). This remarkable work is a large movie disguised as a small one. The story is a quest, undertaken by a triad of sailors, just like the ones in "Sailors" and *Fancy Free* and *On the Town*. There is a war on, but it is worlds away from our heroes, the "old heads" Jack Nicholson and Otis Young, and the kid Randy Quaid, and from the world they share. I may even be cutting corners by putting them into this essay, because they never reach Times Square. We know they want to go there, we see a bunch of fire signs on the night horizon that looks like the Square, but, like Franz Kafka's land surveyor K. in search of "The Castle," they never actually get there. Somehow they remain tangential to the Square. *The Last Detail* constructs one of the most remarkable landscapes ever mounted on the screen, a landscape that shows us a generation of sailors who seem to be tangential to *everywhere*.

The plot of *The Last Detail* is that Nicholson and Young, stationed on a nameless naval base somewhere south of Norfolk and waiting for orders to ship out—it isn't clear to where, but it isn't Vietnam, because they have already been to Vietnam—are inexplicably rewarded by getting a "detail" to

act as cops. They must guard Quaid, a convicted young criminal (his crime
was petty shoplifting), and convey him to Portsmouth military prison in
New Hampshire. Their prescribed route will take them north through
Washington, D.C., Philadelphia, New York, and Boston, and through the
most densely settled and historically evocative parts of America. But this
movie is configured so that, for all the miles they cover, they never connect
with any of the places they pass through. Their journey is an endless passage
from nowhere to nowhere, through barracks-yards, overpasses, corridors, alleys, stairways, men's rooms, dead-end roads, rows of identical bungalows
(they stop off at Quaid's mother's house, but it is hard to find, and then she
isn't there), motel bedrooms (we see only the foot of the bed), buses (we see
the three in the back of the bus), trains (we see them in a train, overtaken by
a faster train), waiting rooms, and station platforms. "We're a navy of three,"*
Nicholson says, and he and Young speak of their love of the sea, but I don't
think there's a drop of water in this movie. The sky is uniformly gray, with
no trace of sun or rain; snow is sometimes on the ground, but we don't see
it come down. There is a scene in Philadelphia's 30th Street Station, but no
trace of its Great Hall; a scene in Washington Square, but no grand arch; a
scene on the Boston Common, but no glorious statehouse. The one building we ever see that is real "scenery" comes at their journey's end: It is the
cupola-covered military prison in Portsmouth that swallows Quaid up.

I was saying *The Last Detail* is bigger than it looks. The sailors we meet
in *The Last Detail* are a travesty of the three heroes of *On the Town*. Those
sailors, at the climax of "the Good War," danced from spectacle to spectacle; they were nourished by all the fabulous places they could go; through
lively dialogue, song, and dance, they transmitted their sense of freedom,
participation in the collective life of their times, sexual yearning but also a
capacity for love (when they found attractive women, they paid attention to
them), and hope for the future—all the ingredients of grown-up well-being.
For the sailors of the Vietnam generation, the grand spectacles and great
hopes just don't come up on the radar screen. Life looks like a road to
nowhere, a sequence without growth or progress, a loop of film that inter-
minably replays itself. These sailors, prisoners and guards alike, live through

---

*Here, as in much war literature, their most serious enemies are competing armed services: in this case
soldiers, whom the sailors bump into and happily fight in a men's room in (I think) New York, and
marines, who run the prison in Portsmouth. Their second line of enemies seems to be civilians.

their lives waiting for Godot.* They can see the bright lights on the night horizon, but that is as close as they'll get.

The Last Detail avoids direct comment on the war in Vietnam, but any work about GIs made in the midst of a war has got to be a war film. Among the eastern urban populations our sailors pass through, there is no enthusiasm for the war. Nobody they meet hugs them to their bosoms, no city offers them its keys. No one attacks them or blames them for the war, though one melancholy longhair says he doesn't see "how you can defend Nixon" and challenges them to "say even one good thing about him." The sailors don't defend Nixon or say anything good about him, and their silence is eloquent. (The movie gets it right: By 1970 the armed forces were all deeply divided about the war; it isn't hard to imagine a group of three GIs in which no one supports it.) But the movie also makes the civilian sound clueless, shallow. It suggests these men in uniform have *been through* something that their critics cannot even imagine. I have never been in uniform, but this sounds right to me. At least it sounds right in a fortunate country that has only once been invaded. It doesn't sound so right in other countries, where millions of civilians have died and lived through terror bombardment. And even in the USA, it doesn't sound quite so right after 9/11. The real gulf is between people who have been under fire and people who have not.

This basic fact of life has been a central theme in war literature since the *Iliad*. But it has often got mixed up with a more dubious enterprise, the propaganda attempt to create justification for wars. The horrors of World War One generated a body of great writing on all sides that sorted these two themes out—being under fire versus fighting to win a war—and created a great gulf between them.[47] But in World War Two, as just a war as Americans are ever likely to fight, they got hopelessly entangled again. The war in Vietnam forced America to draw the line once more. *The Last Detail*, composed in wartime, is part of the drawing process. During the three

---

*"Godot" is more than a cliché signifying cosmic futility. Samuel Beckett was a hero of the Liberation, an activist in the anti-Nazi Resistance in Paris, and a recipient of the *Croix de Guerre*. (See Anthony Cronin, *Samuel Beckett: The Last Modernist* [HarperCollins, 1996], chapters 21–22.) Had there been a Parisian version of our canonical photo (maybe by Robert Doisneau), he could easily have been in it, smiling his wry smile on the fringe of the crowd. But in 1952, when *Godot* was first published and produced in Paris, Beckett found himself an honored citizen of a democracy that was on the wrong side of a bloody imperial war.

sailors' encounter with the hippies, Nicholson boasts to a group of girls that being in the Navy is "doing a man's job." But then, a minute later, by sheer force of free association, his boast turns into a lament: He says, "I've seen men do things I can't even begin to tell you . . ." It may be that the sailor's innocent masculinity, so enchanting to civilians, depends on an unthinking identification with his country's wars. If it does, then this model of manhood may be one of the Vietnam War's first casualties. That war teaches, but also forces, its men under fire to think; but as they do, our carefree studs morph into Ancient Mariners. (Ancient Mariners can be sexy, too, but mostly to people who themselves have been around the block.)

Reflections on masculinity and manhood turn out to be among this movie's strengths. *The Last Detail* shares with Goodman's "Sailors" not only the structure of the sailor trio, but the determination of the old heads to ensure that the kid gets laid. This turns out to be a much taller order for Quaid than for any of the earlier sailors we've seen. This kid, though handsome, is a classic loser. He turns out to be not just a petty criminal, but a lousy petty criminal. He shoplifts ineptly, as if begging to be caught; under guard, he tries to run away in situations where he can't possibly get away. On the voyage north, his depressive gloom is so thick, it looks like it could derail the train. Nicholson and Young worry about what could happen to him in prison. "He's probably glad he's going to the brig. On the outside so many things can happen to him." It's a joke, but seriously, Quaid's character has never mastered many basic skills for living anywhere. They order food, the waiter gets it wrong, Nicholson complains and sends it back, the second time around the waiter gets it right. It is the most routine social transaction—and the kid is incredulous that such a thing is possible: You mean you can ask for what you want, and sometimes really get it? The old heads' hearts sink: The Navy has prepared them to teach kids how to swab the decks, stand patrol, clean and load and fire guns, but not how to recognize their own desires and affirm their own selves. This kid will be crushed by prison unless he can build some basic ego-strength fast. And they are the only ones who can help him do it. These old men, who (they recognize) have used the Navy to avoid the responsibilities of family life, have to reeducate themselves so they can help the kid get himself together and grow up. Movies are magical, so they do.

Before the train trip is over, Quaid orders something and gets the wrong thing. We hold our breaths: What will he do? He sends it back. He isn't quarreling, he's just saying what he wants. But we can see that the act of saying what he wants is a major psychic breakthrough for him. "I'm learning!" he says, with a smile as big as the screen. And it is a breakthrough for his surrogate fathers as well: His growth is their growth; in this Navy of three, all three are learning to be men.

Later on, in a sleazy whorehouse in Boston, he learns more. It takes the help of Carol Kane, who in a lovely performance becomes something like the young sailor's nurse; but also the help of the old men, who become something like his doctors, who explain to her what he needs. But they also act like buddies, in the best U.S. Navy tradition, just like the sailors in "Sailors" and in *On the Town*.* They subdue their own desires and hopes, spend the night on the couch, and use their money to subsidize him for "as long as it takes." Next morning, Quaid is radiant. He says he knows she's a whore, but he feels she was nice to him beyond the call of business. Nicholson agrees, and tries to explain it: "She got feelings, just like everybody else." Here, once more, Ashby and Towne are doing what they do best, advancing a complex idea disguised as a throwaway line. The idea is about freedom within alienation: Even somebody who lives by pretending feelings can still really have the feelings, and can give herself freely, at least for a time. If the kid can grasp that the gift is real, he will know he is not alone; then, even in prison, he will have reasons to want to get out.

The fact that Quaid can have a morning-after shows Nicholson and Young that "the kid's come a long way," and their educational project has worked. Quaid has "made it," and as his teachers they have made it, too. In their "Navy of three" they have done a real "man's work": They have helped a messed-up kid grow up fast. Ironically, now that he is grown up, he is ready to go to jail; now that they have brought him up, they are ready to bring him in. He will make one more hopeless attempt to escape, and all three will get banged up and bloody in the snow. ("They're froze together, see?") The Portsmouth prison is a sad fate, and yet, ironically, it will save him from an

---

*In an earlier encounter in New York, the old men left Quaid alone with a girl, thinking she would take him to bed. Instead she delivered a political lecture, and urged him to desert and escape to Canada. His response, which we heard but his buddies didn't, was, "I couldn't do that—they're my best friends—it would screw them up!" It turned out he was learning more than they knew.

even sadder fate, the war in Vietnam. The old men are still feeling the wounds of that war. But their quest with Quaid has brought them the strength to face their own lives, Young in Baltimore, Nicholson in New York—maybe he will reach Times Square this time. As they leave the prison, we see their backs, like classic movie heroes heading into the sunset (although there is still no sun). There is a new spring in their step, and a full orchestra accompanies them with a big-picture "Anchors Aweigh."

I have been exploring visions and fantasies of sailors over a long time. I am especially interested in an equation that goes back to the ancient times, but that has been highly developed since World War Two: sailors and democracy. Eisenstaedt's, Robbins's, Gene Kelly's young sailors, at the end of World War Two, rejoice in their potency and their grasp. In *On the Town*, it is as if just the act of setting their feet on the sidewalks of New York makes them grow. Fresh off the boat at sunrise in the Brooklyn Navy Yard, they (and we) see the city in a spectacular view. They don't walk, they dance: They bestride the pavement like young Greek gods, nourished by the water and the sun; it seems they could dance over the bay, vault the bridge through the air to the tallest tower, without a break in their step or in their song. Like American democracy as it confronted the world in 1945, they are ordinary nice kids, yet they seem capable of spreading and leaping anywhere and doing anything, at least for the time being.

A generation later, in the midst of the Vietnam War, the Yard is gone, the infinite perspectives closed, the great leaps cut off. New York, America, and democracy are all in trouble. We still can find sailors, but they are wounded or grounded, *geworfen* into claustrophobic railroad cars, men's rooms, and motels. After Vietnam, every last detail of reality seems like a stumbling block to embarrass them and remind them of their limits. They bump into each other; their bodies push and press in on them. They must go through elaborate negotiations just to make elementary moves in a landscape of nothingness. Yet maybe by force of denying the old sailor myths, they will find strength to reinvent them; maybe in this void they can find themselves, and construct a new model of dignity as men and citizens. *The Last Detail* is addressed to a whole generation, the generation that couldn't stop a war but that started a pretty decent counterculture. It offers a dialectic that is a new twist of an old story: *The last will be first.* If our heroes look their powerlessness in the face, they will feel solidarity both with each other and with other others, and they can create a BOND that will bring them some limited but real power in the world. Sailors cut off from the openness of the sea can still make signs, luminous signs, signs of the times, signs in the Square.

The Sailor, The Simpsons, *and 1989*

Our last three scenes, from the 1990s, are drawn from animated network television, from live cable television, and from a song. The song is "Hello Sailor" by Liz Phair; the cartoon is from *The Simpsons* on Fox TV; the live television sequence is from HBO's *Sex and the City*. In "Hello Sailor" and in *Sex and the City*, the subjective voices belong to women imagining encounters between women and sailors. Up to now, nearly all talk about sailors, and about encounters between sailors and civilians, has come from men. (For that matter, nearly all recorded talk about everything has come from men.) One refreshing feature of contemporary life and culture is women, lots of women speaking up and demanding to be heard.

In Times Square today, signs play as crucial a role in people's lives as they ever did. But the BOND sign, which acted as a kind of *chupah*, a bridal canopy not just for the sailor and the nurse but for the whole 1945 crowd, is long gone. What has taken its place is an even bigger and more colorful sign, VIRGIN, for the giant Virgin Records (and books and clothes and food and *tchotchkes*) store that fills all Bond's old space and more. It is ironic, because there are probably fewer virgins in the Times Square crowd today or tonight than at any time in its history. Nevertheless, VIRGIN is one of the stars of both these scenes, indirectly in Phair's song, which actually offers no landscape at all, directly and vividly in *Sex and the City*, where it marks the end of the night. It is the theme of one of the all-time classic Times Square jokes, prefigured by Montesquieu joking about Paris in 1721, told by the pianist and comedian Oscar Levant about the jazz singer and comedienne Doris Day. Day had reincarnated herself in 1950s Hollywood as a late-model *ingénue*, and he was telling TV talk-show host Jack Paar he knew her when. "I knew Doris Day," he said, "before she became a virgin." In both our last two scenes, the heroine is a woman of experience who wishes she could become a virgin, but knows she can't.

Before we get there, though, we have to go through the land of *The Simpsons*. "Bart the General,"[48] produced at the very start of the show's long run (it is still running), has no sailors in it, and it has no Times Square, but it has a cartoon facsimile of our canonical picture, and its magic moment comes at the end of a cartoon version of World War Two. The way its story goes, Lisa has made cupcakes for her teacher and her class. But Springfield Elementary School contains a vicious bully, twice everyone else's size, with his own private army. This guy, Nelson, grabs her cupcakes, partly to enjoy them, partly to destroy them. Bart intervenes chivalrously to protect his sister, but gets beaten up, humiliated, and laughed at by what seems like "the whole school." After it happens twice, he seeks help from his grandfather, a demented veteran (of what war isn't quite clear), from the owner of the local military souvenir shop, and from *Soldier of Fortune* magazine. Bart raises a ragtag army of ex-victims ("If you hate and fear Nelson, meet me . . ."), and for once in their lives these boys learn self-discipline. Bart's advisers teach him to surround the evil army with a pincer movement; they then "commence saturation bombing" with Happy Birthday water bags, and literally engulf the bad guy. After a two-minute battle spectacle, Nelson's army crumbles and flees; he is forced to surrender and sign a treaty of defeat. He gets tied up and carted away, the people flood Springfield's streets, everybody's happy. Then, suddenly a big kid in a sailor hat, apparently a stranger to everyone, appears from offscreen, and throws himself on Lisa. She blows him off nastily, and he disappears as mysteriously as he came. But before he goes, somebody takes a Polaroid of the two of them, and it is flashed before us: My God, it's our 1945 picture! I guess we're supposed to think something like, "*Aha!* so the archetypal image is a phony." That would be a "postmodern" instance of the cynicism for which *The Simpsons* is so well known. But, as postmodern cynicism, this parody fails. The force of the primal picture doesn't depend on the sailor's "real" role in the combat that has just ended, or on the nurse's "real" feeling toward him. Its power is its capacity to symbolize a collective reality that envelops everybody, regardless of how anybody feels. The only way to have made the photo look truly empty and hollow would have been to produce an empty, hollow vision of World War Two. And the makers of *The Simpsons*, even at their most outrageous, are unprepared to do that.

Contrary to what you have just seen [Bart says], war is neither glamorous nor fun. There are no winners, only losers. There are no good wars, with the following exceptions: the American Revolution, World War Two, and the Star Wars Trilogies.

Endless satire and self-satire, yes; total nihilism, no. *The Simpsons'* reenactment of our primal picture shows how far its makers are willing to go in their postmodern skepticism, and where they are not willing to go.[49]

I saw this show because my eleven-year-old son Danny, who since the summer of 2003 has been looking at the big picture from *Life* on our wall, said he had just seen it on *The Simpsons*. I had to sit down right away to see it with him. What we saw was a schoolyard-level microcosm of World War Two; even with all its Simpsonian cynical brilliance, the show's vision of the conflict was amazingly similar to Alfred Eisenstaedt's and Woody Guthrie's and FDR's. I wondered, Where was all this humanist affirmation coming from? Then I realized this was the program's first season: It was in its early days, still feeling its way, not so clear what it was going to be. It was coming to life just a few weeks after the destruction of the Berlin Wall, in the midst of one of the twentieth century's great affirmative moments, a moment best defined by the poet Seamus Heaney when he wrote that "hope and history rhyme."[50] It was a time when, all over the world, people who felt they had experienced too much felt a chance to become innocent again. The time didn't last long, but Heaney's lovely image keeps it alive. So, too, in an unexpected and ironic way, does our DVD that preserves *The Simpsons'* complete first season. Whatever this program and its audience have become through the years, many of us really had a "complete first season" when hope and history rhymed, and when, like that sailor and that nurse, we could enjoy not only the thrill of free love, but the purity of hope.

Girls, Guyville, and the Gulf

In Liz Phair's song, it is just this hope of "free love" that seems to be the target of her rage. Phair is one of the smartest people making pop music today, and also one of the most elusive. If her music has a genre, it must be something like punk-folk. She generally sings softly, in a wavering contralto, in a reflective, conversational tone; but some of the feelings she conveys are crude, gross, pornographically sexual, violently enraged. She has created a persona something like that of Muriel Bentley's First Girl in *Fancy Free*, the sweet homegirl who has learned to act like a brazen slut and walk on the wild side. In many of her songs, her subjects use the word "fuck" as fluently as any sailor. On her latest album cover and liner, Phair is dressed like a stripper on 42nd Street in the 1970s—as if she were reaching for some sort of ultimate nudity, and felt her words were not enough to get her there.[51] But it is her words that we will remember. She has a mind of Jamesian complexity; the relations between her characters and herself are often impossibly dense puzzles that neither she nor we can solve.

The song that best frames her work is the first she ever released, on her first album, *Exile in Guyville*, the brilliantly searing "Fuck and Run." Its heroine wakes up in the arms of a man who, she realizes, will dump her as soon as he wakes up. Then she laments always being seduced and abandoned by men who "fuck and run." But then she realizes she is just like them. What she really wants, she thinks, is a good old-fashioned "boyfriend / the kind of guy who makes love 'cause he's in it." Then she fears: What if a good man loved her? Could she even recognize his love, let alone return it? Or has her heart been deadened by all the years she's fucked and run? Can this be what women's freedom was for? "Guyville" is a primal existential fear, not for women only: to be stuck in a state of being like "the guys" who have no feelings, who trample on love, who sing about loveless sex as they go rolling home.

Phair's "Hello Sailor," written in her early twenties, comes a couple of years after the end of the Wall, in the aftermath of the First Gulf War. The song has never been officially released, yet the lyrics are easily available online.* This creates a peculiarly ambiguous situation, and ambiguity is the realm where Phair is most at home. The lyrics are striking for their violent anger toward the sailor; the song's narrator (and heroine) seems to blame

---

*According to "Biography: Liz Phair" (AOL Music Search, 2003), Phair included it on a demo tape that she called "Girlysound" and sent around to people in the music industry in the early 1990s. I have never actually heard it, and neither has anyone else I know. All I say is based on her lyrics, which her fans have lovingly collected at several richly illustrated Liz Phair websites. The combination of her failure to record the song with her display of its lyrics online is typical of her flair for ambiguity.

the grunt for the war. When I first read this it shocked me, but as a teacher for forty years I recognized it. The girl's total lack of identification with the sailor tells us a couple of things. It tells us she hasn't learned to distinguish between powerful and powerless people. It also reminds us that there are a couple of generations of Americans whose historical memory starts with Vietnam, or even after, and who have no memory traces of America's "Good War," World War Two. If that is this narrator's history, it will help explain why she gives these guys no slack. But since she is a character in a song by Liz Phair, it's too soon to know. Phair is a virtuosa of ambivalence and complex identifications. In "Fuck and Run," her narrator comes to identify herself with the men she spits on. It may be that she never worked through the relationship between herself and her character, and that is why she left "Sailor" in the outtake pile. Or maybe Matador Records put it in the pile because they didn't want politics in her mix, and as a rookie with no track record she had no power of creative control.

Meanwhile, these lyrics alone will tell us some things we should know. It is exciting to imagine an encounter between a woman and a GI where she can both bond with him sexually and say, "No blood for oil!" She asks him many good questions, such as "How does it feel to be hated and loved at home?" But the most striking thing she says is an exclamation she repeats many times: *"Free love is a whole lot of bullshit."* At the song's end, she says it three times, in what looks on the page like a crescendo of rage. It's easy to imagine her girl stamping off, leaving one very puzzled sailor on the street, wondering why this dame is so mad and what on earth she wants.

What does she want? She may not know any more than he knows, but we should know. We need only turn back to points we've been: Times Square, the magic picture, *Fancy Free, On the Town,* a vision of instant harmony between total strangers hot in each other's arms; love that may be fleeting but is real, where men and women pay attention not only to each other's faces and bodies, but to their total lives; love not just personal but civic (as the taxi driver Brunnhilde says in *On the Town*), where you feel a whole city is hugging you and saying "Boys, the town is yours!"; love celebrated and sanctified by a mass public in a democratic public square, in a New York that can symbolize America, in an America that can represent the world. In our perennial American pursuit of happiness, the vision of 1945 is one of our archetypal images of fulfillment. It is a vision of innocent sailors

who could take care of innocent girls, or else, in a more sophisticated version (crafted by writers like Comden and Green), of innocent sailors and
girls who could take care of each other. In this vision, we can love strangers
and they can love us because we have lived together under fire through the
horrors of "the Good War." And such has been America's fate and history
that we really did have a "good war," and it really did give those who had
lived through it an aura of innocence, and it made Times Square feel like
the world's *agora*, and it thrilled multitudes of people, and even a sophisticated lady named Simone de Beauvoir had to melt for a time.

That's what Liz Phair's heroine wants. She wants to melt; she wants to
lean on a man, and let him lead her, and know he will; she wants to feel
hugged and loved by a whole city; she wants the thrills she feels with one
man to be part of a process of liberating the whole world. She wants what
she thinks Eisenstaedt's nurse is getting; she wants what the taxi driver and
the anthropologist and Miss Turnstiles seem to get in *On the Town*. But she
knows that was a long time ago, she knows that since that time America and
Americans have come a long way. She knows that was then, this is now; she
knows what was real half a century ago is bullshit today; that's why she's
mad.

Sex and the City: *Woman Alone in the Square*

On the other hand, or on another side of the brain, Sarah Jessica Parker's
"Carrie," of the comedy cable-TV hit *Sex and the City*, wants very badly *not*
to melt: In fact, she wants not to melt in exactly the way she wants to. *Sex
and the City* seemed utterly shallow when it debuted in 1998, but it has
thrived on the strength of fabulous visual style, brilliant ensemble playing,
and intermittent, unexpected depth. Much of its depth springs from the producers' sensitivity to history as they show history being made by people who
are ignorant of history.

The show presents a vibrant ensemble of "Manhattan women dressed in
silk and satin," just half a century after *On the Town*. Our heroines are working girls, but they are working in the plastic bubble that New York has
increasingly become, propelled by Manhattan's service and spectacle
industries. In law, in publicity, in journalism, in art marketing, they sell

their brains, beauty, charm, and energy, getting generally good deals for themselves and lots of nice designer clothes to display. *Sex and the City* is set in an endless coda to the late-nineties Clinton "boom" (nobody gets out-sourced or downsized here, though a man engaged in kissing a woman's vagina is arrested for insider trading), and part of its allure is women whose sexuality is rather like Clinton's: They don't complain about being grabbed, they get out there and grab, and they feel free to grab anybody they want. One recurrent shot shows our four women barreling down Broadway arm in arm, heading into the camera (and into our laps), flashing their gorgeously colored dresses and purses, and their miniskirted legs, looking like they're dancing in the street. Physically, this shot quotes, or at least alludes to, *On the Town*. But its seriousness and iconic power come from the picture's ironic "post": It is post–World War Two and post-Vietnam, post–sexual-revolution and post-feminist. Our heroines face the world as "a Navy of four," unconnected to any group larger than each other; their looks may nostalgically suggest 1940s sailors' girlfriends, but sexually they are more like the sailors themselves.[52]

The four women we meet are all part of the great diaspora of Liz Phair's *Exile in Guyville*: They know how to "Fuck and Run" as well as any guy. We don't get their CVs (are they on some website I've missed?), but they are pre-sented as children of comfortable suburbs, good liberal arts colleges, and classy city neighborhoods; we are meant to understand that they have learned to be naughty in some very nice places. One of the subtexts of *Sex and the City* is that, in an ultramodern metropolis, among people in the consciousness industry and the spectacle industry, much of the thrill of sex is *talk*. Talking dirty is central to our heroines' dirtiness—their diction is rich in dirty words like "fuck" and "prick"—and montage-style narrative is a mark of their naughtiness. We get to see them naked (or pretty close to naked) in bed with various guys, but it often seems like they get there mainly in order to tell the story to the girls next day at lunch. Their endless lunches (envied by everyone who has to get back to work) work like therapy: They help each other live through painful and even dreadful experiences by situating them in a context of *Bildung*, of growing up. The young Karl Marx, writing about love on his honeymoon in Paris, understood just what they are up to: He said, "human suffering, apprehended humanly, is an en-joyment of self in man."[53]

Carrie, descendant of Dreiser's heroine of Broadway, is the character who carries the burden of all these women's inner lives. She works as a columnist for an "alternative newspaper," and her field is sex. Her voiceovers frame the weekly narratives. Sometimes her narration is smart and even deep, but she is often that archetypally modern figure whom Henry James called "the unreliable narrator." She is the one character on the show who is recognized on the street, and this stirs up all the controversy around her that once swirled around Miss Turnstiles: Is she somebody or nobody? She isn't sure herself. In the grand tradition of Times Square discourse, Carrie is made to interact with her sign. She walks out into 42nd Street just as a city bus turns the corner, featuring *her* as a huge odalisque, advertising her paper; but as she contemplates her image, the bus drenches her with mud and water. She goes home muddy and types a melancholy column. "Can it be," she asks, "that we carefree single girls have missed the boat on love?" Like Phair's heroine in *Guyville*, she yearns for love, dreams of "an old-fashioned boyfriend," but fears her years of sex in the city have disabled her heart.

The incident I will end with, shown in the summer of 2002, could be called Carrie's "Hello Sailor" moment. It is a moment that brings her and us very concretely back to Times Square, where we began. Her sexy sailor is played by the smoldering young African American actor Daniel Sunjata. On a midtown street he helps her get a taxi, introduces himself (as "Louis Leroy from Louisiana"), and invites her and her friends to "a big party for the Navy" that night at the USO just off Times Square. "We have to show them a good time," the super-promiscuous Samantha says, echoing the cabdriver in *On the Town*. "It's our patriotic duty as women of New York." After a hard day, Carrie decides to go. The USO is portrayed as a spectacular panorama of sailors and glamorous girls eating one another up. Carrie meets Louis Leroy once more, they glide together on the dance floor (Otis Redding sings "Try a Little Tenderness"), he touches her back and she sighs, they look soulfully into each other's eyes. For a sophisticated woman on her own, now seems like the perfect moment for sex in the city: If not now, when? But, to our surprise, she turns the sailor down and heads out into the Times Square night alone.

There is some interesting background to this story. When the handsome sailor introduces himself to Carrie, he says, "The fleet's in!" In 1984, the mayor's office (it was Mayor Koch then) entered into a deal with the Navy to create a "Fleet Week" every May or June. For a week or two each year, the city would be decked with ships and flooded with sailors, just like in "the good old days" before the Navy closed the Yard and moved away. Sailors would come off their ships, see the city, act sweet, make friends, spend money (remember the idiom "spending like a drunken sailor"), have sex, make love. Civilians would get to go on board, see spectacular views of the city from the decks, tour the engine rooms, discover the beauty and allure of those big ships, and possibly make nautical friends. The event was a public-relations dream: Everybody would win. (Late in 2003 my son Danny and I "did" the aircraft carrier USS *Intrepid*, along the Hudson at 43rd Street, and we both felt we won.) So Leroy may be presenting himself as a Fleet Week emissary. (Many real sailors in May and June come on just this way.) Or maybe—we don't get to know him long enough to find out—he is quoting Paul Cadmus's delicious painting, and suggesting the two of them would fit right in. Later, when Carrie brings up the sailors' party to her friends, one asks, "Aren't they going to the Gulf?" The women don't seem to care much, but the question does hang in the air. In 2002, "going to the Gulf" meant being part of "the run-up" for President Bush's 2003 invasion of Iraq. The sailors of 2002 were going places that the sailors of "The Fleet's In!" never dreamed of. Carrie's sailor seems to be using images of the Navy's pastoral innocence to promote a very different navy, which is passing through dire straits on the way to some fairly cruel experience. (But maybe not: He could also be expressing nostalgia for the peacetime Navy that is disappearing fast; he could be invoking "The Fleet's In!" as a way of saying he doesn't want it to go out. But he knows, and we know, that when you're in the Navy you've got to go where they send you.)

Carrie and her sailor tear up the dance floor and feel their mutual heat. Then they retreat to a back stairway, where they can share a cigarette and engage in what Carrie believes is the essential form of "sex in the city": intimate talk. But once off the dance floor, this sailor's not so sweet. She asks him how many "great loves" a person can have in their lifetime, and he responds coldly: maybe one, maybe less. Then, as part of the dynamics of flirtation and getting close, she confides to him that until they got together "New York really kicked my ass today." He responds in just the wrong way: instead of drawing closer to her, he stays distant and rips apart New York; it's noisy, it's dirty, people are nasty and impolite (he doesn't notice that he is being pretty nasty and impolite himself), "it's not for me." He dismisses New York in the voice of a schoolmaster expelling a failing student from school; or maybe in the cold voice of President Gerald Ford twenty-five years earlier, refusing a federal loan to save the city from going bankrupt. Any New Yorker old enough to remember the fiscal crisis can recall this chilling voice: I still hear it in nightmares. As the camera focuses on the smiling face of Louis Leroy, it looks like he has frozen into a Southern demagogue, a Madame Tussaud's wax mask of clueless complacency. It seems he has joined the Southern whites who for so long have demonized New York as their "other," and who have dominated American politics for more than two hundred years.

Louis Leroy's disrespect for New York is sad in many ways. One reason people have always loved sailors, going back thousands of years, is their receptivity. Boys from small towns, docking in great ports all over the world, have shown the capacity to adapt, to enjoy what strange places offer them, to ingratiate themselves with people they don't know, to make themselves at home. Eisenstaedt's photo, *Fancy Free, On the Town*—all celebrate the American sailor's sweet openness. I am pretty sure that quite often these qualities have been real. The sweetness of our GIs made America friends all over the world, which, ironically, helped expand American imperial power and control. Is the sweetness still there? It is sad to imagine an American sailor still in his twenties expressing a middle-aged certainty about New York or love or life. He has been here for only a day, he is heading for a war that could kill him, but he already knows it all; no one, not even a romantic and glamorous New York woman, can show him anything new. He's only a kid, but he's existentially closed. Is the show suggesting that from the Good War to the (first) Gulf War our sailors have degenerated? Or maybe that our idealization of sailors has always been a mistake, and if we look close at the real guys in that classic guyville, we will find them no freer, no more loving, no more inwardly harmonious than ourselves?

Carrie knows she's got to bail out of this patriotic gore. "Thanks for that dance," she says, "I really needed that"; she gives him a salute and gets up to go. He suggests it's unsafe (rather than saying he wants to be with her); she assures him she can handle it. She sees there is no point trying to talk with this guy. But she gladly opens up in voiceover to her New York audience, who she feels understands her. "If Louis Leroy is right," she says, "and you only get one great love" in the course of your life, "then New York may well be mine. And I can't have nobody talking shit about my boyfriend." Here, as in "Hello Sailor," the sailor is left puzzled. But we, her loyal audience, can see why she's got to go. She types in a fast file transfer, shifting some of the qualities that figure in the romance of sailors—openness of being, desire to try new things, willingness to get hurt, resolution to bounce back—into a romance of the city. Is there a public space that will bring her shelter from the storm? She runs out into the neon darkness of late-night Times Square, vainly chases one cab, then is ignored by another. The whole ambience of this program seduces us into seeing a quest for a cab as a parable of a search for love. But Carrie's epiphany, that her great love is the city itself, puts daily (and nightly) city frustrations in a more hopeful perspective: From this point, even missed connections are connections. She at once slinks and staggers down one of the traffic islands (lonely woman), down toward 42nd Street. A lovely line of saxophone blue notes appears like a chivalrous late-night escort to keep her company. She is moving toward the Times Square subway station, and for a minute I was thrilled to think: After showing our heroines naked (or pretty close to it) in bed with all sorts of guys, would *Sex and the City* go even farther and actually show these rich girls on the subway? (It's a tease: The program ends before she gets there. Maybe next season?) Accompanied by the blues, she blends into the late-night crowd. The camera follows her in a slow reverse tracking shot, and gradually opens out into the Square's enormity. If this were 1992 instead of 2002, we would worry about her safety, and about her own failure to think about it. In 2002 New York's public spaces are a lot safer, safe enough to worry about loneliness. For late-night Times Square in the 2000s, a lonely woman with an expensive coat trailing behind her is a perfect fit.

At the end of the night, the theater and restaurant crowds have thinned out. Now the electronic signs, saturated with bursts of hot color, bulk larger than ever. As the camera focuses on the great red VIRGIN sign, it takes on the solitary grandeur of a Platonic idea. As Carrie passes under the sign, she throws her coat open to the night. Like Jean-Luc Godard's heroines in the 1960s, she embraces a neon sign as a symbol of what she secretly, hopelessly yearns for. Remember, Carrie worried, "That ship has sailed," with respect to sailors like Leroy; modern women like herself "have missed the boat on love." If she could trade in her sophistication for what she imagines as a new innocence, maybe her ship could come in? After separating herself from a sexy sailor, she uses the whole class of sailors as material for allegory: "Maybe the past is an anchor holding us back," she tells us in voiceover. "You have to let go of who you were to become who you will be." As she tells herself to let go, all the Square's colors melt and her world becomes black-and-white; then it disappears and we fade to black.

In this show's last minute, the heroine stumbles on a primary modern fantasy: If we can only forget all we know, all we have done, and all we are, we can reach a state of primal innocence and a new pinnacle of innocent joy. Nietzsche called it "creative forgetting." The camera caresses the giant VIRGIN sign: It is the allure of the pole star at the end of Carrie's journey to the end of the night. *To become a virgin again:* This is the consummation that Doris Day might have dreamed of forty years ago, the El Dorado of perfect Americanism that Jerome Robbins tried to impress on HUAC and on himself, the seven-eleven throw of the dice that another friendly witness, Abe Burrows, imagined for his crew of men who knew too much in *Guys and Dolls*. I think it's the primary hope that has propelled the gigantic, twenty-year, multi-billion-dollar, endless "Cleanup of Times Square."

But *Sex and the City* won't buy it. Their Square is a wine-dark sea where people cling to their anchors, and people recognize each other as grown-ups with intense, complicated needs. Here the blue notes in the background are actually part of the foreground, acting not only as company for everybody in this lonely crowd, but as a kind of Times Square souvenir that they can take home with them and that will continue to bind them together. Our last look at Carrie shows her blending into the liquidity of the Times Square night, in a moment of solitude that is also a moment of community: a community of yearners, a community of others.

CHAPTER 4

Times Girl and Her Daughters

The electricity flows in rivers . . . disports itself in a great spectacle. . . . I ascend to the top of the "Times" building, which is one of the boldest of the skyscrapers. . . . The most diabolical [sign] of all is the face of a woman, which occupies as much space in the sky as the Great Bear. During the few seconds she shines, her left eye winks as though in enticing appeal. . . . What on earth can they be selling down there?

—Pierre Loti, "Impressions of New York,"
Century Magazine, 1913[1]

. . . her earning capacity fell short of her yearning capacity.
—title describing Babs Comet,
switchboard operator in Times Square,
heroine of silent movie *Classified* (1926)

To understand the history of women in Times Square, we have to note its startling trajectories. It started in the 1890s, around the new electrified theaters that opened on and near Broadway, a living spectacle that presented a few women as stars and invited many women to present themselves in public as spectators. Then (there is much argument about when), with a minimum of change to its façade, the spectacle split into two radically different places, the bowtie and the deuce: The bowtie developed into a festival of signs where generations of men and women could interact and grow, and where, at "the great noon" of 1945, strangers could embrace and love; the deuce became a shock corridor where images of women were degraded and real women repelled. For a time, you could say a kind of delicate balance subsisted between the spaces. But in the 1970s, as the city teetered near bankruptcy, the balance collapsed: The deuce grew nastier, its violence spilled over and stained the bowtie, whose great signs went dark, whose open spaces seemed to close, and whose women felt abandoned and alone. In the 1990s, in a travesty of Hegel's dialectic, "the negation of the negation," a giant private-public real estate deal removed the scene that had removed the women, and a new generation of women, now for the first time in the top ranks of government and corporate management, engineered and produced the deal. "The deal" is Times Square's greatest-ever work of living theater, and all of us who are trying to grasp and judge it are living inside the deal now.

Some of the women in this chapter are real women who have passed through the Square and passed their lives around it, like my mother and her sister Idie. Some are women characters in books, plays, movies, and cartoons set and sometimes made in and around the Square. Some are singers of songs, and some are subjects and objects of those songs. Some are figures in several generations of electric signs. Sometimes they are portrayed in relationships with men, sometimes with other women, sometimes as parts of large collectivities—like Times Square itself—and sometimes alone. I know I am mixing all sorts of languages, styles, and cultural genres. But this is a place that has always been a mix of different and often sharply clashing planes of life and reality; most of the books about it, even the smart ones, haven't been mixed enough.

For a tremendous assortment of women, the Square has been a workplace, a source of entertainment, a source of work in the entertainment industry. But it has also been more. It has played a large role in women's *Bildung,* in their moral education, their work of finding themselves, of identity formation, of growing up. It was a place where they could conduct what John Stuart Mill, in his book *On Liberty,* called "experiments of living."[2] Of course this has been true for plenty of men as well. It helped both my parents move beyond the horizons of the Lower East Side ghetto where they grew up. But places like Times Square have made more of a difference for women, because the experience of being here is so intensely *public.* In most societies through the ages, men's lives have been largely defined by roles they have played—sometimes chosen, usually imposed—in their society's public life. Women, on the other hand, have been mostly locked up in a variety of domestic cocoons, unable to participate in any sort of public life at all. There is a nursery rhyme that every kid learns which puts the gender polarity just right:

> *Peter, Peter, pumpkin eater,*
> * had a wife but couldn't keep her.*
> *He put her in a pumpkin shell,*
> * and there he kept her very well.*

For centuries, the only socially recognized "public women" were whores. The long-term process of modernization, and modern phenomena like great cities, mass democracy, popular culture, the Jazz Singer's "my name in electric lights," have created significant openings in public life for both sexes. But women, before they could be there, had to break out of the pumpkin; they have had to come a longer way, make a bigger leap, pay a higher price.

In the 1890s, in Sister Carrie's generation, when the neighborhood was still called Longacre Square, it was already full of girls breaking out of the pumpkin. Look back to our Times Girl montage: Look past her and past the big building, and see all the five-story houses on the Square's far (west) side. From the 1890s to the 1920s, when big office buildings replaced them, they were what people called "theatrical boardinghouses," mostly for young people (or young families) hoping to make it on one or another plane of "Broadway." Eugene O'Neill was born in one of these houses (his father spent twenty years playing the Count of Monte Cristo). Theatrical designer Aline Bernstein, remembered as Thomas Wolfe's lover and muse, grew up in one. She uses a lovely phrase to describe the crowds of young actresses in the summer, setting out from these houses in their most colorful dresses, going round to agents to look for work: "They embroidered Broadway with themselves."[3] American popular culture has built many splendid comic and tragic monuments to them: *42nd Street*; the *Gold Diggers* films; the Betty Boop cartoons; *Stage Door*; *Dance, Girl, Dance*; *Guys and Dolls*; *The Band Wagon*; *A Chorus Line*; and many more. Susan Glenn, in her book *Female Spectacle*, portrays girls like this as the source of a new model: "the reflection of a new generation of striving urban women. [They] symbolized the emergence of modern women into the twentieth century."[4]

Back to Times Girl: Her postcard seems to work in a more complex way than postcards usually do. Instead of saying, "Here I am, the same person you've always known, in front of this grand palace," it says something like, "I'm changing myself, I'm becoming more like this girl, this brave new building is helping me change." The act of sending this card through the mail is a psychic adventure, an advertisement for the self the sender wants to be. Times Girl is propping her left leg against a space across the street where another building should be (the Condé Nast Building is there today). Its façade is blank except for the message: "Talk about hard times? Send me a cushion! Yours," and a space left blank for the sender's name. Now many people knew in 1900 that *Hard Times* was a classic modern book, and that it brought home the misery of the urban working class. This has to be a force in the card's human background. But anyone who looks at the Times Tower in the foreground has to notice that "hard times" also has a crudely comic sexual point. Both meanings, the Dickensian tragedy and the Mae West comedy, are in the card. To identify yourself with Times Square in the 1900s is to imagine yourself playing both, or being both. If we can imagine people who might have sent Times Girl, or might have received her, we should be able to get a feeling for Times Square's poignancy and depth.

Times Girl is not only Sister Carrie's kid sister; she is the twentieth century's first comic hero. (Chaplin's tramp, who resembles her, may be the second.) She exposes and stretches and spreads herself out over an abyss. She looks undefended, like an open city. But somehow, with her hand on the Times Building, she is not only keeping her balance but having a good time, and maybe even laughing at herself. But the force of her comedy depends on her closeness to tragedy. She is too close! She kicks her legs up with the exuberance of a girl on a swing; but even as we feel enthralled, we know that although Times Square may be a place to play, it's no playground, and it's a long way down. She knows it herself, and puts her appeal in the mail. She shows the world her spirit along with her flesh. Look at her again, and you will see a classic archetype of a modern woman on her own, inhabiting the city center but living close to the edge, surrounded by men and institutions who want her lights, but wouldn't think of recognizing her rights. By virtue of her verve and nerve, she incarnates what Baudelaire in the 1840s called "the heroism of modern life."

In the 1900s, thanks to extensive lobbying by the newspaper, Longacre Square metamorphosed into Times Square. The *Times's* new corporate headquarters opened with an extravagant fireworks display on the stroke of midnight, on New Year's Day 1905. It was a twenty-five-story skyscraper with a dashing modern form like the triangular Flatiron Building, and handsome detailing that evoked the Florentine Renaissance. The building was universally praised, and its image, beaming floodlights over the city, was reproduced on mass postcards and in Sunday rotogravures. (The floodlights shone on special occasions till sometime in the 1930s.) In 1904, the Square became the terminal point for the new IRT and BMT subway stations. The subways brought tens of thousands of people every day; they not only instantly made 42nd Street and Broadway the most crowded place in New York, but connected it directly with every far-flung immigrant neighborhood in Brooklyn, the Bronx, and Queens. The enormous neo-Baroque Astor Hotel opened in 1905. It was instantly beloved, especially by producers and consumers of show business, but also by tourists looking for a New York "flavor"; it stayed beloved even after it was abruptly destroyed in 1965. These buildings expanded the architectural scale, and paved the way for more big buildings, mostly office towers. They not only expanded the architectural scale, but enlarged both the day and the night populations. The thousands of people who worked around the Square every day became a primary market for the theaters, restaurants, dance halls, and cabarets that thrived by night; these entertainments in turn could expand radically, now that enlarged markets were just outside on the streets. Meanwhile, the development of electric power in the 1900s made it feasible to install enormous electric signs, sometimes mounted on the roofs of shorter older buildings, sometimes on the façades of big new ones. Years of conflict between Broadway and Fifth Avenue owners' associations led to a plan to restrict electric signs in most of Manhattan, but to concentrate them around Times Square. In 1909, a state court overturned a city law that limited their size. Nearly overnight, a new generation of huge, bright, kinetic signs came to life.[5]

The new signs gave the Square a new scale of expression. All through the twentieth century, and into our own, the electronic billboard became a prime metaphor for the expansion and magnification of the self. And Times Square emerged as a utopia for men and women and children all over the world who dreamed of "making spectacles of themselves."

In the great crowds that poured out of the subways, down from the elevated trains, off the trolleys and into the Square every day, there was an amazing variety of women, women of all classes and ethnicities: cooks, bakers, waitresses, seamstresses, milliners, maids, office cleaners, salesgirls for all commodities, actresses and singers and dancers, wardrobe mistresses and costumers, switchboard operators, fashion models, theater ushers and dressers, nightclub hatcheck girls, office clerks, typists, stenographers, bookkeepers, and on and on. Many of the neighborhood's boardinghouses crossed a sexual frontier, and became home to thousands of working girls. Richard Harding Davis wrote about them in 1892:

> The girl bachelor, who is either a saleslady or a working girl . . . can and does walk alone. . . . She has found her hall bedroom cold and lonely after the long working day behind a counter or at a loom, and the loneliness tends to homesickness . . . so she puts on her hat and steps down a side-street and loses herself in the unending processions on Broadway, where, though she knows no one, and no one wants to know her, there is light and color, and she is at least not alone.[6]

And thousands more every day and night came into the Square as customers for all its infinite varieties of entertainment. There may never have been such a vast variety of women thrown together in any one place before. A small proportion of these women were prostitutes, professionally offering many varieties of sex, and appealing to customers in every class.* Other women, sexual amateurs (though often fairly sophisticated), offered themselves to coworkers, bosses, or customers, sometimes in hope of a respectable marriage, other times settling for cruder satisfactions like furs, jewels, and rent money. Some would have died rather than give up their premarital virginity, yet sought alluring ways to present their sexuality in the ways they dressed and moved and spoke.

All this gave the Square an aura of tremendous sexual promise. And it frightened the hell out of many moralists, who agitated for laws that would

---

*"From the beginnings," says Lawrence Senelick, "the Times Square region was ringed with red lights." This is from his essay "Private Parts in Public Places," in *Inventing Times Square*, 330. See also Timothy Gilfoyle, "Policing of Sexuality," in *Inventing Times Square*, 297–314, and his fascinating book, *City of Eros: New York City, Prostitution and the Commercialization of Sex, 1790–1929* (New York and London: W. W. Norton, 1992). Gilfoyle shows, in rich detail, how prostitution followed the movement of respectable entertainment uptown. The great leap came in the 1880s, with the opening of the Metropolitan Opera House on Broadway and 39th Street. Gilfoyle accepts the estimate of "antivice" activists, the Committee of Fifteen, that the neighborhood in 1901 contained at least "132 different addresses housing some form of prostitution"—brothels, tenements, apartment houses, and hotels—and provides a block-by-block map. He mentions the proliferation of streetwalkers near public places, and cites a complaint by the Reverend Adam Clayton Powell, Sr. (later father of the Congressman from Harlem) that his West 40th Street Church was "in the most notorious red-light district in New York City." On Sunday nights after services, Powell said, streetwalkers with their dresses open would stand across the street from the church and solicit men as they came out. Gilfoyle adds that the West 43rd Street block that would later house the *Times* was known in the 1900s as "Soubrette Row." (*City of Eros*, 207ff.)

create curfews, establish early closing hours for theaters, restaurants, and cabarets, shut down the subways, and generally "clean up Times Square." It is important to understand that the enemies of Times Square have always been a very diverse group of people. Some of them, in Lewis Erenberg's words, were "traditional moralists, often of evangelical background, who believed that play itself was an affront against God."[7] But many others were secular intellectuals with left politics—people like Jane Addams, Walter Lippmann, Lewis Mumford—who wanted the masses to be radical and militant and to struggle for their rights, and who believed that commercial mass culture was corrupting their minds.

As much as moralists detested prostitution, they were probably even more upset by New York's new wave of cabarets, which clustered around the Square in the 1900s. These cabarets seem to have been modeled on the Parisian *café-concerts* of the late nineteenth century. (For the originals, see Degas, Manet, Lautrec, and Zola's *Nana*.) Unlike already-existing saloons and dance halls, patronized by male customers who flirted with women employees, the cabarets were "places where men and women went together," and they were "open to everyone." The Raines Law of 1905, which regulated drinking in New York, made crucial distinctions among public spaces. It established some boundaries, but tore other boundaries down:

> What set cabarets apart . . . was the removal of overt and blatant prostitution from their premises. Men wanting to purchase sex now went to hotels for the actual intercourse. This enabled cabarets to cultivate an atmosphere of subtle sensuality, allowing middle- and upper-class women to join in the fun.[8]

These turn-of-the-century cabarets helped turn Times Square into "a dangerously open environment." Respectable women were seen as an especially endangered species: Places like this could drive "women out of control." A decade later, the great fear was dance halls. Julian Street, a social commentator and author of *Welcome to New York* (1913), lamented

> the hodge-podge of people in which respectable young married and unmarried women, and even debutantes, dance not only under the same roof but in the same room with women of the town.[9]

It wasn't for nothing that they called Times Square "the capital of dangerous love."[10]

What were these angry moralists afraid of? "The principle of the modern world," Hegel wrote in the 1820s, "is freedom of subjectivity."[11] Let's think about public spaces: A great public space puts everybody in it on display. In traditional cultures, "women of the town" are routinely displayed for sale or for rent, but respectable women are displayed only at specified times (e.g., festivals), and then only under the control of others: parents, husbands, elders, priests. Very early in its life, even before it got its current name, Times Square emerged as a place where respectable women could have the freedom to be "going to see and be seen,"[12] to *display* themselves. When women walking through the Square looked at each other, or at female characters and actresses (and at fellow audience members) in plays or movies, or at singers and dancers and hostesses in clubs or in cabarets, or at figures on the giant signs around and above them, we should try to imagine their glances as part of their *Bildung,* their growth as human beings. Visions of other women suggested people they might want to know or imitate or assimilate or hope to become. (A different but similar spectrum opened up when they looked at men.) For women looking at ways to be modern, to change themselves, to become sexual subjects as well as objects, to engage in sexuality in ways that could engage their subjectivity, the Square was a great fair or bazaar or *agora* of human possibilities, an exemplary democratic space.[13] Of course, for women or men who do not want to change, or who want not to change, Times Square was a far more problematical place.

Sister Carrie: *Lonely at the Top*

The first serious vision of "dangerous love" in Times Square appears in Theodore Dreiser's *Sister Carrie.*[14] The book starts on a train to Chicago: Dreiser's heroine is on her way to the big city, where she hopes to find a better life. She has no marketable skills, except for her youth and her charm. But in the cities of the Gilded Age, these qualities turn out to have more market value than she thought. She is not conventionally beautiful, but people notice her; they are struck with her soulfulness and yearning. She

falls in love with one man, then another. This second man, George Hurstwood, throws over his own life and moves with her to the metropolis of New
York. At first, she doesn't know what to do with herself. But before long, she
finds work in New York's rapidly expanding entertainment industry. In the
1890s, that industry is just coming to be centered in Times Square.

Times Square marked New York's uptown boundary for most of the
nineteenth century. In the 1870s, its main use was as stables. But after the
invention of the lightbulb in 1879, it quickly became the city's prime entertainment district. Dozens of theaters, restaurants, and cabarets soon opened
up or moved uptown; all were newly and elaborately wired, and all offered
electric light as a spectacle. By the 1890s, "the gay nineties," the whole
neighborhood was bathed in light, and had an aura of spectacle. That light
show generated two of the twentieth century's triumphal images: "the city
that never sleeps,"* and the individual with "his name in lights."† At the
book's end, Carrie has risen from the chorus and become a star; not only
does she have a new name—she is born again as "Carrie Madenda"—but
her name is in lights. Intellectually, *Sister Carrie* towers above the products
of Broadway, but it defines what will become one of Broadway's strongest
traditions, celebrated in the 1930s in *42nd Street* and in the 1970s in *A Chorus Line:* The leaders come from the line; the chorus is a school for stars; the
theater incarnates democracy's primal myth.‡

Dreiser situates Carrie's theatrical company on 39th Street and Broad-

---

*This image sounds ultramodern, but actually goes back to the Bible, specifically to the prophetic vi-
sion of Second Isaiah in the sixth century B.C. This writer's utopian prophecy also contains one of the
earliest mentions of the idea of the "world city": "Arise and shine, for your light has come. . . . They all
gather together, they come to you . . . the abundance of the sea shall be turned to you, the wealth of
nations shall come to you. . . . Your gates shall be open continually, day and night they shall not be
shut, that men may bring to you the wealth of nations." Isaiah 60: 1–13.

†The actress, producer, and diva Maxine Elliott may be the first person in New York with "her name
in lights." In 1908, shortly after the opening of the Metropolitan Opera, she opened "MAXINE EL-
LIOTT'S THEATRE" diagonally across from it.

‡This tradition flies in the face of the dualism that defines Susan Glenn's argument: "the spectacle of
female self-assertion" versus "theatrical spectacles that worked to obliterate the notion of female autonomy and personality" (*Female Spectacle*, 8). Glenn's aim may be to expose the tradition as a lie. Any
current or former chorine, and any lover of theater, would agree that it is *mostly* a lie. But the kernel of
truth in the myth accounts for much of theater's aura, leads smart and talented women (and men) to
throw themselves into it, generation after generation, and keeps theatrical production alive. Glenn
specifically cites *Sister Carrie*, along with Willa Cather's 1915 novel *The Song of the Lark*, for using
"the performing woman to explore the theme of female self-production through stage spectacle" (7).

way, just below the Square, and calls it "the Casino." Dreiser appears to have been friendly with several of its real-life eponym's members, to whom he was introduced by his brother, the Broadway songwriter Paul Dresser. (Dresser had changed his name from Dreiser.) In Dreiser's autobiographical memoir, *Newspaper Days*, he speaks of "the far-famed Casino, with its famous choruses of girls, the mecca of all night-loving Jonnies and rowdies."[15] The Casino's longest-running and most spectacular chorus starred in the musical comedy *Florodora*, which appeared in the same year as *Sister Carrie*, 1900. *Florodora*'s chorus was a sextet of ingenues who sang "Tell Me, Pretty Maiden," a song that for decades was one of operetta's greatest hits. (It sounded pretty sappy to me in the 1950s when I heard it on "Your Show of Shows.") Within a couple of years, Atkinson says, "all had married millionaires."[16] Their track record helped to create a stereotype that thrived all through the twentieth century: young girls who put themselves on show in the hope of attracting rich men who will not only marry them but get them out of show business. In their instrumental and pragmatic display of charm, the *Florodora* girls paved the way for the protagonists of *Gentlemen Prefer Blondes*, "Diamonds Are a Girl's Best Friend," and *How to Marry a Millionaire*. They may be stars of the theater, but the society page is where they want to be.

The most famous alumna of *Florodora*, not a member of the sextet but part of the larger chorus, was Evelyn Nesbit. Atkinson describes her as "a stunning girl of sixteen from Tarentum, Pennsylvania." She had an affair with the great architect Stanford White, designer of Penn Station and Columbia University, but married a coal millionaire, fellow Pennsylvanian Harry Thaw. (In fact, White, too, was from Pennsylvania; the state's inner dialectics, hard for outsiders to grasp, are a subtext of this affair.) Thaw was widely regarded as a dolt, barely capable of a coherent English sentence. I don't know if he originated the stereotype of the brain-dead millionaire who parks his limousine in front of the stage door, but he certainly helped to nourish it. Inept as he looked, he still managed to confront White and shoot him three times in the head. There was a sensational murder trial which brought out endless details of money, romance, and intrigue on Broadway. Thaw was found insane, but his crime gave his stereotype new depth: millionaire-dolt-murderer. Nesbit stayed in circulation for years, but apparently nothing gave her an inner depth to replace her lost youth. She came to be known by the name of a toy (a sex toy? a sentimental toy? a mix of both?) that White had made for her: "The Girl in the Red Velvet Swing."*

Near the end of the book, Carrie becomes a star, and fan mail starts to pour in. Much of it comes from men who claim to be millionaires. The first time it happens, her friend Lola urges her to follow it up: "Why don't you see him. . . . He couldn't hurt you. You might have some fun with him." Although Carrie is lonely, she is adamant about this: "I know what he'd say. I don't want to meet anyone that way" (48, 456).† As *Sister Carrie* ends, her character is still open, not fully defined. But at least we know she doesn't want to market herself like a Florodora girl. One way we can know her is by what she does *not* become.

The name of Carrie's company, "the Casino Players," dramatizes Dreiser's whole view of the world. It shows the randomness of human fate. With Carrie's rise comes George Hurstwood's fall. First he can't hold a job; then he can't get a new one; then he takes to drink; then he plunges into ever-deepening depression; then he kills himself. But first he leaves Carrie, knowing there's nothing she can do to help him. In charting the downward spiral, Dreiser has perfect pitch. He is deft in avoiding moralism: There's no "reason" for Hurstwood's downfall, nothing we could mark as a tragic flaw. One up, one down: In a Casino world, that's life.

Dreiser felt the same scorn for late-nineteenth-century theater that Bernard Shaw conveyed so powerfully. The plays Carrie sees, and then acts in, are foolish and shallow: "They have the charm of showing suffering under ideal conditions" (35, 325). They make no demands on either the cast or the audience. Nevertheless, once she gets onstage, she displays an ex-

---

*The movie *The Girl in the Red Velvet Swing* appeared in 1955, directed by Richard Fleischer, written by Charles Brackett, and starring Ray Milland as Stanford White, Farley Granger as Harry Thaw, a youthful Joan Collins as Nesbit, and the great magisterial Yiddish actor Luther Adler as the lawyer whose dialectics save Thaw from death. So far as I can tell, it has never appeared on videotape. (I can remember the reviews from my childhood: They all agreed it was dumb, but also said it was dirty. Why did I pass it up? A fifteen-year-old boy at Bronx High School of Science, I wanted dirty, but not dumb. I looked up to women like Marlene Dietrich, Lauren Bacall, Lena Horne, Simone Signoret, who looked both dirty and smart.)

E. L. Doctorow, in *Ragtime* (Random House, 1975), may be the first to treat Nesbit with sympathy and respect. He brings her to the 1910s Lower East Side, and brings her together with poor Yiddish artists, neglected children, and Emma Goldman. He portrays her as a complex person capable of spiritual growth and self-development.

†Numbers in parentheses designate chapter and pages of the edition of *Sister Carrie* used throughout section. See note 14, page 240.

pressive power that transcends her material: a quality that Dreiser calls "emotional greatness," a soulful "longing for that which is better" (40, 378). She is innocent of the Gilded Age bombast and pretension that drive most of the people around her. She feels empathy for poor people. "Carrie had experienced too much of the bitterness of search and poverty, not to sympathize keenly" (47, 457). As she sits for the first time in a good restaurant in New York, she has a flashback, and "in that flash was seen the other Carrie, poor, hungry, drifting at her wits' ends, and all Chicago a cold and closed world" (35, 324). Even after she becomes a Broadway star, "She remembered the time when she walked the streets of Chicago" (45, 435). But before that, when her middle-aged lover starts to falter and fail, her empathy and soulfulness dry up fast. Unemployed, Hurstwood spends a brief interval as a house-husband. When he remarks on the high cost of butter, she snaps, "You wouldn't mind it if you were working" (39, 365). When he says he can't get a steady job in New York, she responds not just with impatience but with a condescension that is brand-new and startling: "You couldn't have tried so very hard," she says; "*I* got something" (42, 401). Soon she uncouples herself from him, concentrates on her career, and manages not to see the drama that she knows must be going on just offstage.

The Square is where they meet for the last time. It isn't clear how much time has passed, but Hurstwood has caved in and crashed. He is dressed in rags and shaking from the cold. He, and many like him, drags himself through the cold from one end of Manhattan to the other all day long. Hurstwood still can read, and even as he falls, he sees stories of Carrie's rise. Finally, one icy day, after trudging through the Square, he stops in front of the backstage entrance to the Casino and waits for her.

> "George," she said, "what's the matter with you?"
>
> "I've been sick," he answered. "I just got out of the hospital. For God's sake, let me have a little money, will you?"
>
> "Of course," said Carrie, her lip trembling. . . . "But what's the matter with you anyhow?"
>
> She was opening her purse, and now pulled out all and the only bills in it, a five and two twos.
>
> "I've been sick, I told you. . . ."

"Here," she said. "It's all I've got with me."

"All right," he answered softly. "I'll give it back to you some day"
(49, 477).

People stare at this odd couple. What are they doing together? She doesn't
know enough to be able to explain, but she feels enough empathy to be par-
alyzed with grief and guilt. He is openly, desperately needy, yet he doesn't
seem angry, just very, very sad. He tells her he lives on the Bowery now. Now
that he has got her to connect with him, he turns solicitous, almost courtly
toward her.

"Better go on in," he said. "I'm much obliged but I won't bother
you any more."

She tried to answer but he turned away and shuffled off toward the
east.

Carrie and her audience know where he is going. "Toward the east" signifies
the East River, and in the language of 1900—Stephen Crane's 1893 novel,
Maggie: A Girl of the Streets (A Story of New York), marks the spot—this
river means death. In poor people's New York a century ago, the sun set in
the east. We can see she would give and share more if she could, but we can
see, too, that nobody can help him now. (Given the overpowering depression with which Dreiser afflicts him, probably no one could have helped
him then, either. But she learns what we knew all along: She got off the
death train too soon.)

This is one of the most heartrending scenes in all American literature.
But it isn't over yet: A chapter later, Dreiser hits us with a crushing coda.
Hurstwood, even more wrecked than he was a little while ago, heads for the
Square's bright lights like a moth seeking flame.

"I'll just go down Broadway," he said to himself.

When he reached 42nd Street, the fire signs were already burning
bright. Crowds were hastening to dine. Through bright windows at
every corner might be seen gay companies in luxurious restaurants.
There were coaches, and crowded cable cars (50, 493).

Earlier in the book, Dreiser describes Carrie's first visit to Broadway. She is
bowled over by the grandeur of its shops and signs and the glamour of its
people. Many of these people want to isolate it as a kind of upper-class
ghetto. Their hopes will be frustrated in the 1900s, with the coming of the
subway. But meanwhile, Dreiser mentions a hit song that describes a poor
and shabby man, and demands: "What Right Has He on Broadway?" (34,
323). Hurstwood comes to stake out a claim, a right to be there, "going pur-
posely to see and be seen," wrecked as he may be. He stops in front of

> an imposing restaurant, before which blazed a fire sign . . . through
> the large plate windows could be seen the red and gold decorations,
> the palms, the white napery and shiny glassware, and above all, the
> comfortable crowd.

He proceeds to make the outsider's gesture that became classic in the course
of the nineteenth century: He sticks his face against the glass to look inside.
In one of the primal scenes in nineteenth-century literature, in the midst of
the grand masked ball, "Madame Bovary turned her head and saw the peas-
ants peering in from the garden, their faces pressed against the glass."[17] *Sister Carrie* urbanizes this primal scene: It is an everyday (or every-night)
event in Times Square; but then, Times Square is a place where there is a
grand ball every night. (In the 1990s, Mayor Giuliani baptized Hurstwood's
gesture a "quality-of-life crime.") So close to the "gay companies" who fill
the Square in the 1890s, he gets mad at last:

> "Eat . . . That's right, eat. Nobody else wants any." People turned to
> look after him, so uncouth was his shambling figure. Several officers
> followed him with their eyes to see that he did not beg of anybody.

He realizes he has called attention to himself more than he can afford to.
"In his weary and hungry state he should never have come here. The contrast was too sharp."

> Then his voice dropped even lower, and his mind half lost the fancy it
> had.

"It's mighty cold," he said. "Awful cold."

"What's the use," he thought. "It's all up with me. I'll quit this" (494).

That very night, he will find a Bowery lodging house where he can turn on the gas and make a "fire sign" all his own (499).

But before we come to this grisly ending, Dreiser twists the knife in Hurstwood, in Carrie, and in us once more. While still on Broadway, he drifts past the Casino again. This time he is too wasted to wait for anyone or ask for anything or even know where he is. But suddenly, surging up before him, filling the frame, here Carrie is again! Can it be she? Yes and no: It is "a large gilt-framed poster-board on which was a fine lithograph of Carrie, life-size." It isn't the woman—the lost love of his life—it's her *sign.* That sign not only brings him back to life, it awakens his dormant resentment and repressed rage:

> "That's you," he said at last, addressing her. "Wasn't good enough
> for you, was I? Huh . . ."
>
> "She's got it," he said. . . . "Let her give me some" (494).

He starts for the stage door, but an attendant pushes him away, and he slips and falls in the snow. He looks up at the Square's shimmering lights and fire signs from the perspective of down on the ground.

> Now a fierce feeling against Carrie welled up—just one fierce, angry
> thought before the whole thing slipped out of his mind. "She owes me
> something to eat," he said. "She owes it to me."

"Hopelessly he turned back into Broadway again and slopped onward, begging, crying, losing track of his thoughts." Dreiser leaves Hurstwood and us in an uncertain state: We never learn whether he understands that it isn't Carrie, it's her sign. This is nearly his last night, but he will not go gentle into it. He affirms the right of even the lowest of the low to be "on Broadway." The fire signs fill him with hate, but also, ironically, as he moves closer and closer to death, they pull him toward life.

She owes it to me. Carrie would probably agree. One of her star qualities is her feeling for all the people out there who will never become stars. Great actors and actresses in the nineteenth century tended to repress low origins and give themselves aristocratic genealogies; Dickens was the striking exception. Carrie incarnates a new type, distinctive in twentieth-century mass culture: the star who has come from the bottom of society, but who remembers where she (or he) came from. In the twentieth century, the audience for popular forms is much expanded: It is full of people who started low; once movies and other forms of electronic entertainment get going, it will be full of people who are still low. Many twentieth-century stars have the distinctive power to incorporate their early poverty into their auras, to turn their lowliness into an intimate bond with "their people." Charlie Chaplin, Louis Armstrong, Al Jolson, defined this twentieth-century form. (Sarah Bernhardt somehow embodied both forms, and figures as a transition.) During the Great Depression, it was developed by figures like Billie Holiday, John Garfield, and Woody Guthrie. After World War Two, it was spread round the world by Edith Piaf, Evita, Elvis, Pele, John Lennon, and rappers like Tupac Shakur and Biggie Smalls. In figures like Bruce Springsteen and Eminem, the form lives on; they *won't* escape their origin, which gives them an obsessive depth that transcends the celebrity that might otherwise flood them out.*

Carrie's last scene, with her friend and roommate Lola, reminds us of different ways to remember the past. They are sitting in the comfortable hotel suite they share, while a blizzard rages outside. They see a man fall down in the snow. Carrie asks, "Aren't you sorry for all the people who haven't got anything tonight?" Lola says no, she's not sorry; in fact, as the man falls, she laughs. She says, "people never gave me anything when I was hard up"; she seems to think that is enough to explain why she has no empathy for people who are hard up now (50, 495). Lola's language echoes fictional characters like Bounderby in Dickens's *Hard Times* and Becky Sharp in Thackeray's *Vanity Fair*, along with the many real-life "self-made

---

*If this were a different book, I would argue that the first up-from-the-bottom modern star was Jean-Jacques Rousseau. His mother died at his birth ("Motherless Geneva"), his father abandoned him; he was passed from relative to relative, and got in endless trouble in his hometown; he ran away at sixteen, he got arrested as a homeless vagabond in two different countries—and somehow, through this dreadful mess, he developed not only a sense of his own lonely subjectivity, but a gut feeling for "the people" and a vision of their collective sorrows and hopes and history. Overall, he created a body of work, full of contradictions, that goes farther than anybody else's work in defining "modern thought."

men" and "Social Darwinists" who bulked large in the culture of the 1890s. Dreiser sympathizes with poor people, but he doesn't sentimentalize them. He shows how the memory of one's own poverty can lead to greater empathy and generosity, but it can also lead the other way. When *Sister Carrie* came out in 1900, although the author made little money from it, it made him a star. It shines not just in its powerful narratives of rise and fall, but in its insight into the ambiguities of life at the top. Carrie is special not just because she gets to be a star, but because Dreiser has imagined her in a way that makes us feel she *deserves* to be a star.

It isn't her, it's her sign. This encounter defines a classic Times Square moment. One of the Square's great qualities, since the 1890s, has been its plethora of signs. In 1900, thanks to electrification, the signs are more radiant and luminous than ever. Their scope is *mass* communication. Leaps forward in photographic technology have made it possible to put super-life-size images of people on display. These signs help transform the Square's public space into a mass medium. Once the signs are there, a great collective leap in perception and awareness takes place. García Márquez, writing of Macondo, manages to see Times Square: "In that state of hallucinated lucidity, not only did they see the images of their own dreams, but some saw the images dreamed by others."[18]

What will the new "hallucinated lucidity" do for twentieth-century men and women? Its effects will be paradoxical and contradictory. Hurstwood's old love for Carrie reawakens when he meets her in the flesh, "the image of his own dream"; but he feels enervated and even violated by her sign, an "image dreamed by others." As for Carrie, she loves her work as an actress on the stage, but she can't adapt to the state of celebrity, where everyone wants to be seen with her or near her, but no one gives a damn what she actually thinks or feels; critics praise the sense of inwardness she projects, but nobody ever asks her what is going on inside her. The one exception is a critic named Ames, reminiscent of Dreiser himself, who suggests to her that her inner loneliness resonates with a great many other people's out there (35, 333ff.; 47, 479ff.). She lives in a "celebrity suite" at the Hotel Wellington: The landlords charge her a "celebrity rate," which is "anything you think you could afford to pay" (42, 451); they know her presence will create "a buzz" that will bring more business in. In her celebrity suite, looking out at her name displayed to the world in lights, she is lonelier than ever.

Her very sadness magnifies her melancholy allure. Lola is irritated: "You oughtn't to be lonely," she says. "There's lots would give their ears to be in your shoes" (47, 458). In fact, "her lonely, self-withdrawing temper" makes her a new form of "interesting figure in the public eye" (49, 478). But being interesting doesn't amount to being humanly happy.* She feels crushed by her sign, even though it is a sign of her success. She may be the first American character to be convincingly lonely at the top.

Theodore Dreiser was a cultural journalist before he became a novelist. Starting out in the small towns of the Midwest, then working in Pittsburgh, he found himself instantly at home on Broadway. Younger brother of the songwriter Paul Dresser, Dreiser in 1897 created one of the great archetypal lines in the history of American popular music: "I long to see my mother in the doorway." (This is the key line in the song "On the Banks of the Wabash," which, before sound recording, sold half a million copies in a year.)[19] Dreiser was instinctively at home with the ironies of the twentieth-century mass media world: the world that Guy Debord, in the 1960s, would call the "society of spectacle."[20] Dreiser made his debut as a novelist just at the moment that a society of spectacle was growing up along and around Broadway. If we get into the flow of his writing, he can help us feel at home in an environment that constantly nurtures experiments in self-display and in self-alienation, a place where these human antitheses intertwine and flourish together in the same bright light.

The 1920s: "Hallucinated Lucidity"

As time has gone by, the energy I had hoped to expend in a general chapter on Times Square in the 1920s got channeled instead into a chapter-long essay on Al Jolson and *The Jazz Singer*. One theme that is salient in the Jolson essay is the arrival of Jews in Times Square, especially East European Jews, "from the other side." They enriched vaudeville and popular comedy,

---

*That it's "lonely at the top" is one of the enduring themes in twentieth-century mass culture. Many people far from the top find this idea ridiculous. The suicides of Marilyn Monroe and Judy Garland suggest some of the reality that underlies it, a reality that may be graver for women. Compare suicide-to-be Janis Joplin at the Fillmore East in the Summer of 1968: "Listen to me," she implored. "I make ten thousand people feel sexy, and I go home alone." Balzac's Coralie in *Lost Illusions* and Zola's Nana strike this chord. Carrie may be the first to strike it in America.

which flourished in the Square. In the "Tin Pan Alley" of the Brill Building, on Broadway and 51st, they created innovative forms of popular song. They worked easily with black performers, and assimilated black music. (This is a central theme of *Show Boat* as well as *The Jazz Singer*.) They manifested their presence by obtrusively "hanging out" in delicatessen-type restaurants like Lindy's, or directly on the street. People who didn't like them said they treated the Square like the ghetto. They made the neighborhood far more informal than it had been before World War One. They elaborated a kind of jive-talk that American youth immediately took to heart. They moved easily between media—vaudeville, theater, cabaret, movies, radio—and imagined "mass culture" before sociologists did; they created a press and a language to talk about it. The Jewish men who contributed most to language include Jolson, Irving Berlin, Walter Winchell, and Sime Silverman, editor of *Variety* in its prime, and Billy Rose. The Jewish women include Dorothy Parker, Edna Ferber, and Fanny Brice.[21]

In the 1920s, the emplacement of giant office buildings around the Square—the Paramount Building was the biggest and most striking—triggered a tremendous expansion in the group of working girls. My mother was one of these, first an ace stenographer, then a bookkeeper, and finally, long after her husband had died and her kids grown up, "chief financial officer"; all her life, she worked hard to get jobs in offices near Times Square, so she could be near the theaters and Town Hall, and see, in every season, what "smart women" were wearing. (Note that the women of Times Square, rather than Fifth Avenue, defined her idea of "smart.") These girls are the subject of Christopher Morley's *Kitty Foyle* stories, which my mother and Aunt Idie knew by heart. (They felt the 1940 movie with Ginger Rogers was charming but shallow.) Then there is *Classified*, a 1926 silent movie, which I saw at the Film Forum in the 1990s, and hoped to write about here, but I couldn't find a video for detailed scrutiny. The heroine, "Babs Comet," is a switchboard operator who takes calls for classified ads in a *Times / Tribune*-style newspaper in the Square. She is configured on the Florodora model of working girl, not the Betty Boop model: She dreams of (and eventually gets) a Prince Charming who will take her away from her work, rather than one who will help her with her work. But the movie contains one knockout line that will live forever in the literature and lore of working girls: "Her earning capacity fell short of her yearning capacity."

The 1920s also saw a tremendous brightening of Times Square: my mother's "bath of light." People increasingly spoke of the Square as a kind of psychedelic environment, "Dream Street." The great bath of light flooded many people's minds in an ecstatic way. Other people worried about the power of the spectacle to render people—usually young people, often female people, but really all people—"blinded by the light." One of the most imaginative celebrants of light was Paul Morand, a French surrealist poet who worked in New York as a diplomat.[22] Morand moves and lives in the same cultural tradition as Pierre Loti; his writing, like Loti's epigraph, shows an appreciation of Times Square, and of New York itself, that often comes more easily to cultivated Europeans than to our fellow Americans. "Today, on a winter evening, I arrive in Times Square about six o'clock. It is Broadway's finest hour. Here, until midnight, New York takes its bath of light." Morand offers a lyrical catalogue of all the colors of light, and all the forms of its motion: "tumbling, running, turning, zigzagging, rolling, vertical, perpendicular, dancing, epileptic; frames are whirling, letters flash out from the night." He examines the various flaming signs. "In 42nd Street it is a glowing summer afternoon all night," a world of "undiscovered prisms," of "rainbows squared."

> In rain, or when there are mists floating around, it is still more beautiful; the rain becomes golden water; the skyscrapers vanish halfway up, and nothing more can be seen but the haloes of their cupolas suspended in a colored mist. . . . The great searchlight atop the Times Building is sweeping up the remains of the sky.

> The Great White Way! All America dreams of having a Broadway. The craving for amusement breaks out like a revolution. . . . The festival offers all the false promise of the city festival, but . . . false only on the morrow. There is but one truth—the truth of tonight! . . . This is life at its most spectacular.

> Here the class war no longer has any meaning. This is victory! The electric lamp is no longer a lighting device, it is a machine for fascinating, a machine for obliterating. . . . This weary throng [is] determined not to go home, determined to spend its money, determined to blind

itself with false daylight. . . . 42nd Street is a conspiracy of commerce against night . . . there is only one latitude left, the latitude of pleasure.

Morand's lyricism is thrilling, but it is hard to know what it means. Does it mean that the mass craving for amusement is itself revolutionary, as in the pursuit of happiness that Thomas Jefferson canonized in the Declaration of Independence as an "inalienable right"? Or is Morand echoing his contemporaries, Ortega, Lewis Mumford, Walter Lippmann, Aldous Huxley, and, prefiguring the Frankfurt School, the Situationists, and all the "Mass Culture" writers of the 1950s, in saying that "the truth of tonight" is disabling the masses from thinking about tomorrow? Is he saying, like Le Corbusier, "Architecture or Revolution. Revolution can be avoided"?[23] And if he is, is this because "life at its most spectacular" is an outright victory for the producers or financers of spectacles? Or is it because, as Marshall McLuhan will suggest, that this great array of machinery, programmed to "blind [people] with false daylight," can inadvertently endow them with a second sight, an insight into "the truth of tonight" that is deeper than the truth of the working day? It is hard to know. But then, not even the most ardent celebrants of Times Square have ever claimed that its bath of light could make thought clear.

When *The Jazz Singer* created a sensation in October 1927, it almost buried what is probably the greatest film ever made in Hollywood, F. W. Murnau's *Sunrise*, which had opened just a couple of days before. Murnau's hero is a family farmer who falls for a city girl (who is vacationing in the country) in a desperate need to raise cash, as the farm is close to bankruptcy. Enraptured with her, he dreams of an abstract psychedelic cityscape with a bowtie shape a lot like Times Square. He attacks his wife (Janet Gaynor), aiming to kill her (as in Dreiser's *American Tragedy*, which had just come out), but she flees him into the woods. There, in the middle of the forest, like a spirit in a fairy tale, a streetcar materializes. Magically yet realistically, it transports the shaken couple to what looks like a real city. They spend a tourist day exploring it, and Murnau makes the trip transform them both. It is the wife whose changes we really believe in. She begins the story totally absorbed in farmwork and in child care, and emotionally dead. In the city she comes to life; she metamorphoses into an animated, vibrant, intelligent, radiantly sexual person. The husband no longer dreams of a city girl because his wife, exposed to the city, has become that girl. Murnau's symbolist version of Times Square is the medium of her growth. This movie may be the first authentic romance of tourism. This movie imagines *regeneration* by tourism, at just the historic moment when tourism, propelled not only by railroad but by ocean liner, is coming to play a crucial role in the economic life of New York.

The Depression and the Working Girls' Class

In the Depression decade, all writers on Times Square talk about its economic depletion and increasing sleaziness. It becomes a living parable of decline and fall—and, simultaneously, a kind of language laboratory for developing a discourse of decline and fall. Listen to the Federal Writers' Project Guide to New York, published in 1939. The writer of this morose appraisal is believed to be the young John Cheever:

> The depression emphasized the midway side of the Times Square district. Theaters closed one after the other, and contract bridge, chess tournaments and sideshows occupied the vacant stores and restaurants. Long before, however, decisive popular support had shifted from dramas and musical plays to motion pictures. Hollywood had taken over the most desirable locations, relegating the legitimate theater business to the side streets. Only two legitimate houses remain on Broadway.
>
> On Forty-second Street west of Broadway, once the show place of the district, famous theaters have been converted into movie "grind" houses devoted to continuous double feature programs or burlesque shows. Among cut-rate haberdasheries, cafeterias, and bus stations are tokens of a not-so-distant past—the photographs of the Ziegfeld Follies in the lobby of the New Amsterdam, the exterior of the Republic, and the names above the brightly lighted marquees: Eltinge, Wallack's, Sam H. Harris, Liberty, Times Square, the Selwyn, the Lyric.*

*WPA *Guide to New York City* (new edition, Pantheon, 1982), 175. These theaters have never ceased to be intensely contested space. They became pornographic showplaces in the 1960s and 1970s, central to the world of Martin Scorsese's 1976 film *Taxi Driver*. In the late 1980s, they were forcibly closed by the city, and became the object of competing development plans. In 1990–91, for a little while, they were to be showcases for various forms of mordant conceptual art. Soon after, they were torn down or

Cheever is writing a parable of urban grandeur and decay. He organizes it around the collapse of "legitimate theater." His idea of "legitimate" is wider than some: It includes vaudeville, in the form of the defunct Ziegfeld Follies ("tokens of a not-so-distant past"). His point seems to be that Broadway was a grand showplace for "dramas and musical plays" only yesterday, but it has turned into a tawdry "midway" today. What are the symptoms of this decay? On one hand, "cut-rate haberdasheries, cafeterias and bus stations"; on the other hand, movies. Speaking of West 42nd Street, he highlights the decline of formerly grand theaters into what he calls "movie 'grind' houses," a word that enables him to blend movies with burlesque. Is the idea supposed to be that sex is an agent of pollution and degeneracy? And that modern modes of culture—both movies and burlesque shows—are infected by it, in some way that "legitimate theater" is not? (This idea will amuse readers of the great sexy fiction that Cheever had not yet begun to write.) Of course, this view leaves out the more respectable incarnations of Hollywood in the neighborhood: the great movie palaces whose premieres, magnificently lit from both the Times and Paramount Buildings, may have been the central cultural events on 1930s Broadway. Here is a phobia shared by many intellectuals in the 1930s: If we don't talk about mass culture, maybe it will go away.* Or rather, he mentions the movie palaces only as real estate operations, and incursions on New York from outside—"Hollywood had taken over the most desirable locations"—without allowing them or their products any aura of their own.

From the perspective of Cheever and the *WPA Guide*, the collage that was Times Square in the 1930s looked like a disaster. But if you were coming at it from the other end, from out of town and below, it could look great.

---

completely transformed. By the late 1990s, they were enshrined in the canon of New York culture as nostalgic symbols of "the old 42nd Street." This vision is portrayed in the magazine *GRAND STREET* (#57, 1997), and in Samuel Delany's *Times Square Red, Times Square Blue* (1999). All this will be discussed later in the book.

The best brief narrative of 1930s transformations is probably Lawrence Senelick, "Private Parts in Public Places," in *Inventing Times Square*, 335–38. The downgrading of grandly decorated theaters into burlesque houses was routinely turned into gallows humor by the idiom "It went the way of all flesh." Times Square burlesque was especially dingy and tawdry, Senelick says. Its prosperity "depended on low salaries and secondhand scenery, abetted by the curiosity of the man in the street." But if Senelick knows a burlesque tradition that *wasn't* dingy and tawdry, he doesn't tell us when or where, or how to find it.

*The great 1930s exception is Nathanael West's Hollywood satire, *The Day of the Locust* (1939; New Directions, 1962), in which a movie premiere erupts into an urban riot. But the narrator of this brilliant book could almost share the view that his subject is impossible to talk about.

Gypsy Rose Lee's autobiographical memoir evokes her first taste of 42nd Street in 1931. She had spent her whole life on the road on vaudeville circuits, riding in buses, living out of trunks. But she had recently switched to burlesque, achieved tremendous overnight success as a sophisticated stripper, and got the long-dreamt-of call to Broadway. She was booked into the Minsky's flagship Republic Theater, and into a room overlooking it, just on top of the Nedick's Orange Drink and Hot Dog stand, on the corner of 42nd and Seventh Avenue.

> There was an exciting flamboyance to 42nd Street that early summer of 1931. Legitimate theaters were sandwiched in between Hubert's Museum, hot-dog stands and burlesque houses. Fred and Adele Astaire were starring in *The Band Wagon* at the New Amsterdam. *Private Lives* was playing next door to Minsky's Republic. The Eltinge Burlesque, with a four-a-day grind policy, faced *The House Beautiful* at the Apollo. Upstairs, a beauty salon advertised three items, shampoo, finger wave and manicure, for one dollar.[24]

Rose Lee showed a fine feeling for the Square's contradictions: Here the Astaires, the most aristocratic act in the history of American popular culture, could fly through the air amid crashes of downward mobility and smells of fast food. The weird juxtapositions that many people denounced as signs of breakdown looked to her like thrilling urban creativity.

Nedick's, at the Square's south end, the Horn & Hardart Automat in the middle, and Howard Johnson's at its north end typified the 1930s fast-food chains that supplanted the gourmet restaurants of the 1920s glory days. Many people who know nothing of Nedick's, which died in the 1980s, will remember Nedick's billboard, which stood into the 1990s, and said WELCOME TO TIMES SQUARE, CROSSROADS OF THE WORLD. In fact, the 1930s Square became a "crossroads" of classes and ideas and values in ways it had never been before. The new people in the Square had a lot less money to spend than the crowds of the 1920s; the new forms of commerce were pitched toward cheap ways of hanging around. But many of the new people were more focused, active, and intense. The Square in the 1930s became not only democratized but politicized.

One primary source for Times Square crowds was now the garment center, whose factories and workshops had only lately moved uptown from around Union Square. Far more than most American labor unions, the big garment unions—the ILG (for women's clothing), the Amalgamated (for men's clothing), the Hatters (a big union—it's hard to remember now that up to the 1960s, most adults wore hats; the shedding of hats is as radical as anything else people did in the 1960s)—were ideologically aware and radically ambitious. Socialists and Communists within these unions let loose dreadful fury against each other, and, long before 1945, laid out the whole Manichean vocabulary of the Cold War. But there were a few things they agreed about. After 1935, when the Comintern proclaimed the Popular Front, they agreed that Seventh Avenue should be draped with banners that urged all Americans to SUPPORT DEMOCRACY FIGHT FASCISM. They all loved mass demonstrations—and Times Square's expanses and enclosures, its continuous baths of light and publicity, made it a perfect place for them. Many of these demonstrations were about union recognition—"recognition" was one of the key words in Depression mass politics—and a living wage. Others were more abstract and ideological: They featured groups that were more diverse and blended, and capitalized on the neighborhood's abundance of mass media—papers, magazines, theater, radio, photo agencies, journalism, popular songs, movie newsreels—to transmit their words and ideas around the country, and, sometimes, the world.

In Brooks Atkinson's history of Broadway, his chapter on the Depression is called "The Paradox of the Thirties." The paradox was that, in the Broadway theater, quantitative loss nourished qualitative gain. The number of new productions plummeted steadily throughout the decade—close to 250 at the end of the 1920s, less than a third of that by the end of the 1930s.[25] But historians agree today that 1920s numbers were lopsided, indebted to the bull market, and especially to a stream of bootleg money in need of laundering, "rather than an indication of artistic vitality."[26] The Depression concentrated many people's minds, and focused their brains and imagination on the question of how to bring to life the suffering and overcoming that America was going through. For the first time in its history, Broadway got serious; it got to where it could be a source not only of pleasure and of spectacle, but of self-knowledge.

Stage Door: *New York as Underdog*

It is important to see how much smarter and more serious the Broadway theater grew during the Depression. Ironically, though, the medium's growth
in intelligence helped to undermine its self-confidence. In those years, even
as the theater industry was collapsing, the movie industry, in the first years
of sound, was going through spectacular growth. The sharp contrast placed
everyone who stayed in New York on the defensive. People who had grown
up with a vision of New York as a cultural metropolis had to adapt to a reality in which, all of a sudden, New York's culture seemed truncated, underdeveloped, minor-league. Compared with the rest of America, the city's
culture still looked pretty grand. But in the theater more than anywhere,
people who believed in their creative powers felt a new need to explain
themselves: What on earth they were doing here? Virtually overnight, here
became "there." New York's culture was suddenly culture on the defensive.
To belong to it meant to be an underdog. To *decide* to belong to it was to
make a life decision that seemed, on the surface at least, quixotic and absurd.

   Stage Door is a classic 1936 play that became a classic 1937 movie. Stage
and film versions differ in important ways, but the most striking thing about
both is the environment they both create: "The Footlights Club. A club for
girls of the stage." The club is located just off the Square, in "one of those
old houses whose former splendor has departed as the neighborhood has
changed."[27] Its residents are young or not-so-young women, looking for
work. They heckle one another as they compete for parts in the theater,
nearly always small parts. In harder times, they compete for work that they
see as "below" the stage, such as dancing in nightclubs and burlesque, or
reading recipes on radio. They never stop competing for men, men who can
help them get serious work onstage, or men who can marry them and take
them away—Appleton, Wisconsin, and Seattle are among the places that
signify "away"—from their daily grind. When they think about their future,
they are often close to despair. Yet they hold each other's hands, share
dresses and stockings, swap boyfriends, help each other with their lines, and
wisecrack at the world, and their boardinghouse overflows with in-spite-of-
everything *joie de vivre*. Both versions of *Stage Door* carry on the "Times

Girl" tradition of the showgirl as Times Square's Representative Man. None of the *Stage Door* writers—Edna Ferber and George S. Kaufman on the play, Morrie Ryskind and Anthony Veiller on the movie—uses any explicitly Marxist language. Nevertheless, they all shift consciousness in what we have to call a Marxist direction. They portray their heroines as members of a class, as victims of collective forms of suffering, as human subjects with a collective awareness, and as heroines in a collective struggle. We could call it the working girls' class.

One issue that is crucial in the play, but that disappears from the movie (it's not hard to see why), is this: What should a New York worker do when New York offers no work? Does the concept "New York worker" mean anything at all? Terry, the best actress of the lot (Margaret Sullavan onstage, Katharine Hepburn onscreen), proclaims her passion for the stage. "But I can't act if they"—the owners of theatrical capital and the directors they hire—"don't let me." She works behind the counter at Macy's during the day and goes to auditions at night. But nothing leads anywhere. Then her friend Jean arranges for screen tests for them both. The studios love them, and Jean prepares to buy train tickets west for two. But Terry says she won't go. Why not? "That isn't acting—that's piecework. You're not a human being." Terry, like the Marxists of the Frankfurt School, is updating Marx's "alienated labor" so it fits twentieth-century mass culture. Jean's reply is to turn a similar indictment against the theater. She asks, what does theater do to its workers? "I suppose you call *this* being alive? Sleeping three in a room in this rotten dump? It builds you up, eh?" Terry, defensive, says she sees the Footlights Club as "only the beginning" of a long career. Jean says "You can't play ingénues forever," and Broadway is no more generous to women than Hollywood: The media centers on both coasts crush them in procrustean beds, and spit them out before they have a chance to grow old.

There are problems in Terry's rap. It's one thing for an actor to say that "Broadway" acting, on a stage before real people, is nobler, more fully human, than "Hollywood" acting in a studio. It's much more of a stretch for an unemployed actor—and Terry is unemployed when this exchange takes place—to say *not acting at all* is better than acting in Hollywood. But our heroine stays in New York, works at Macy's, goes to auditions, keeps the faith, and hopes something will turn up. One of the nice things about the stage version of *Stage Door* is that it's a comedy, and comedy is a genre where things do turn up. At the end of Act Three, she walks into the sunset with not only a star role in a good play, but a good guy who's handsome and smart and rich and who owns the play. The moral is, you don't need to go to Hollywood to have a Hollywood ending.

What can we say? "Nice work if you can get it!" is what the Gershwins say in their 1937 song. But we can also say that we can see New York's popular culture in the process of going on the defensive and turning in on itself. This is a time when the growth of the culture industry is precarious, uncertain, blowing in the wind; for now, only the movies seem immune to the blight. More and more writers, actors, designers are driven by the same cruel imperatives as riveters or grape pickers or longshoremen: *Go where the work is*. The conditions of work are likely to be dreadful, but the drain on the self who doesn't work is even worse. This is an era when millions of people are migrating around the country in search of work; there doesn't seem to be much reason for anyone to be anywhere, if they can't get work. Or is there? From now on, everybody involved in culture in New York will have to work overtime to wrestle with the question: Why are we still here? In the stage version of *Stage Door*, we can see the "I Love New York" campaign getting under way. Ferber and Kaufman are clearing the road to *Annie Hall*.

Betty Boop, Symbol of Resistance

Why are we still here? Unlike Hollywood's feature films, which displayed many different and competing visual styles, its cartoons, like Model T Fords, came in just *one* visual style: Disney's. Disney studio productions strove for—and, to a remarkable extent, achieved—a vision of a smooth and homogenous universe. There were plenty of evil creatures and dark forces in the Disney world. But beyond their reach was a preestablished harmony, an aura of total integration, that ruled the Disney world itself.

One girl on Broadway who did give the big boys a fight was Betty Boop, star of dozens of animated cartoons and hundreds of newspaper comic strips.[28] Between 1930 and 1939, she was created right in this neighborhood, at the Fleischer Brothers Animation Studio at 1600 Broadway. (The studio is long gone, and the office building has been replaced by luxury condos.)* Betty's persona is in the "Times Girl" tradition: a grown-up woman's sexuality combined with a hometown girl's sweetness and innocence. The Fleischer studio at first intended her for a minor, supporting role (in a cartoon where a dog was the star), but her presence delighted people, and there was an instant demand for more of her. In the early 1930s, the Fleischer Brothers presented her in a number of roles: a flapper in a fancy car, a jazz singer—sometimes the glamorous star of a Ziegfeld-type revue on Broadway, sometimes the banged-up chanteuse in a dark and dingy cellar club—a mother, a nanny, a schoolteacher, a geisha in Japan, a working girl applying (along with hundreds of other girls) for a job, a nurse, a judge, the President, Mother Goose, and more and more. Her dark hair, dark eyes, brisk but sexy walk—she has places she's got to get to, fast—and abundant curves evoked a whole generation of girls, often Jews, generally immigrants or their daughters, who grew up poor in America's big cities. As soon as they could, they took the subways downtown and went "out to work," to escape their families, but also, often, to support them.

One striking feature of Fleischer cartoons is their use of live jazz for soundtracks. (This is one of their sharp differences from Disney Studios, which created a loathsomely sweet musical world all its own.) Betty is portrayed as a white girl from an immigrant family (her parents' accents are a variety of stage-Jewish) who is completely at home with urban black music, and whose singing is often accompanied by musicians like Louis Armstrong and Cab Calloway. (Calloway sings "Minnie the Moocher" for her.) In her affinity for jazz, Betty looks like an ideal modern citizen: the self who is at home with the other. But here, as elsewhere, the Boop persona radiates ironies. Her ingratiating sweetness, which seems to have reminded many people of their daughters, may well have not only intensified people's anxiety about what might become of their daughters (or what had already become of them), but struck darker chords of forbidden feeling around those

*In the 1980s, Broadway's nadir, this building became the scene of a stark, neo-Hopper night scene painted by Jane Dickson. Actually, it is the sidewalk in front of the building, and a couple of the neon signs hanging from it, that she paints. There are only three people in the painting, and we can't see any of their faces: an apparently old man and an apparently young one talking to each other, and a man who could be a cop, and could be reaching for his gun, and could be trying to stop what could be a drug transaction. The vast and frightening ambiguity in this spare scene may be one of the painting's themes. The biggest piece of the building in the painting is an open window, a windowsill, and the invisible painter herself. Did she know she was looking from Betty's perch?

girls out on the town. ("Minnie the Moocher" is, among other things, a commercial for drugs. And not only for drugs, but for forbidden neighborhoods where people go for drugs, "to kick the gong around.")

As the 1930s progressed, Betty became more and more of a girl under fire. Paramount Studios, who distributed the cartoons, were subject to increasing pressure from the Hays Office, and they passed the pressures on to the Fleischers. They were told to tone her down, flatten out her curves, raise her necklines and lower her skirts so she couldn't spill out of her clothes (one of her signatures), drop that single garter from her wardrobe (another signature), flatten the inflections in her voice, mute the *double entendre* in her dialogue, make her more remote and less inviting. These pressures increased after 1934, with the ascendancy of "Code." If we rent Boop videos today, and try to look at them in chronological order (this is often uncertain), we can imagine what nervous wrecks the Fleischers and their animators must have become, and we can admire them for giving Betty as long a run as she had.

There is another way to read these cartoons more than half a century later. Consider "Betty Boop's Big Boss," created in 1933, at the Depression's nadir, and at the same historical moment as *42nd Street*. Betty, surrounded by a crowd of girls and women like herself, takes an elevator to the top of a skyscraper, in search of a job as a secretary. For her audition, she sings, in baby talk, a song that disparages her own work skills, "But when you get me home alone / you'd be surprised." The boss, who could be a cartoon Boss from the *Daily Worker*, is enchanted and hires her on the spot. Then it turns out that in fact her secretarial skills are formidable. But it also turns out that when the boss wants to kiss her, she is "shocked, shocked." She calls the police; but instead of the police, a whole army arrives, and they bomb the building; the tower crashes; at last, when Betty and the boss hit the ground, she is on his lap, and they seem to be locked in a loving embrace. What is supposed to be real here? And real in what way? Is this a satire on "sexual harassment" as it was sixty years ago, or as it is today? Whatever, Betty is an impressive character. She looks like many of the working girls in Times Square: forced to get up every morning and take the subway to a job that may be grueling and humiliating; singing to herself all day—"They can't take away my Boop-Boop-a-Doop" is one of her refrains—and, responding to the signs and stereotypes that surround her, entertaining fantasies of spectacular success, with gowns, jewels, limousines, bright lights, that symbolize her power to conquer the city all through the night.*

We know the changes in her appearance over the Depression years reflect pressures of censorship on her creators; but if we think of Betty as her creators hoped we would, we can imagine a real subject, living through history, working on herself: struggling with her appearance—less self-display or more, trying to look youthful or grown-up, weight problems (within a range of twenty pounds or so), more talk or less talk, baby talk or adult talk, acting vulnerable or acting resourceful, playing the ingénue or the wiseguy, dreaming of a good solid man or dreaming of the moon; trying to figure out which of her metamorphoses will "get over" in the personality market she works and lives in, but also what she really feels and which of her desires are real. Against the nostalgic discourse, fully alive in the 1930s, that conducts a funeral service for the good life in Times Square, Betty stands up for the present and the future, and insists that the young men and women here are just coming into their own.

There is one Boop cartoon I've seen only in fragments, the print is cracked and discolored, I don't know the name, but I know the song. Betty appears, dressed in what looks like a Japanese kimono, and sings, waveringly, tremulously, first in English, then in what sounds like a pastiche of Japanese. I haven't the least idea why this song is being sung, but it's both sweet and serious, and moreover its arc leads upward:

> Got a language of my own, known in every foreign home.
> You'll surely know it, Boop-Boop-a-Doop.

Betty incarnates a power that is individualized, "all [her] own," and yet that moves and lives everywhere; that men and women, blacks and whites, Americans and everyone else in the world, can share in harmony; that emanates from this time and that place, Times Square in the 1930s, and yet that is somehow primal—"You surely know it," even if you don't know you know. This sweet young thing is fighting for a life force that holds the whole world together.

*The videos of Cyndi Lauper's "Girls Just Wanna Have Fun" and Madonna's "Material Girl," great hits of the 1980s, quote Boop cartoons explicitly; the uncomprehending immigrant family in "Girls" is a pretty exact replica of the family in "Minnie." If I watched more rap music videos today, I know I would find more quotations and connections. Betty at her best offers a female variation on the Jazz Singer theme, a story close to the hearts of many girls and boys of the hip-hop generation.

Gold Diggers: *Broadway in Hollywood*

"Hollywood has taken over. . . ." During the Depression, while Hollywood movies flourished as Broadway theater collapsed, some people wondered why there should be any continuing need for Broadway to exist at all. However, one of the outstanding things that Hollywood did all through the Depression was to produce brilliant representations of Broadway: *42nd Street, Stage Door,* the Busby Berkeley *Gold Diggers* series, and, at the very end of the 1930s, Dorothy Arzner's *Dance, Girl, Dance.* Why should this be? One reason may be that, at a time when the movies were on a roll of spectacular prosperity, many people benefiting from it had begun their careers on the stage, and still believed that the theater, so much more precarious and vulnerable, was infinitely more "real," more "authentic." Another reason is that these films are all about the backstage world, the world behind the world of illusion; they are about how theatrical illusions are created by real people, members of real hierarchies of power, men and women who are willing to sell themselves in exchange for real money—but who usually can't find buyers. The deuce in the Depression is a street full of people who desperately need work; if the star doesn't shine, they can't pay the rent.[29]

Since the year 2000, a theatrical revival of *42nd Street* has been playing on the deuce, in the newly reconstructed American Airlines Theater. The current revival reproduces 1930s Broadway decoration very well. But although the play is set in 1933, this production is totally insensitive to the meaning of 1933, the worst year in the Depression, and the year that both Roosevelt and Hitler came to power. It occludes the economic pressure, shared by actors, directors, stagehands, and audiences—and even by the backers—that gave the plot its human urgency, and gave the show's triumph its big thrill. The revival never even uses the word "Depression," or any number of other words it could have used instead, to convey that the whole country was in trouble. But it was this trouble, so damaging to Depression Broadway, that made Broadway qualified, maybe for the first time in its history, to represent a real world. To get a bead on today's vision of *42nd Street,* try to imagine *South Pacific* without World War Two.

One of the most poignant 1930s meditations on individuality and collectivity is Busby Berkeley's "Lullaby of Broadway" number from *Gold Diggers of*

1935. The star of this number, playing Times Girl in the 1930s, is the actress and singer Wini Shaw. She is its star, not only in the sense that she does more acting and singing and gets more screen time than anybody else. She is the star in the sense that the whole number, with its cast of hundreds, is about her, her *Bildung*, her inner life, her fantasies about herself, her quest for identity. Everything is dramatized as if it is her dream. So far as I know, this is the one place in Berkeley's *oeuvre* where he focuses on an individual and her inner life. Of course, he brings us his usual Piranesian vistas and gargantuan choruses; but now they mean more than usual, because, instead of just dropping these tropes on our heads from some Olympian sky, he shows us how they can spring organically from a woman's life, from her desires and her dreams and "her yearning capacity." People who don't like Berkeley's work have always called his landscapes "Fascist," but Fascism is never at home with human inwardness, or with anyone's struggle for identity, certainly not a working girl's. (Indeed, the seductiveness of Fascism has always been its promise to deliver modern men and women from the struggle for identity.)*

The most famous shot in this number comes at its dramatic climax, when, pressed by a great crowd, to our horror, the heroine plunges over a balcony—or does she fall, or is she pushed? (The uncertainty is as disturbing today as it was to its first generation of viewers.) But the image that is richest and most profound comes at the very start of her dream. First she sings the "Lullaby" slowly, with only a faint accompaniment; her face is luminous against a background of total blackness. She puts special stress on

---

*The psychological critique of Fascism is developed very brilliantly in three classic sources: Dostoevsky's "Legend of the Grand Inquisitor," in *The Brothers Karamazov*, Part 3, Chapter 5 (1881); Sartre's short story "Childhood of a Leader" (1938); and Erich Fromm's *Escape from Freedom* (1941).

This critique goes over the top when it starts to blame Fascism, which after all made its great successes and conquests in Europe, on the USA. One way of doing this, a cliché in my youth, was the idea that the Nazi Party's Nuremburg rallies (see *Triumph of the Will*) were "based on" or "rooted in" American football halftime shows and chorus lines. Here is the great culture-critic Siegfried Krackauer in 1927, commenting on a popular cabaret ensemble called the Tiller Girls in Berlin: "These products of American distraction factories are no longer individual girls, but indissoluble girl clusters whose movements are demonstrations of mathematics." See *The Mass Ornament: Weimar Essays by Siegfried Krackauer*, translated and edited by Thomas Levin (Harvard, 1995), 75–76. In language like this, we can understand exactly where Susan Glenn is coming from when she says, half a century later, that "theatrical spectacle . . . worked to obliterate the notion of female autonomy and personality" (*Female Spectacle*, 8). Berkeley's "Lullaby of Broadway," which develops a mass spectacle out of an ordinary girl's dreams and inner life, may have been a defense against no-longer-individual-girls and obliteration-of-personality talk that found him guilty by association.

one of the last lines: "Your baby goes home to her flat / to sleep all day."
Then the camera zooms in, and settles on her face at close-up range. She
smiles up at us, her black hair curls over her face. Then she lights up, and
suddenly, magically, *her face becomes the city*: Her eyes, nose, mouth metamorphose into a landscape of midtown New York. Now she sings the same
song again, but at a jazzy tempo, backed by an inner big band. Gradually
her dream unfolds; a metropolitan crowd surrounds and envelops her; she
alternates between merging with this crowd and emerging from it. She
imagines herself in an immense ballroom: Sometimes she is part of a huge
chorus; then she is a soloist, whirled through the air by a man whose moves
suggest Fred Astaire; then she is on a balcony having drinks and watching
the action with a movie star, who turns out to be Dick Powell. Powell plays
a distinctive role in her dream life, in fact the role he created in *42nd Street*:
an empathetic and unselfish mentor who is happy to teach a woman all he
knows and work to help her become a star without making sexual or romantic demands of his own. In American culture, this is a new form of "Mr.
Right." When Powell urges her to join the crowd that is gathering just below
them, his word carries weight. She agrees, sings alluringly, "Why don't you
come and get me?" and then instantly (remember this is a dream) becomes
not just a face in the crowd but its leader. She leads a mass dance up and up
a grand spiral staircase, till she reaches the roof of a penthouse with a spectacular view of Times Square. She and Powell have a passionate kiss that
somehow goes through the terrace's glass door. As they kiss, a great wave of
people pours through all around her. These are the people she led up the
stairs, doesn't she remember? It looks as if she has forgotten, she looks confused and tries to turn away, even if only for just a second. But as she turns,
in the midst of this crowd, their sheer momentum plunges her off the roof.
Then comes the classic horrific "plunge" shot, in which we see the roofs
and streets getting bigger and bigger, closer and closer. Just before the crash,
we fade to black. The narrative reverses itself, and the city becomes her face.
Home again, she climbs the stairs to her room. Her neighbors are all smiles.
"Your baby goes home to her flat / to sleep all day." We know she will wake
in time for another night on the town.

This is one of the most memorable scenes in American cinema. But its
star, Winifred "Wini" Shaw, was dropped almost as dramatically as the girl

she plays. She appeared in twenty-six films from 1934 to 1937, then nothing at all until her death in 1982.[30]

Miss Sarah Brown: Crossover Love

A Times Girl from the same period who enjoys a happier ending is the heroine of Damon Runyon's 1933 story, "The Idyll of Miss Sarah Brown." This may be the most famous story Runyon ever wrote; it is the basis of the dearly beloved and perennially revived 1950 Broadway musical, by Frank Loesser and Abe Burrows, *Guys and Dolls*. Yet editors seem to be uncomfortable with it: I was surprised to find that it has not been reprinted in any of the posthumous Runyon anthologies (*The Best of Damon Runyon*, 1967; *The Bloodhounds of Broadway*, 1981; *Damon Runyon on Broadway*, 1999). It isn't even in the original 1942 edition of *Guys and Dolls*.[31] I got the text below out of a collection called *Great American Love Stories* (1988).[32] Runyon fans may have problems with this story because, although vividly situated in his familiar Broadway world, it has a psychological complexity and depth much more familiar to the world of Edith Wharton and Henry James.

Sarah Brown, aka Sister Salvation, plays cornet in the Save-a-Soul Mission band on the corner of Broadway and 49th Street. The verve with which she plays and the incandescence of her orations, urging the Square's night people to repent and change their lives, endear her to the man who will become the story's romantic hero: gambler Sky Masterson, who gets his name from his flair for bets and games where "the sky's the limit." When they meet, the narrator tells us in Runyonese, "The Sky is a goner, for this is one of the most beautiful young dolls anybody ever sees on Broadway" (220). He hangs around her and sends the mission a portion of his winnings. She enjoys his presence and at first feels grateful for the money, because the mission is poor. (Remember, in the Depression, this whole neighborhood, along with most of the country, is poor.) But then she is attacked from inside her organization, and turns icily righteous in self-defense: She says she doesn't want his dirty money, and blows him off. The narrative languishes, but not for long. Suddenly, with amazing *chutzpah*, she steps up and makes her move. She breaks into Nathan Detroit's all-male crap game and challenges Sky to a kind of existential duel: Does he have the guts to shoot craps with her for his soul? The game becomes the story's dramatic climax: "This two dollars against your soul, Mister Sky. It is all I have, but it is more than your soul is worth." She then executes the classical hustler's gambit: acts as if she doesn't know what she's doing, and then abruptly, with a quick six and a five, cleans up and walks out.

> Naturally, the Sky follows Miss Brown. . . . [She] turns on the Sky and speaks to him as follows:
> "You are a fool," Miss Sarah Brown says.

But then, just as she astonished him by breaking in on his crap game, he astonishes her by invoking her Bible:

> "Why," the Sky says, "Paul says, 'If any man among you seemeth to be wise in this world, let him become a fool, that he may be wise.' I love you, Miss Sarah Brown" (227–8).

The story's happy ending depends on a double crossover: She becomes a woman of the night to denounce the values of the night; he becomes her fool for love to force her into profane love; in ways neither would expect, they change each other and are changed themselves. Their mutual crossover leading to happy convergence definitely makes this, as Rosenthal says, one of the "Great American Love Stories." The climax is staged by Runyon with Bojangles-like dazzling footwork. His last twist, at the story's very end, is the narrator's announcement: "The dice with which she wins the Sky's soul . . . are strictly phony"—and they know it. Here as in much Depression romance, there is a bittersweet happy ending. Love conquers all, but only because it fixes the fight. The lovers learn that they can't win unless they learn not only to fight but to fix themselves.

Guys and Dolls: *From Crossover to Double-Cross*

When Abe Burrows and Frank Loesser transformed Runyon's story into the book for a musical, it was the late 1940s, a completely different time. World

War Two and what radicals called "the permanent war economy" had pumped up Broadway and made the Square more frantic than ever. There were more high rollers around—many of them defense contractors and their agents—with big money that had to be spent fast.[33] Midtown New York was overflowing with nightclubs and a whole new scale of conspicuous consumption. Times Square and Broadway were ready to symbolize America's postwar "affluent society." The change in historical context gives Sarah's character a new critical largeness and resonance: a Broadway icon who denounces the whole culture of Broadway. "Someday," she says, "I'm going to take a pick-ax and rip up Broadway from end to end."[34] What does she have against Broadway? Above all, its incessant preoccupation with *style*. She vilifies style, but she vilifies it stylishly. Her stylishness is unconscious, but everybody who has ever thought about style agrees that's the best kind.

Miss Sarah Brown's most important theatrical precursor is Bernard Shaw's 1913 *Major Barbara*. This heroine appeared on the screen in 1941, played luminously by Deborah Kerr in her film debut. But Burrows and Loesser excised not only Sarah's breakthrough in violating gender conventions, but also the crooked contrivance that creates the happy ending. In *Guys and Dolls*, onstage and onscreen, Sarah and Sky are bonded not through surreptitious mutuality, but by magic: It happens the dice fall the right way. The show's great climactic number, "Luck Be a Lady," belongs in the hymnal of magic realism.

Guys and Dolls is one of the most brilliant, delightful musical comedies ever made. Some of its virtues are very traditional, in the traditions of Broadway and Times Square: It shows us a world full of people who are flamboyantly weird, and yet makes us feel we are like them, we are all part of the same (as Baudelaire called it) "family of eyes." It seems petty for me to complain about it, and I won't complain long. But we need at least to ask, Why did Burrows "clean up" Runyon's ending? Is it sheer paranoia to connect it with Burrows's own action in "coming clean" and acting as a friendly witness for HUAC?

I don't think this "cleanup" project messes up the whole show. Michael Kidd's opening street montage, the gangsters' crap game in the sewer, and the love scenes between Sarah and Sky (with several terrific love songs), all flesh out the Times Square dialectic—Embrace Your Opposite: "Side by side, they're glorified"—and bring it fresh new life. Sarah's part is done wonderfully. She deepens Runyon's dialectical vision of the Times Square heroine: a woman who throws herself into the night in order to smash the night, but who is driven by the force of feelings she tried to deny to become the person she set out to overcome. But there are places where the desire for cleanup cripples the process of fusion that makes the show great.

In the Mission at midnight, we hear Burrows's travesty of McCarthyism. It's hard not to be troubled by this scene. Nathan Detroit abruptly gets the authority of a mob boss (or a committee chairman), and he pushes people around. He starts by demanding that Benny South Street confess his depravity. Benny refuses, and says, "I plead the Fifth Commandment." But after more pressure, Benny caves in. The scene unfolds as a prolonged orgy of self-abasement, featuring a confessional aria by Nicely-Nicely (Stubby Kaye), backed by soaring harmonies from the gangster ensemble. "I dreamed last night I got on the boat to heaven," he starts. He brings his usual kit of dice, whisky, and worldly skepticism. His fellow passengers reprove him; he laughs at them; they say "And the people all said, 'Sit down / Sit down, you're rockin' the boat.' " Finally, a wave washes him overboard. He screams for salvation and awakens.

Now comes the crucial line in the scene, the proof of Nicely-Nicely's redemption:

And I said to myself, "Sit down / sit down, you're rockin' the boat . . ."

He testifies he is grateful not to have been killed, and he will sit down and shut up; the other passengers won't have to tell him to be like them; he will tell himself. Can there have really been a time when people thought this scene was *not* about McCarthyism? The movie (1955) is easy to rent, it makes few changes in the script, and paying attention to this text will tell you a lot about that time.* Just in case the politics aren't clear enough, director Joseph Mankiewicz adds some small touches to make them clearer. In the last minute, after a double wedding before a mass crowd in Times Square, Sky and Sarah and Nathan and Adelaide leave for their honeymoons in police cars.

---

*Burrows testified before HUAC as a friendly witness in 1951 and again in 1952. Eric Bentley has collected his testimonies, both in his long anthology, *Thirty Years of Treason* (1972; Nation Books, 2002), 533–68, and in his short one, *Are You Now or Have You Ever Been?* (Harper & Row, 1972), 81–97. Both these selections highlight Burrows's genius as an ironist.

Examining the Cold War linkages to 1950s culture can get tedious. Anybody tired of the Cold War is welcome to try a different link. Take this one: I don't see how any Jew can avoid embarrassment today when we see how the show's all-Jewish production team, Cy Feuer and Ernie Martin, Burrows and Loesser, Michael Kidd and George S. Kaufman, play up the Jewish flavor of the gambling subculture all the way through—the guys take bets on Mindy's sales of cheesecake and strudel, they sing love songs that go "So sue me" only to close it with a mass "conversion of the Jews" to the harsh WASP fundamentalism of the Salvation Army. What on earth could have possessed these guys to ring down the curtain on themselves? Would anybody like to testify on the dialectics of Jewish self-hatred? Yet I wouldn't have thought to find it on theatrical Broadway, one of the most vibrant Jewish scenes in the world. This only shows the depths of my ignorance, even in my own hometown. (So sue me!) All I can say is, if the book had been by Mel Brooks, at least we would have known it was a joke.

Another place where I missed the joke: the Times Square setting in the 1955 movie. It's as if the designers strained themselves to produce a Times Square environment that looked absolutely nothing like New York's. At ground level all the buildings are uniformly white, suggesting stucco, the Sun Belt, White Towers, or Burger Kings, alternating with the color scheme of airport plastic pastel. What could be the point of this denatured environment? It was especially startling for movie lovers like my father and me, who knew Hollywood as the source of so many romantic and glamorous visions of New York (think of *42nd Street!*).[35] Why did the adaptors of this New York–signature work design a setting that turned its face 180 degrees from New York? Those were Cold War days, and Hollywood as much as any American institution had suffered from the blacklist. I wondered if the survivors were trying to highlight *echt* "American" folklore, and disengage it from our "un-American" city? I was starting to worry then about a polarization between "New York" and "America." In fact, something like this really happened. For thirty years or more, the mass media bought it without a thought. It meshed with the "Southern strategy" of the GOP. It reached its zenith in the 1970s, during the city's fiscal crisis, in President Gerald Ford's "New York Drop Dead" speech, which said "the American people" would not be affected if New York went down. As it turned out, the American people didn't buy this bullshit for a minute. But the *Guys and Dolls* movie could have been part of a bizarre project to color *noir* Technicolor and take Times Square out of New York. I wonder what think tank devised that thought experiment, and what they are thinking now.

Dorothy Arzner and the Depths of Dance

At the very end of the Depression, in Dorothy Arzner's little-known but re-markable 1940 movie *Dance, Girl, Dance,*[36] the figure of Times Girl is split in two. *Dance, Girl, Dance,* like the 1937 film *Stage Door,* takes place in the Times Square neighborhood, the West Forties, in and around what used to be called a theatrical boardinghouse. Arzner offers a daylight pastoral es-tablishing shot of the Square, featuring the majestic old Times Building. She goes on to show us a cross-section of dance forms and venues that have developed in this neighborhood, from ballet theaters to "interpretive-dance" studios to big and small revues to chorus lines in Broadway plays to nightclub acts to burlesque. (The great jazz ballrooms are below her radar.) She also shows us the fluidity of New York's dance culture in the 1930s, which made it possible for a dancer to cross over from one form to another.

The first time I saw *Dance, Girl, Dance,* I was startled by a big sign in its first Times Square shot: DISNEY SALE. What could the Walt Disney Com-pany be doing in the Square in 1939? And what could it be putting on sale? In fact it isn't Walt at all: It's the "Disney Hat Co., Fifth Avenue and 42nd Street," manufacturers of very classy ceremonial top hats.[37] Arzner puts these hats on sale, suggesting that the upper-class ceremonial world where Disney Hats were status symbols is *kaput.** But then she picks them up and puts them on her stars, who look ravishingly gorgeous in top hats in the movie's first scene, a risqué dance (on the road—in Akron) rudely inter-rupted by the cops. With this hat trick, Arzner makes clear the lasting beauty and power of burlesque.

Dance, Girl, Dance is very explicitly framed by the 1930s world depres-sion. In America a great deal of the labor force is unemployed, under FDR

---

*The fact that this is a dance film points us toward Fred Astaire, who put top hats on the dance map forever. What is Arzner suggesting about Astaire? Maybe that his great hat dances presuppose the top hat's social obsolescence, but reconstruct it in an existential way, as a prop for a glorious but socially un-embodied and lonely artistic identity.

the welfare state is only in its infancy, millions of people every night go to bed hungry, and the categorical imperative and constant obsession for every man and every woman is: *Get work.* Any girl or woman who wants to work as any sort of performer will have to sell herself—her body, her verve, and her sex appeal—to a bunch of sleazy guys with cigars; she, and maybe her whole family, will go to bed hungry if she can't make a sale. That is the over-riding fact of life that underlies *42nd Street, Stage Door,* and all the *Gold Diggers* films, and that forms the context for *Dance.* Here, when a young dancer gets a job as a "Gaiety Girl," and people talk, a producer's secretary speaks up for her: "Don't condemn a girl because she has to earn her own living." The girls in the house are in constant competition for prime roles and for rich men, but nevertheless, like the young actresses in *Stage Door,* they feel an underlying solidarity, share scant resources, and find ways to help one another out, especially to find work.[38]

The poles of the *Dance* world are two Times Girls who are dedicated not only to very different styles of dance, but to radically opposed modes of being. "I decided," Arzner told a friend, "the theme should be 'The Art Spirit' (Maureen O'Hara) versus the commercial 'Go-Getter' (Lucille Ball)."[39] Arzner sells herself short in this self-presentation; the polarity she develops is actually deeper than she seems to think. Ball plays "Bubbles," a queen of Times Square burlesque; O'Hara is Judy, a "serious" dancer who only at the movie's end finds a proper venue for her talent and her desires. When we meet the two stars, they are wearing identical tophats, short span-gled skirts, and boots, but they project sharply clashing personae. Bubbles's strategy is basically to say "Yes": She is at home in the breezily cynical fe-male tradition that stretches from Mistress Quickly to Defoe's Moll Flan-ders to Mae West to *Gentlemen Prefer Blondes* to "Anytime Annie" in *42nd Street.* (Recent incarnations of this character include Marg Helgenberger in *China Beach,* Madonna's 1990s "Material Girl," and Kim Cattrall's Saman-tha in *Sex and the City.*) She routinely puts out, especially for rich admirers; she doesn't expect to be loved or to fall in love, but she is never alone for long. Judy's strategy is to say "No," look cold, and turn away from anyone who is interested in her in any way. At first, Judy may simply look frightened, or frigid, and we may not even realize she has a strategy. But when, in scene after scene, people she rejects eagerly follow her around, we realize there is more to her than meets the eye. Ever since the early days of Christianity, expressing indifference and disdain for the world has been one of the primary ways to conquer it.

Arzner seems to feel no idealism about romance, but she is full of idealism about work and art. Her sense of mission is crystallized in Judy, who says she "only wants to dance." What she apparently doesn't want is to please or entertain an audience: When she talks about the audience, she talks as if their very existence degrades her; she preserves her artistic integrity by dancing abstractly, as if they aren't there. Ball, at the other pole, as "Bubbles," is expansive with and ingratiating to her audience. She simultaneously acts sexy and parodies sexuality, and has a great laugh with the guys in the seats. She does a neo–"Heatherbloom Petticoat" routine, wearing a modern evening gown and using a wind machine to blow it up and away. From the way Arzner frames her two heroines, it is clear that Judy is the character who speaks for her and the role model we're supposed to admire. Alas, O'Hara's performance is pallid; she doesn't even begin to make Judy matter to us as we can see she matters to the director. Meanwhile Lucy fills the screen with overflowing life and steals the show.

In the Times Girl tradition, both heroines are self-made women, always struggling to make a living. They share contempt for people from "high society"—though there is a drunken and degenerate playboy who courts them both, and whom both are drawn to more than they care to admit. Solidarity between the two women is the emotional glue that holds the film together. When Bubbles becomes a millionaire's mistress and a burlesque star, she remembers where she came from, and goes back to the boardinghouse, weighed down by expensive jewelry and a dog, to recruit Judy and her mode of dancing into her act. Judy reacts to the idea of burlesque with haughty disdain, but both Bubbles and the landlady (who hasn't been getting her rent lately) point out that it's steady work.

The two women go to work together, and create a gimmick that forms the heart of the movie. The gimmick is about Art, one of burlesque's perennial themes, and it reflects on how to incorporate "high art" into "low art." It is presented with a deliberateness that suggests a directorial self-portrait. The role of Judy in Bubbles's show may be Arzner's parable about the relation between herself, a director of soulful "B" pictures marketed for women, and mainstream "A"-picture blockbuster Hollywood. Judy performs as a curtain-raiser, executing her ballet moves in solitude, sublimely indifferent to the people in front of her. The audience gets restive, not only ignorant of Judy's ballet language, but also put off by her coldness, and increasingly hungry for personal contact; then Bubbles sweeps in, only too glad to give them the appreciation and human warmth they crave. The audience turns out to be hip enough to appreciate Judy and her role, and the act even attracts a page-one story in *Variety*, "Bubbles and her Stooge." But then, for complex plot reasons, the chemistry between the rivals breaks down and their act unravels. Judy's dress rips, props fall on her, and the audience abruptly turns cruel. In this scene, the audience is shot from above and lit in a particularly lurid way; in Hollywood terms, it suggests the Colosseum audience in 1930s Roman epics, shouting for the hero to be eaten up. Judy has simply been (or at least has acted—we never really know) oblivious till now, but she can't ignore them any longer. She faces them down with a director's set piece of articulate abuse:

> Go ahead and stare. I'm not ashamed. Go on. Laugh! Get your money's worth. Nobody's going to hurt you. I know you want me to tear my clothes off so you can look your fifty cents' worth. Fifty cents for the privilege of staring at a girl the way your wives won't let you. What do you suppose we think of you up here—you with your silly smirks your mothers would be ashamed of? And we know it's the thing of the moment for the dress suits to come and laugh at us too. We'd laugh right back at the lot of you, only we're paid to let you sit there and roll your eyes and make your screamingly clever remarks. What's it for? So you can go home when the show's over and strut before your wives and sweethearts and play at being the stronger sex for a minute? I'm sure they see through you just like we do.[40]

This is the most emotionally intense moment in the movie. It made Arzner a hero for a later generation of feminists, who understood it as a diatribe against men, and male pleasure, and "the male gaze."[41] I agree that Judy's speech is a powerful attack, but the object of that attack is more complex and ambiguous than it may seem. Look at these men (mixed with a few women): What are they doing to deserve her scorn? They are doing exactly what every mass audience in history has always done: seeking pleasure, looking for a good time, wanting the performers to cater to them and make them feel good. When Judy calls up images first of mother and child, then of husband and wife, she is making it clear that she recognizes the deep emotional roots of the performer / audience relationship. But if this is so, then her abuse cuts deeper than she knows, and certainly deeper than the sexual politics on the surface of her speech. If she doesn't want any part of the mother / child dyad, and she doesn't want any part of the husband / wife dyad—or rather, I think we should say, the adult love dyad—what does she want? And what's she doing on a stage? (Or in front of a camera?) If she hates entertainment that depends on making audiences feel good, doesn't this rage undercut *all* entertainment, all mass culture, everything produced around Times Square and on Broadway and in Hollywood, including the movie that Arzner is producing right now? "I know you want me to tear my clothes off . . ." This isn't the first time, and it won't be the last, that an entertainer tears her clothes off, only to reveal raging nihilism underneath.

But there are ironic wheels within wheels here. Judy is turbulent and distressed, but the audience applauds tumultuously. Arzner is aware that part of the audience in Times Square, at the end of the 1930s, is glad to turn against itself. There is a newly sophisticated audience out there: It derives from Ibsen's audience, and Manet's, and Bernard Shaw's, and the Armory Show's, and Weill and Brecht's. These are men and women who feel exploited and bored by art that is made to make them feel good, but they can get a thrill from art that calls them names or treats them as if they aren't there. This is the audience for plays like *The Cradle Will Rock* and *The Threepenny Opera*, and for plenty of modern poetry and painting and music, even jazz, which is turning from swing bands that make people get up and dance into bebop psychodramas of lonely soloists playing for their lives. Arzner knows this modernist audience is out there, somewhere, and she fights all her life to reach it.

Arzner makes us feel the fury of the performer's nihilism. But she doesn't want it to burn up the performers themselves. (And we can see she knows it can.) She gives the movie a scheme that, unbeknownst to Judy, will rescue her and liberate her furious energy in constructive ways. Arzner introduces Ralph Bellamy, as "Steve Adams," a dance-company impresario, a kind of

Lincoln Kirstein figure who wants to produce something new in American dance. He says he wants a form of dance that will provide "an interpretation of American life—the life of shopkeepers, mechanics, aviators." Bellamy's recipe situates us rather klunkily in Popular Front country. And the brief scene we see of his company in motion, choreographed by Ernst Mazay, is a sort of Popular Front mobile mural. The strength of art with a Popular Front sensibility has always been its great horizon, its human inclusiveness, its largeness of vision; its weakness is a tendency to flatter the audience and give them a prefabricated easy ride. Bellamy's character is underwritten, but he is inserted very clearly into what we come to recognize as the movie's scheme: Everything moves toward a synthesis of Judy's negativity with Steve's positive energy. He pursues her, she runs away from him (though we know he is producing just the sort of dance she wants to do). After endless plot devices to avoid it, they finally make contact, and the movie ends with a vintage Hollywood romantic clinch. We are gently shoved into feeling that we are present at a great historic moment. American culture is about to make a great leap. O'Hara's art for art's sake and Bellamy's art for shopkeepers, mechanics, and aviators are about to converge, and a new dance is going to be born. *Dance, Girl, Dance* lays out all the artistic and social forces that in just a little while will bring us Jerome Robbins and Leonard Bernstein's *Fancy Free*, and Martha Graham and Aaron Copland's *Appalachian Spring*, and Agnes de Mille's choreography for Rodgers and Hammerstein's *Oklahoma!*, stage and screen incarnations of *On the Town*, and George Balanchine's postwar modern New York City Ballet.

All this is happening in 1940, just as America is gearing up to enter "the Good War" against the Nazis. Arzner's contribution to the war effort is a utopian vision of a form of dance that will both unite and ignite the American people. Yet her hope is undercut by her own savage indictment of all art that makes people feel good. Yes, maybe the new company will light new fire signs in Times Square. But who can keep both tomorrow's artists and their audience from being blinded by the light?

One sad thing about Arzner's dialectical synthesis is that it leaves Bubbles out. Ball has been by far the strongest human presence in *Dance, Girl, Dance*, up to the *dénouement*. But the movie's scheme seems to demand that O'Hara be promoted over her, so that Bubbles and her spirit of burlesque simply get dumped.* I have been arguing that Arzner disapproves of Bubbles. The literature says she was comfortable with Ball offscreen. But it is important for us to pinpoint what she signifies when she is on. Bubbles doesn't share the standpoint of Judy's diatribe at all; even if Judy could explain her nihilism, Bubbles probably wouldn't get it. She sees no need to (in Judy's words) "see through" her audience, because she doesn't think that they are in disguise: With her, both their sexual desire and their embarrassment about their desire—which provokes their raucous laughter—are out in the open. She doesn't feel degraded by their lustful looks, and she doesn't consider herself morally superior to them. She has a knack for moving fluidly in and out of both the mother / child and the wife / husband (or lover / lover) dyads, without being dissolved by them. Ball's achievement in *Dance, Girl, Dance* is to create a call-and-response dynamic with a mass audience that enables them and her to feel equal, mutual, and at home. This is a political as well as an artistic achievement. It fleshes out the Popular Front. Can Times Square, or dance in America, live without it?

Ball's performance here is popular culture and Popular Front at its best; so it is sad to see Arzner drop her from the vision of future dance. But Lucy will get her revenge. Within a decade she will be back, liberated from Broadway, and from Hollywood, and from everyplace else, in a new mass medium that will be a new incarnation and a new travesty of the Popular Front, and there—where?—she will dance circles around everybody.

---

*In fact, in the late 1930s and the early 1940s, New York's populist mayor Fiorello LaGuardia was conducting a fervid campaign against burlesque, with lavish support both from the Catholic Church and from Protestant NGOs—often directed against a vision of greasy, lecherous Jews—and with covert support from the 42nd Street Property Owners and Merchants Association. By the 1930s, mass culture was getting some First Amendment protection from the courts, so a government could not shut down theaters simply because it was offended by what they put on the stage. But the city planning agencies of this period, which "sought to contain outdoor activity of all sorts," including arcades, street musicians, and sidewalk cafés, helped devise forms of real estate zoning that eventually empowered New York and other cities to bypass constitutional issues by closing burlesque houses on zoning grounds. See Senelick, "Private Parts in Public Places," 336–38, and Friedman, *Prurient Interests*, 73–77, on the anti-burlesque claim that its presence was "cheapening the street." This zoning strategy would work again in Times Square at the end of the 1980s.

CHAPTER 5

The Street Splits and Twists

Take a walk around Times Square
With a pistol in my suitcase
—Marianne Faithfull, "Times Square," 1983

One way to see Times Square in the later twentieth century might be this: *That sailor and that girl got split up.* West 42nd Street, "the deuce," became a place where the sailor and his male friends and fans could feel more than ever at home, while the girl and her friends came to feel that where they had once danced on taxi roofs with Ruby Keeler, there was no room for them anymore. Those sailors, glamorous, patriotic heroes of 1945, stars of *On the Town*,[1] were themselves displaced, as the Department of Defense closed the Brooklyn Navy Yard and moved its large facilities to the South and the Gulf Coast, while the Port Authority shut down nearly the whole New York part of the port. The PA moved its cargo traffic to New Jersey, and concentrated its New York budget on speculative real estate, notably the World Trade Center downtown.[2] Meanwhile, the dynamics of the real estate market subjected the Square to devastating assaults: It lost its two most glamorous buildings, the gorgeous neo-Baroque Hotel Astor and the turn-of-the-century Times Tower, which had defined not only the Square's optical focus but its social identity. This is the structure Times Girl clings to; what could she cling to now? It was a pity that when the *Times* sold its building to the Allied Chemical Co., none of its competitors had the guts to run a headline, TIMES SELLS OUT TIMES SQUARE. (Of course they had their own properties and their own real estate departments, always in search of deals.)³ The developers did not obliterate the tower as they obliterated the hotel. Its new owners sheathed it in white marble. Many New Yorkers were puzzled by this new look. I liked to say it was actually a public service, to enable the modern public to keep in touch with its biblical values, to give us direct experience of what Jesus called "whited sepulchers," monumental symbols of inner emptiness and death.* Yes, Times Square was losing life and fullness. And yet, for generation after the war, the Broadway theater, the Square's core industry, was at its creative peak. Think of *Death of a Salesman*, *A Streetcar Named Desire*, *South Pacific*, *West Side Story*, *A Raisin in the Sun*, *Long Day's Journey into Night*. You could learn a lot about where America was going, and about what it was losing, if you went to shows and watched the signs.

Ethel Merman: The Woman Who Filled the Sky

New York homegirl Ethel Merman, née Zimmerman, is one of Times Girl's most flamboyant descendants. She made a Broadway career that started in the Depression and ran into the 1970s. Unlike many other divas who used Broadway as a springboard to Hollywood, she seems never to have been comfortable outside the theater's eight-days-a-week routine, and never at home outside New York. This made card-carrying New Yorkers like my parents especially fond of her: As New York became increasingly isolated and embattled, she was *our* voice.

Merman was the star of the first Broadway show I ever saw, *Annie Get Your Gun*, where my parents took me for my eighth birthday.⁴ (It was a Sunday matinee; afterward we admired the lights and went to Lindy's.) She could belt out a song at top volume and yet make it sound like casual conversation, and I became her fan the minute she opened her mouth to sing. *Annie Get Your Gun* became an instant classic. It was universally beloved, reproduced in all media, endlessly revived. It is always on the short list when people talk about Broadway's gifts to world culture. They remember Mer-

---

*Matthew 23:27. I got laughs, but for years I couldn't bear to look. I still can't bear it, but the space is so enveloped with billboards today, it's hard to tell there ever was a building there.

man, and also Irving Berlin, both working at the top of their forms. What gets forgotten in most of this talk is what got remembered in my family: its feminist plot.[5]

Annie Get Your Gun presents a woman—a girl, really, at least at the start—who is a great "natural" sharpshooter, with overflowing talent but no training or sophistication. Writers Herbert and Dorothy Fields posed two dramatic questions, one about the heroine, one about the world. Would the world recognize this woman's talent? Would she find the inner strength and balance to confront the world? The Fieldses made the issue more complex and interesting when they made her fall in love with the only man whose talent approached hers, and when they made Frank Butler a man—a typical man, my mother used to say—who could love only women he could dominate. The issues then became: Would she stand up for herself? Would he stand by her, a woman he knew was more talented than himself? And could they learn to love each other on those terms? If they didn't learn to work together, the plot said, the show would fold. I, and the other kids in the audience, were learning, too. One thing we were learning was that this play was a musical *comedy*, and that in a comedy, whatever trouble might unfold in the middle, the answer would be Yes in the end. With help from leading backer Chief Sitting Bull and producer Buffalo Bill, the hero overcame his need to be on top, the heroine learned to trust a man, he became her manager, and they looked into each other's eyes, embraced, and faced the world together as fellow performers in Buffalo Bill's Wild West Show. The play's last line was sung not only by all performers in chorus, but also by the whole audience on its feet: "Let's go on with the show." I learned that show business was there to *show* what justice, freedom, respect, and love were all about. (It's hard not to say: Those were the days.)

It has to be a tribute to the spirit of Broadway, including the receptive spirit of the Broadway audience, that people like my parents could instantly see *Annie Get Your Gun* as a play about them. They had no trouble merging the Fields/Berlin/Merman Annie Oakley into their own lives. They sang its songs, as solos and duets, while waiting for the bus, doing dishes, putting us to sleep; they adapted lines from these songs into their endless ongoing conversation. "Doin' What Comes Naturally" was about the two of them as a couple and the way they spontaneously clicked. "My Defenses Are Down" was about their mutual inner resistance to being swept away, and the thrill of overcoming their resistance. The heroine's childhood as a hillbilly stood for their own impoverished childhoods (and Irving Berlin's) "in the ghetto," as they called the Lower East Side. Neither of my parents would have dreamt of picking up a gun (my father was rejected by the Army for his heart condition), but when Annie said, "I'm a girl, but I can shoot like a man," it was obvious to them both that "shoot" meant "think." When Frank Butler left the show about halfway through, hadn't he said "You're too smart for me"? But after another hour of plot, he learned to live with it. His struggle to love a woman who could shoot better than he could symbolized my father's struggle to love a woman who was smarter than he was. He was smart in some ways, he knew—"I know the streets," he liked to say—but he always told me "your mom's the brains of the family." The smartest thing he had ever done, he said, was to grab her and hold her and listen when she talked. (That was the comedy of their life together. The tragedy was that they never found a Buffalo Bill.)

"Anything You Can Do, I Can Do Better" was one of their favorite duets. I worked hard to get the words, to sing along, to know both parts, not to break down in laughter. This was a problem, because even as the singers were dissing each other—as my students would do in freestyle rap battles half a century later—they were also laughing at themselves:

Anything you can buy, I can buy cheaper,
I can buy anything cheaper than you.

They hold a pseudo auction and bid each other down. They finally come together on an activity that neither can perform: bake a pie.

Can you bake a pie? No! Neither can I . . .

As I grew up, I learned how *Annie Get Your Gun* proclaimed America's very own romance of self-promotion, and how it expanded and deepened the romance by insisting on women's right to participate in it.[6] But this show's comic genius lay in its capacity both to promote women's self-promotion and to recognize that the whole promotional enterprise was absurd.

And yet, I saw as I grew up a little more, the fate of those who were excluded from the industry and denied promotion was a lot worse. In fact, the great postwar feminist comedies like *Annie Get Your Gun,* and like *On the Town,* and like *Adam's Rib* and *Pat and Mike,* had marked a false dawn. As Cold War America made its first great leaps forward, a generation of terrific women got left back. In 1964 or so, when I brought my mother *The Feminine Mystique,* she was glad to read it, but she said that she and the women who had been my teachers already knew it by heart. The people who canonized *Annie Get Your Gun* as an American classic achieved what canonizers always achieve: They lost track of what the work was all about.

I was in college when *Gypsy* came out (1959). I felt Merman's live performance was the greatest I'd ever seen. It was also a musical comedy, but it seemed to me about as dark as comedy ever gets. (Maybe tied with *The Threepenny Opera,* which played Off-Broadway—you could even say, *defined* Off-Broadway—at the end of the 1950s.) It was ostensibly based on the memoirs of the intellectual stripper Gypsy Rose Lee. Anyone who reads that book will find a smart, funny, ebullient, self-ironic sensibility, reminiscent of her friend Anita Loos (*Gentlemen Prefer Blondes*), and thoroughly in control of her material.[7] All those who saw Merman's *Gypsy* found themselves in a very different, far scarier world.[8] Merman, as the heroine's mother Mama Rose, took over the play as brutally as Captain Ahab takes over *Moby-Dick.* In fact, *Gypsy* and *Moby-Dick* share quite a lot: the polarity between the captain and the crew; the frightening ease with which the crew, symbol of "the people," is bullied into total passivity and submission; the demonic force of the central character, who as the story progresses moves ever farther away from labels like "hero" or "villain," and ever closer to labels like "beyond good and evil"; the lack of inner balance in the work, and our uncertainty about where it is going, till it lurches on; the brooding darkness of the whole environment, which carries us back to a vulnerable and crumbling country that is a world away from the world empire we live in today.

The dark world this play throws us into forces us to think in ironical and allegorical ways. When Merman sings "Everything's Coming Up Roses," it is hard not to think something like "Yeah, in the graveyard." All her big numbers in *Gypsy* invite—really, demand—that kind of jaundiced response. Mama Rose gets a new boyfriend, Herbie, who undertakes to manage her act while he pleads (in vain) for her hand. When the featured and favored sister, June, elopes (she will become the actress June Havoc), and then all the boys in the act defect, Herbie and Mama Rose are clearly in trouble; but if they feel troubled, they aren't telling us. They define their new situation in a cheerful, rousing dance trio, "Together Wherever We Go." If we grasp the human context of this number, we may want to rename it "Together Over a Cliff," or at least "A Dance to Delusion." Nevertheless, thirty years after Zimmerman morphed into Merman, Merman was finally getting a chance to do something that those who loved her had always known she could do: She was filling the sky.

When the family's various vaudeville acts collapse, as we know they will, Rose pushes Louise out onto the runway, and then is horrified to see Louise use it to run away from *her*. As Rose becomes Gypsy Rose, and has a brilliant success with the Minsky burlesque on 42nd Street, her mother rages against her and calls her degraded. But we can see that what really bothers Rose is the sight of her daughter *up*graded, that is, growing up.

One of the show's memorable numbers, sung by three rank-and-file strippers, is "You Gotta Have a Gimmick." Louise/Gypsy's gimmick, which gets her over more than any physical charms, is sophisticated irony. From the moment she goes out onstage, she speaks and moves with a self-assurance and a self-irony that people usually get, if they ever get it, only after years of good therapy. Where did she get hers? It seems that, all through the years she was sewing the costumes for her favored sister, she became something like her own shrink, learning to scrutinize herself, her family, and the world. All her inner growth went on below Mama Rose's radar screen because it never occurred to her mother to ask or notice what she thought. Louise is like a Soviet satellite that has developed an elaborate dissident subculture, but is unnoticed by the KGB until its first general strike. Her mother vilifies her and tries to tear her down, but she is strengthened by the world's recognition and acclaim. Her audience doesn't know her so well—certainly not in the primal way we know Mama Rose—but we can recognize her and love her and want to help her get over because we can feel her desperate struggle for identity as something like our own.

Merman dominates the last act, as she has dominated all the rest. Only now she is faced with a newly complex existential task: giving up her power. (I remember wondering whether Merman was a powerful enough actress to remove herself from power; later, I wondered how I could have wondered.)

The final scene starts with Louise/Gypsy dressing for a party in her honor. Rose bursts in, in full armor, to attack, assault, and perhaps disable her. But then, in a moment of unbearable intensity, the suddenly grown-up child looks into the Medusa's eye and doesn't blink. *She wins!* And then, from the height of her victory platform, she invites her mother to come to her party, and even offers her own fur coat. Mama accepts her daughter's coat with ill grace—she mutters, "It looks better on me"—but still she takes it and puts it on. She is going through a shock of recognition, recognition not only of her daughter but of herself. She is recognizing that Gypsy has broken free of her; that her freedom has become a source of power, to the point that now Gypsy is going to be the power in the family; and that Rose's own identity from now on will have to be as part of Gypsy's supporting cast. The act of giving up power gives Rose insight into the life she has supposedly lived all for her daughters: Now she can see, "*I did it for me.*" *Gypsy* begins as a backstage musical, but becomes a declaration of human rights. It affirms the right of children to grow up, to pull away from their parents and their parents' plans for them, and to make plans of their own. For Laurents and Sondheim, this is "life, liberty, and the pursuit of happiness." These kids can take care of their parents. But their parents must let them, by recognizing them as adults.*

Gypsy is one of the most grueling of American plays. It's amazing how many of the greatest American plays ran on Broadway in a single decade—*Death of a Salesman, A Streetcar Named Desire, Long Day's Journey into Night*—heartrending ordeals, every one. *Gypsy* is the one great ordeal with a happy ending. Its climax, where Gypsy offers to take care of Rose and her mother lets her, is a rare utopian moment when we can actually see tragedy metamorphose into comedy. Our history doesn't offer many moments like

---

*In Bernadette Peters's revival in 2003–04, she sang beautifully, with a far greater range, both musical and emotional, than Merman's. *But she did not fill the sky.* She did not strike terror into everybody in the theater. When she played scenes with other actors, she projected herself as their fellow human being. It was clear from the start that her *Gypsy* was going to be a comedy. When she finally recognized her daughter as an adult, it didn't seem that she would be crushed by this act of human decency. As Peters's *Gypsy* unfolded, the gulf between the two versions grew. Ironically, this revival served to revive a much more tormented and troubling play that ran alongside it, haunted it like a dybbuk, and threatened to rub it out. Thus a live star with a lovely human presence brought a dead star's far more menacing presence back to life.

this. Imagine, if we could see King Lear settle into a retirement cottage in Cordelia's kingdom; or see Captain Ahab at the very last minute turn the ship around and return to Nantucket, where he could get drunk, try on new clothes, and tell tall tales; or see the Red Army refuse to fire on the people and join in the jubilation of the Prague Spring. Alas, we can't see any of these things. But Laurents and Sondheim and Merman have brought us a stirring vision of how somebody who used to fill the sky can learn to share the earth. It is an impressive political as well as a theatrical moment, and a crucial moment not only in Times Square's and Broadway's history, but in America's.[9]

It is fitting that Merman's *Gypsy* should overlap so well with the Kennedy presidency. I saw it in the winter of 1960–61, just as the Kennedys were coming to power. I remember reading, maybe in Leonard Lyons's Broadway column in the old *New York Post*, that the Kennedy family was very fond of this play, and would often command a block of twenty or thirty seats of an afternoon. It made perfect sense to me. After all, the great leap forward in Kennedy history had come when Jack and Bobby had freed themselves and their descendants from their own Mama Rose, the billionaire Fascist patriarch and Hitler groupie Joseph K. People of my age, remembering the Kennedy moment, are apt to feel a sense of tragic waste. It's true; but we can't really grasp the tragedy unless we can admire the Kennedys for their great leap from Fascism to liberalism, a leap that made it possible, for two minutes, to experience American political life as a comedy.

The later 1960s were hard times for Ethel Merman. After you have filled the sky, where can you go? What role could she have played that wouldn't be trivial? Could somebody have written her a Broadway musical version of Racine's Phaedra? Or of Lady Macbeth? Could the woman who morphed from Zimmerman to Merman have morphed into Aretha Franklin? Was there a Buffalo Bill in the wings who could have helped her grow? Bill Graham once said he would love to play Merman at the Fillmore East, but he feared her most ardent fans would never find the place. Possibly true, but sad, since so much of the Broadway bravura that Merman embodied was born on Yiddish Second Avenue. (It was a pity that Holocaust survivor Graham, who knew so many of American culture's buried treasures, didn't supply the public with more treasure maps.)

One of Merman's last roles was a Lincoln Center revival of *Annie Get Your Gun* in 1966. There were many layers of irony in this performance. I didn't go, but my mother did (my mother would have paid good money to hear her read the phone book). She expressed the same unease that some reviewers did: Merman's voice and her sheer presence were still a thrill, but it was like seeing a woman with grown children go back to school and go to the head of the class. So, why shouldn't she go back to school? I asked. What was the point of having Broadway, if its own stars couldn't be reborn in it? Yes, yes, by all means, my mother said; it just felt strange. But the diva's desire for rebirth is one of the great theatrical traditions. Sarah Bernhardt at the Hippodrome would have got away with it a century ago: She would have died tragically—coffins were among her favorite props—and then triumphantly risen from the grave; people who doubted her deaths and resurrections just wouldn't see the show. Sister Carrie at the Casino would have urged and enticed us to believe in her, but she would have telegraphed her own inner doubts. (Of course her sign would have brushed the doubt away.) Judy Garland at the Palace would have signaled that rebirth was impossible, but she was going over the top, maybe for the last time, and her late-1960s audience would have loved her for trying even as they mutually acknowledged the hopelessness of hope, and wept with her for her impending early death.[10]

People talked in 1966 about how much Ethel Merman had changed. But what about the ways *America* had changed? Many of the biggest changes had to do with guns. Think of the assassinations (more were coming); of the Vietnam War, and what it did to the people in it—"We had to destroy Ben Tre to save it"; of Frantz Fanon's romance of murder as inner liberation (eat your heart out, Raskolnikov); of the Black Panthers on page one, "pickin' up the gun"; of the enormous increase in everyday homicide, which *quadrupled* in a decade in New York (and many other cities' numbers were worse). When *Annie Get Your Gun* opened on Broadway, America was at peace, and people could argue peaceably about what guns and shooting might signify. Twenty years later, it was hard to see guns as anything but machines for killing people. Starting in the middle 1960s, there was a heroin market thriving in the alleys just off the deuce, often spilling out into the street. At night, when people came out of the theaters and out of the great 42nd Street Public Library, you could often hear what sounded like gunfire pretty close by. I still had a hard time believing it was real, but sometimes the eleven o'clock news would show the body bags and the blood on the streets, and the next morning's Metro section would tell the story and name the names (when they could find them). They were rarely people we knew, but before long we knew we were in a crossfire. Inside the crossfire, it was hard to see guns as comic props, or to buy our kids toy guns.

Since we are talking about Times Square, we should be able to assay the changes by seeing the signs. Look at *Annie Get Your Gun*'s original 1946 fire sign. In fact it is a reproduction of the program. It portrays Ethel Merman who is armed but eminently respectable, sort of a gun-packing matron.

In the play she is promoting here, her character is sloppy, unstable, a bit scary, full of *chutzpah* and punk allure. But from the playbill and from the billboard, you would never guess: Her character has been cleaned up for her sign. A woman who not only carries guns but knows how to use them, and knows how much she knows, is potentially a dangerous character; the play's promoters try to neutralize the danger by bathing their star in an aura that is corny as Kansas in August and normal as blueberry pie. Earlier on, I cited Oscar Levant's classic Broadway wisecrack about the metamorphoses of Doris Day: "I knew her before she became a virgin." This fire sign shows a Merman who has become a virgin, that is, who has constructed an artificial innocence and purity that she flamboyantly displays. If she is sexy (and many reviewers felt she was), it is in the image of what art critic Thomas Hess calls "the pinup girl . . . the healthy American cheerleader type," featuring "an open, friendly smile that discloses perfect white teeth . . . the friendly neighborhood sex symbol Americans know and love."[11] Postwar Times Square filled up with giant images of women like this, frequently in bathing suits, selling soda or cigarettes, chewing gum or toothpaste (does anybody remember the "Ipana smile"?); over the years the commodities moved gradually upscale, toward perfumes, whisky, expensive clothes, and cars. Merman's 1946 Annie Oakley is like them, radiant in her wholesomeness. She could be a recruiting poster for the WACs.

But American culture at mid-century was dynamic and full of contradictions. A thesis generated an antithesis: An imposed abundance of "good girls" created a widespread yearning for "bad girls." Images of those girls— nasty, aggressive, disheveled, often violent—pushed themselves into the foreground. Their sexuality was often ambiguous, but it was close to the surface and close to being out of control. Early in the 1950s, in the Abstract Expressionist paintings of Willem de Kooning, raucous women with toothy smiles suddenly thrust themselves into the center of his picture plane; his art was never pure again.

Thomas Hess calls these women "icons," and sees them as "violent intellectual and emotional criticism, in visual form, of the contemporaneous situation of the American woman, as reflected in the pinup."[12] Anti-pinup women were also featured in one of the most dynamic cultural forms of the mid-century: *film noir.* There they were always endangered, but they could be sources of danger as well. Their images ignited the covers of some of America's earliest paperback books: *Night in the City, The Amboy Dukes, Knock on Any Door.* I can remember being stirred by the images but disappointed by the mostly tepid and turgid texts. There was something about these women, some violent anger, some immense promise, that the authors of those genre books just didn't get. To use an expression from the boys' playground, these girls were "in your face." But why? Did anybody know the name of the game? Here were women demanding attention and stirring up intense feelings in people of both sexes, but there was a serious mystery about what they were up to, and about what was up.

Annie Get Your Gun's 1966 fire sign, already discussed in our "Signs" chapter, featured one of those iconic women embracing the Square. The sign was memorable in a way the production itself was not. This woman's presence revived some of the emotional fire at the play's core. It portrayed an Annie Oakley who was a "bad girl," more like a punk rocker than a WAC. At the same time, it reminded us that the star of this production was not a kid: She had played Mama Rose; she had filled the sky; she was a woman who had been around. Alas, I have not been able to find an image of this sign; you will have to imagine it. Ethel Merman, over a forty-year career trajectory, had the genius to magnify and sanctify Broadway roles and songs, to the point that she could make herself incarnate America, and make Broadway become the world. In *Annie Get Your Gun,* she was an innocent America that not only wanted but deserved more power in the world. In *Gypsy,* she was an all-too-experienced America that needed to learn to give up power and learn to share power in the world.

The Deuce Overflows: The Dirty Boulevard

He's going out, to the dirty boulevard . . .
And fly fly away, from this dirty boulevard . . .
—Lou Reed, "Dirty Blvd." (1989)

I have been trying to show how Times Square, over most of the twentieth century, created an ambience where women could be not only commercial sexual objects but, at the same time in the same place, authentic human subjects. But then things happened that wrecked the place's remarkable inner balance. Over a twenty-year span, it went through not only material impoverishment but spiritual collapse. Paradoxically, as often happens in history, the collapse triggered all sorts of cultural creativity—you can feel it in Lou Reed's song just above. But it's vital to see that it really was a collapse, because the Square's collapse yesterday paved the way for the gilded corporatization that envelops it today.

First of all, the deuce "tipped," and its sex businesses, which had been part of the scene since the 1880s, came to flourish on a spectacular scale, and to attract a greatly expanded all-male public. Forty-second Street had been sexually segregated and overwhelmingly male since the 1930s,[13] but the new men on the street displayed a new aggressive edge. Women in the 1970s came to feel not just excluded, but directly menaced by this block, and then the menace seemed to spill over. It got so, all over the Square, a woman had to *prepare* for being there.

In the 1970s and 1980s, the *Times* came to sound more and more like a tabloid as it highlighted horror stories in its backyard. ("A Nether World: A Block of 42nd Street," by Josh Barbanel; "Childhood in Hell: Growing Up on Times Sq.," on the Carter Hotel, by Maureen Dowd.) I had no doubt the stories were mostly true, but I felt the paper's perspective was skewed: It was oblivious to equally horrific stories in other people's backyards. (In Harlem, say, where I taught; in the South Bronx, which for years, from week to week, was burning down; in L.A., where drug gangs seemed a lot better organized and better armed; in cities like Washington and Miami and Houston, which always were, and still are now, a lot more dangerous than New York.) In the short run, I think I was right. But the *Times*'s perspective, though skewed, was right, too: The Square's deterioration meant something not just to them, but to people from all those other neighborhoods and cities, because Times Square had always been "a bath of light," a refuge from and alternative to their neighborhoods and cities.

Some of the bad stuff that happened was on both a national and a global scale. After the 1973 oil embargo, American industry crashed; giant firms like GM, whose names had always defined the Square, lowered their profiles and put their fire signs out. Huge billboard niches went dark, and empty spaces opened up in the Square that no one had ever seen. Some people ascribed apocalyptic meaning to those black holes. Others, like me, described them as transient and transitional. But really, who knew? And no one could deny that the darkness and emptiness were real.

There were obvious, blatant changes in the neighborhood's demography and infrastructure. It filled up with poor people who a generation earlier would have worked in the garment industry, next door to the Square on the south, or on the docks, next door on the west, and who would have lived in housing projects built with federal money. But the process that economists called "deindustrialization" hit old cities first.[14] Symptom One was a working class without work. The West Forties were full of large hotels. In the 1960s and 1970s, many landlords collected bonanzas from the Welfare Department by converting their hotels into SROs, "single-room occupancy" buildings, warehouses for the new generation of urban poor. (The metamorphosis of the Art Deco grand Hotel Carter, which went through from West 42nd to 43rd streets, was especially grim.) This was a generation with lots of jobless men who spent their days standing around, and with lots of kids who spent their lives on streets that weren't built for kids. Lou Reed, darkest of rockers, saw the SRO world pretty clearly:

> *No one here dreams of being a doctor or lawyer or anything*
> *They dream of dealing on the dirty boulevard.*

Some of these kids dreamt beyond the song, found adults who could take care of them, kept their lives in focus, stayed in school, and made it to college. In the 1990s, at CCNY, I got to know a few ex–"hotel kids"; except that, as one told me, "You're never an *ex*–hotel kid." They told stories of siblings or friends who became lookouts or mules for local drug dealers, or who were discovered by scouts from the dirty boulevard's various sex industries. Those kids could find themselves making a lot more money than their parents—especially the ones who "looked innocent." But after a year or two of ceremonies of innocence with arrays of anonymous Humberts and Quiltys, kids could get burnt out or worse. One kid half my age said he bet he'd been to more funerals than me; I didn't want to bet him.

In those rough years, the Broadway theater district stayed frayed but surprisingly intact, and, if we include "Theater Row" on 42nd Street between 9th and 10th, Off- and Off-Off Broadway, the neighborhood's theatrical capacities may actually have grown. But other forms of culture suffered. As the Square's all-night bookstores morphed into all-night pornographic bookstores, and as many of its venues for late-night theater turned into venues for live sex shows, I felt that lights were going out for me—and not just for me. Some of those pornographic bookstores were former secondhand book and magazine shops, often with their old proprietors, some of whom I had known since high school. (In ninth grade I had gone to the Square, which then was rich in old book and magazine shops, in search of 1938 editions of *Popular Mechanics*, which had plans for a shortwave radio that my friends and I wanted to build. When they dissed me as an inept builder, which I was, I reminded them who had found the plans.) At first I enjoyed browsing through them, in pretty much the way I've always enjoyed bookstores. But soon the pattern of merchandising changed. Everything got wrapped in plastic, to preclude browsing. Customers had to know in advance exactly what they wanted. The rhythms of hanging out were replaced by the rhythm of fast food: in and out. These customers tended to be middle-aged men with short haircuts, business suits, and raincoats; I thought they looked as if they came from "Meadowville, Indiana." I wondered, How come they always seemed to know exactly what they wanted? If they couldn't look, how could they find out? I never had the guts to ask. (After a few years, the merchandise itself changed: Printed matter was flooded out by a far more expensive article, videos. Most were videos that no one who lived in a family with children could bring home. A few more years, and consumers could stay home: In the 1990s, the Internet emerged as a vessel big enough to hold floods of pornographic stories, images, Websites, chat rooms, and blogs. Surfing the Net, you could not only indulge your favorite fantasy, but refine it into an addiction, and affiliate with fellow addicts, without going outside, without even leaving your chair.)

The most serious discussion of the deuce in its last wild years is *Times Square Red, Times Square Blue* by the poet and novelist Samuel "Chip" Delany.[15] Some of it is a vivid, detailed, but pointedly unsensational account of what sexual and social life were actually like in the Square's pornographic cinemas and its gay bars. Some of it is a sophisticated public policy argument, *à la* Jane Jacobs, that a modern city needs the modes of friendship and sociability that were nourished there. After all the hypocritical sanctimony of the Giuliani era, Delany's narrative is a breath of fresh air. He knows how to create "ordinary" characters with whom ordinary straight readers can identify. His men tend to be middle-aged, as he is, and to have stable proletarian occupations like taxi dispatcher and lunch-wagon operator. His book includes photographic portraits of many of them, and his evocative images have an iconic solidity that recalls Edward Hopper, Walker Evans, the best Popular Front murals. Port Authority Bus Terminal "taxi dispatcher Anthony Campbell" could fit comfortably on Mount Rushmore. His portrait could be an item in the James Earl Jones scrapbook—how did we miss that show? Delany's implicit appeal is *Attention must be paid to this man.* How can we be so cruel as to deny such a man his human right to pleasure and friendship?

But nobody ever felt the 42nd Street problem was people like *him.* They felt the problem was kids like the ones in the photo on page 168, flashy, slinky, like snakes, coming at you, in your face.

Ironically, the most dynamic choreographer on Broadway at just that moment, Bob Fosse (*Cabaret, Chicago, All That Jazz,* etc.), cultivated this "look," at once sexy and menacing, in his dancers of both sexes. More than once, late at night, he must have crossed the deuce and wondered whether those kids snaking their way along the street hadn't all come out of his head.

The other problem, which led Marianne Faithfull to think about packing a gun, was the street's aggressive hostility to women. For twenty years, I had to walk my women students to the bus terminal or the subway, and we had to avoid the deuce. It wasn't just a male cruising strip: it was an *all*-male cruising strip. Delany acknowledges this tacitly. "Our literature," he says — he probably means gay male literature —

> Our literature is full of such all-male scenes similarly structured that its charms, sociality, and warmth — if it has any — depend entirely on the absence of the woman — or at least depend on flattening "the woman" till she is only an image on the screen.

In the scene that follows, he describes an all-male pornographic cinema where some men jerk themselves off and others give blow jobs to others. A woman friend of his is fascinated by his story and wants to see the scene for herself. "What would happen," she asks, "if you took a woman in there? Probably everybody would get all upset and angry." Maybe she fears an inversion of Euripides' *The Bacchae*, where a man tries to sneak into the Dionysian women's secret rite but is recognized as a male and torn to pieces. Will Times Square's male maenads erupt against the one woman in the house? One Thursday afternoon, he takes her to the Metropolitan — not, however, in Times Square, but on East 14th Street. So they go in to-

gether, and she does what she does, and the guys do what they do, and noth-ing happens. That's the joke, the comic *dénouement*: N-o-t-h-i-n-g![16] They could have been George and Elaine on the *Seinfeld* show. But Delany wants the story to mean more: He wants us to see these steady customers as paragons of John Stuart Mill–type liberal virtue. (You can leave your daugh-ters with them!) I'm sure this episode happened just as he said it did. But then why did he shift his scene from West 42nd Street to East 14th? So many of the men behaving badly on the deuce were trying to stake a claim to an all-male *street*. For Delany to change the scene in a way that leaves out the worst is to conduct a cleanup of his own.

We can get an idea of what is missing on Delany's street map if we take a look at Bruce Benderson's. Benderson is Delany's sometime lover; the deuce was where they met. Here he acts as Delany's shadow, his Slim Shady, his antiself. He rhapsodizes "the heroin-high hustlers of Times Square"; he promotes a street that will be "the groundless, treacherous ter-rain of today's underclass." On Benderson's deuce,

> everybody is a "nigger." There is a certain depth of need or disorgani-zation at which a person will stick it in anybody or let anyone at all stick it in. . . . This repressed, disaffected, overprotected class in Amer-ica is yearning for the extremes of experience and knowledge. They are suicidally restless. They must be the new sacrificial lambs. . . . They fear the violence of the inner city but they imitate its surface.
>
> Wannabee homeboys and homegirls, rebel! It's time to sacrifice yourselves to the dangers of the new degenerate narrative![17]

If Delany's afternoon in the dark reads like a canceled *Seinfeld* episode, Benderson's sounds like a continuous performance of *Naked Lunch* at "Show World NY." If Delany is working to create a stable and sophisticated gay urbanity, Benderson is fighting for a city that will crash the Richter scale. (Could Frears and Kureshi, or Zwick and Hershkovitz, capture this couple's inner drama? Or would it take another Shakespeare to do justice to the comedy of their inner contradictions?)

If gay historians like George Chauncey (in *Gay New York*) can be be-lieved, men had been pushing the deuce that way for decades. Probably many felt it was male "turf," the way Italians in Bay Ridge and Irish in South

Boston had felt their neighborhoods were *their* turf: If outsiders came in, they got pushed out. Note, too, that "rough trade" was the deuce's primary gay style: It was just as nasty to fairies as to women, and to men who didn't want to be part of the cruise. I worked a block away from the deuce for thirty years, and I got plenty of free-floating nastiness over the years, but for myself I didn't much care: I grew up in a rough neighborhood (rough for kids, at least; nicer for grown-ups), and I learned the moves a guy needs to keep his place on the street. But on West 42nd Street, sexual segregation and aggression enveloped a public space that for generations had been an oasis of integration, in a neighborhood where the spectacle of the crowd was the street's big thrill. This was a disaster for the city. Much of the allure of Times Square, from the 1890s through the 1960s, was its gold mine of possibilities for women. But in the 1970s, as real women felt under crushing pressure on the streets around the Square, extremely crude images of women surged up to take their place.

When I talked about the 1966 *Annie Get Your Gun* fire sign, I described a movement toward increasing complexity, ambiguity, and richness of meanings. It is pretty dispiriting to see what came next:

This was the north side of the deuce, right next door to the Eighth Avenue subway arcade. Look close and absorb the shock. This is a "reduction" of woman in so many different senses! Look at her blank eyes, the holes in her mouth, her nail polish job that leaves out the thumb, the pathetic ornaments on her breasts, the youthful body that doesn't seem to have been through anything played off against a face that looks like it's been through everything. The cosmic emptiness of this face makes the faces of *Playboy* and *Penthouse* nudes, and of the pinups on the billboards on Broadway, look like Rembrandts or Vermeers. The most chilling detail here is the word "Complete": The sign doesn't tell us what it is we can do to or with this woman for $10, but it assures us that for $10 that will be all, there will be nothing left. Shall we call this woman "Ms. Complete"? King Lear had a word for her: "Thou art the thing itself, unaccommodated man . . . a poor, bare, forked animal."[18] The deuce's most dismal legacy is a vision of naked and sexual woman as "a poor, bare, forked animal," stripped of the aura that makes sexuality a human adventure and a form of transcendence. The experience Ms. Complete invites us to share, two thirds of the way through the long twentieth century, is a nightmare life-in-death that seems to bring down the curtain on the high-stepping, the vast horizons, the ebullient hopefulness embodied by Times Girl, and by Times Square, when the century was young.

I had thought "Ms. Complete" was the worst. Then I remembered my *King Lear*, where Edgar says that so long as you can say "This is the worst," you can be pretty sure there will be something worse.[19] And indeed there was something worse—how could I forget?—and it stood there for years, first at the east end of the deuce, then later at the west: a giant reproduction

of a cover of *Hustler* magazine. The caption said something like "Let's not treat woman as a piece of meat." The picture showed a naked woman, upside down—you could see only her legs—apparently being thrown headfirst into a gigantic meat grinder. There was no way this image could make us feel anything but horror; but *Hustler* seemed to be saying, "It isn't ours, we hate this stuff, we're displaying it so you can reject it; if it horrifies you, blame everyone else out there who mistreats women, but don't blame us." The magazine's honest intentions entitled it to saturate its covers with evil. By 1980 or so, everyone I knew knew this image. But they didn't find it in *Hustler*, which few New York intellectuals read. They found it on the corner of 42nd Street and Broadway, magnified many times its original size, at the table of an organization called WAP, "Women Against Pornography." WAP dedicated itself to closing sex shops and putting the owners of pornographic magazines in prison. To arouse hysterical rage against its enemies, it displayed horrific images, greatly enlarged. It claimed that its desire to eradicate evil entitled it to drench the Square with evil, in extra-large spectacular visions, year after year, "in your face." (Of course, that was the great Times Square tradition; not that WAP cared.) It specialized in belligerent marches and demonstrations; Times Square was its favorite staging area. Its motto, brilliantly conceived, was "Take Back the Night!" I could sympathize with WAP's desire to fight the pressures that led women to fear the urban night; I believed its night marches and demonstrations gathered crowds, increased the density and safety of the streets, and helped women— and not only women—feel at home. But WAP's ambitions reached far beyond this point. The women who maintained its tables, who led its marches, who handed out its leaflets and flyers, and who began to appear in American graduate and law schools, all seemed to believe they were fighting for exclusive possession of the night, and that there was only a very limited amount of night to go around. I felt they had all lost touch with Times Square's basic truth: There is enough night and enough light for us all.

"The Male Gaze": Twisted Sister, Twisted Street

If WAP could be said to have a metaphysics and an ontology, they were developed by an array of 1970s art and film historians. Even as American movies lost their connection with the experience of "going downtown," and (thanks to the Federal Highway System) even as thousands of spectacular downtowns crumbled into ghost towns,[20] America and the UK experienced a tremendous boom in "film studies," rooted in the public university system, especially in the newest universities, and in the extraterritorial technology of VCR and DVD. One of film studies' first great bursts of energy went into the "deconstruction" of classic and canonical films. As it happened, one of the strongest currents in feminist film criticism developed around the idea of "the male gaze."

The classic anatomy of "the male gaze" was performed by the British film critic Laura Mulvey in her 1975 essay, "Visual Pleasure and Narrative Cinema." Mulvey didn't invent the "male gaze" concept, but "Visual Pleasure and Narrative Cinema" raised it to a metaphysical intensity.[21] Even a hostile reader like me can be impressed with Mulvey's intellectual power. But I think her essay gets some primary human experiences spectacularly wrong. Moreover, I think it has had so much intellectual influence *because* of the way it gets things wrong. Mulvey mentions casually that her favorite film genre is melodrama, and after reading her theory of "the male" it's easy to see why. Her understanding of sex and love has a definite melodramatic pathos. But the word "melodrama" may be too weak to encompass her vision of the predatory man. Maybe we should think of her as the Grimm Brothers' long-neglected twisted sister.

In the ambience of the late-and-post-1960s counterculture, Mulvey feels free to let pent-up malice loose. Her language is both deadened and deadly:

> It is said that analyzing pleasure or beauty destroys it. That is the intention of this article.

Did she just say she wanted to destroy everybody's sense of pleasure and beauty in films? Yes, she did: Give that woman a gold star for sheer *chutzpah!* But it isn't much compared with what comes next: She wants to destroy "the ego."

> The satisfaction and reinforcement of the ego that represent the high point of film history hitherto must be attacked. [The author's aim is] a total negation of the ease and plenitude of the narrative fiction film.

There is something uncanny about this language in the 2000s. But it was easy to find on the left at the end of the 1960s, when the New Left disintegrated into mutually hateful sects of *enragés* and *enragées*, promoting competing but overlapping forms of nihilism. It's a declaration of war on pretty much everybody.[22] I don't know Mulvey's biography, but I recognize her language. It's the language of nice hopeful kids who grew up with the Vietnam War, and learned to celebrate death.

Mulvey's theme is ostensibly limited to Hollywood-type cinema and its widespread human appeal. But she writes in a dogmatic, left-Heideggerian mode appropriate for proclamations about the nature of Being. Thus, she asserts, the gazing subject is universally male. "In a world ordered by sexual imbalance, the pleasure of looking is split between active/male and passive/female." The essential male pleasure is "scopophilia," a philosophical word that means something like pleasure of the eye, pleasure in seeing. Mulvey puts this pleasure through a Lacanian grinder; she chops it up and sorts it out into a mix of voyeurism and fetishism, sadism and masochism. I don't see anything inherently wrong with analyzing one thing as another; why else did God give us these big brains? And don't we all agree that there's more in life than meets the eye? But Mulvey's special talent was to make psychoanalytic language sound like schoolyard abuse. She canonized the word "voyeur" as a new-age obscenity. Alas, French words can't be said in English without sounding smooth and graceful; but "voyeur" has often been used by people whose inflection showed they wished they could spit it out. (On the other hand, expressions like "fetishistic scopophilia" could be spat out, and they were.) Mulvey's analysis of "the male gaze" became canonical in a new academic field, postmodern "cultural studies." The field got crowded fast, and turned into a street with 180-degree turns. There you could hear radical intellectuals, who only last week prided themselves on their "transgressive" insights, turn on one another this week and abuse themselves for the transgression of wanting to see.[23]

Take a look at Mulvey's archetypal male. Everything this guy does is sinister. If he looks at a woman, his gaze is "controlling." Indeed, he "controls events," "makes things happen," "is a representative of power," and enjoys "a sense of omnipotence." Women's "image [is] continually stolen" by him. In fact, the very act of a man looking at a woman is itself an act of theft. Why does he want her image, anyway? Only for the purpose of "gaining control and possession." But this cyclops is dumb. He doesn't see that once a woman "becomes his property," she "los[es] her outwardly glamorous characteristics [and] her generalized sexuality." When I first read this riff, I knew I'd heard it somewhere before. After a while I remembered where: It was part of the timeless wisdom that so many girls' parents in my youth in the 1950s still inflicted on their daughters. *Don't give it up,* they said: once a woman surrenders she's *ruined,* she's *damaged goods.*

Mulvey's dogmatic style rarely stoops to give examples. Her one example of a movie star ruined by surrender is a surprising one: Lauren Bacall. Bacall's ruin, presumably in Humphrey Bogart's arms, is so plain to her, she doesn't seem to notice she's making a controversial interpretation, and she sees no need to defend or support it. But in fact Bacall's aura on the screen, as fresh today as it was half a century ago, comes from her capacity to embody adult love, where a woman in love *doesn't* surrender either sexuality or autonomy, and *isn't* damaged or ruined. She knew how to be part of a romantic couple where there was mutual respect and both people could win. Bacall, who has always talked openly about herself, has felt damaged by all sorts of things—by the culture of Hollywood, by anti-Semites, by alcohol, by McCarthyism—but never by love. Mulvey might say that if Bacall doesn't feel damaged, it only shows how damaged she is; and if a mass audience loves her, it shows how damaged they all are, and how much they require "the total negation of [their] ease and plenitude," which would damage them even more.

Meanwhile, the women on Mulvey's street don't look back. Not even wise guys like Bacall look back: There is no female gaze in her script. Women are here—on the screen, in the world—to exhibit a quality she describes in a proto-Heideggerian word: *"to-be-looked-at-ness."* But they cannot be looked at too closely, not even by the men who want to steal their image, because just beneath their gaudy surface lies the horror: Women are, in Mulvey's most haunting phrase (does it betray a Catholic background?), *"bearers of the bleeding wound."* The wound, she says, is castration. She imagines women entirely in terms of what they don't have, what they are not: Her women don't want, don't fantasize, don't project, don't identify, don't even dream, they just look to-be-looked-at, they bear, they bleed.

Mulvey dimly remembers something she calls "the magic of the Hollywood style at its best." In fact, this was the force that created and nourished

"America's Movie Center" as it thrived for decades around Times Square. In those days, the Square was a place where generations of ordinary men and women went to movies with each other, and where mass culture helped bind them together. In the Square, the private languages spoken by Gable and Colbert, Powell and Loy, Bogart and Bacall, Tracy and Hepburn, enabling them to be intimate in the midst of the Code, became raw materials that millions of ordinary couples took back with them across bridges and through tunnels, and used to create their own secret codes of pleasure and intimacy in the midst of intrusive parents, neighbors, bosses, children. Movies and other mass media—for my mother it was the novel, for my father jazz, for my Aunt Idie dance—gave them a radical dream of music and dance and love beyond the bounds of the social world they lived in; at the same time, it worked as a prime conservative force that bound them to that world. That contradiction and complexity was the real "magic of the Hollywood style at its best." But Mulvey doesn't seem to get it. Her constricted perspective works just right for the deuce of the 1970s, when the magic broke down, the horizon collapsed, the male gaze turned aggressively nasty, women passing through were relieved not-to-be-looked-at, and only a flattened image of a woman like "Ms. Complete" could be at home. Maybe the way to appreciate Mulvey is to say that her lurid vision of the world was a perfect fit for a street that had collapsed into "the dirty boulevard."

WAP anticipated the "Dworkin-MacKinnon" laws of the 1980s, which tried to exempt pornography from First Amendment free speech protection by redefining it as a violent action, a form of rape: not as speech that might lead to rape, but as action that in itself *was* rape.[24] It also prefigured Mayor Giuliani's 1990s attempts to close the Brooklyn Museum because he and his allies found some of its art "indecent."[25] I have always thought that attempts to police culture are sinister and dangerous to the people they claim to protect. People who say they believe in democracy need to see that it means letting people make their own decisions about what to look at, what to read, what to think, what spectacles to be thrilled by. Nevertheless, the phrase "the degradation of women" is not hallucinatory. Think of "Ms. Complete"; think of the woman being thrown into the meat grinder in that *Hustler*-WAP multimedia coproduction. Think of the depth and dread impacted in those images. Whatever we think of the social policies that followed from the degradation of women in the Square, we will be clueless and helpless if we don't see that the thing itself was something real; for a time, Mulvey's twisted perspective had a real address.

If we can keep this reality in focus, it can help explain something that at first struck me as thoroughly irrational: a generation of women's fear and hate for the Square. For fifteen years or so, virtually no woman I knew would go there. Over a thirty-year span, starting in 1970, I taught at the CUNY Graduate Center on West 42nd Street, across from Bryant Park, a block from the Square. My graduate classes were always in the late afternoon or evening, and most of the time they ended after dark. It turned out that many of my students were jittery about the streets, and escorting them to the West Side subways and the Port Authority Bus Terminal became a fascinating aspect of my job, not mentioned in the Job Description. If they were women, we would have to take elaborate detours to avoid 42nd Street. This was equally true if I was going with a woman to a Broadway or to an Off-Off-Broadway play. Of course the detour blocks—40th or 41st streets, Ninth Avenue—offered plenty of sleaze in their own right. But none of those streets had an *aura*, the way 42nd Street did, and none of the others made so many women feel under assault.

I said earlier that women had to prepare for being there. There was a range of ways to do this. My mother worked very close to the deuce, and when she went to the theater, or went to buy tickets (this was long before the net), she used it without complaint. I asked her if she got any abuse from guys. She said most of it was in Spanish, and she knew what to do: "I just freeze them out." Her freeze: She could walk down a street as if the nasty men not only weren't there, but didn't exist. There were other strategies. One of my graduate students showed me her brass knuckles, which she had bought in the Square and always wore when she went there. If a man called her "cunt," and made dirty sounds—this had happened several times—she flashed "my knucks" and let loose a rhetorically amazing torrent of abuse. "Now they know me," she said, and flashed her teeth, "I get respect. I'm prepared." I had another grad student, a pretty tough woman, a community organizer on the Lower East Side. Once I mentioned a show I thought her ten-year-old daughter might like. "Bring her here? I'll see Times Square bombed before I bring my daughter here." That was well before the city had announced any of its giant plans. But when I heard someone like her say something like that, I felt sure that "bombed" was what Times Square was going to be. A large array of women, who stood for very different things in nearly every other way, came to share the belief that West 42nd was a one-way street aimed personally against them. If we don't see the reality of that feeling, we won't grasp the forces that finally blew the deuce away.

Taxi Driver: *The Male Maze*

Martin Scorsese's classic 1976 film *Taxi Driver* unfolds a nightmare vision in which the dirty boulevard envelops the world. The movie starts inside the cab of Travis Bickle (Robert De Niro). It is late on a summer night as he glides through Times Square. The crowds of people have thinned out, but the signs are still on fire, the colors splash red and blue (*à la* Minnelli), the ambience is melancholy but sublime. The audience feels comfortably enveloped in the classic Times Square landscape, the world first designed by Vincente Minnelli for MGM's *On the Town*. But then he hits the deuce, and it is almost like a crash. Suddenly the street jumps out at him: The color base turns garish yellow, camera movements speed up and become jagged, the street seems to ooze people, they look almost naked, they snake and shake their bodies provocatively at one another and at the world. It is an explosive paranoid nightmare of the dirty boulevard, a primal vision of the city as a threat, the street as a threat, the crowd as a threat, sex as a threat, other people as a threat. He shakes with rage. "Someday," he says in a voiceover, "a real rain will come and wash all the scum off the streets" (7).[26]* We don't understand what has happened to him, but he has turned very abruptly scary, and we have to be glad we're not in his cab.

This twisted travesty of public health turns out to play a central role in the taxi driver's mind. Charles Palatine, a presidential candidate, gets into his cab and asks him what the next president should do. He answers with a tirade:

> Well, he should clean up this city here. It's full of filth and scum, scum and filth. It's like an open sewer. Sometimes I can hardly take it.
>
> Some days I go out and smell it, and then I get headaches that never go away. We need a president that would clean up this whole mess. Flush it out (28).

The "hygiene" metaphor has a notorious history in modern times. In 1908, in the "Foundation and Manifesto of Futurism," F. T. Marinetti wrote in praise of "war, the world's only hygiene." Here is the sentence he wrote it in:

> We want to glorify war, the only hygiene of the world—militarism, patriotism, the anarchist's destructive gesture, the fine Ideas that kill and the scorn of women.[27]

Marinetti was writing after nearly a century of peace in Europe. He was hoping to make young men eager to go to war, and hoping for a war something like World War One. His manifestos were brilliant, and his twisted idea of public health established itself right away as one of "the fine Ideas that kill." The Nazis picked it up and ran a long, long way with it. But we

---

*Parenthetical numbers designate page numbers in the published version of the screenplay *Taxi Driver*. See also endnote 26, page 245.

should not be Eurocentric: In our time, people in every part of the world, and at every level of development, have proved themselves capable of genocide; wherever they have done it, this metaphor has come to their aid. It has helped them perform a spectacular act of remapping, to frame the act of killing people as a process of cleaning up solid waste. In Rwanda in 1994, in the genocidal outbreak against the Tutsis, one of the most fervid promoters of mass murder as hygiene was the lady who was the Rwandan Minister of Health. That metaphor has a lot to answer for. *Taxi Driver* puts it squarely on the Times Square map.

Driving around the town in his cab, De Niro spies Betsy (Cybill Shepherd) working as a Palatine volunteer. She turns out to be a flirtatious but respectable middle-class woman of his own generation. "Like an angel out of this open sewer," he writes in his diary. (13) At first he stalks her, and she has to call coworkers to get rid of him; it's clear to her (and everyone else) that he is dangerous. But her smile, her body language, her tone of voice, her flirtatious innuendoes (she compares him to the hero of a Kris Kristofferson hit song), all make it clear how exciting she finds Travis. She agrees to go out with him. He takes her to the only kind of entertainment he knows: a pornographic movie on the deuce. As the screen shows a pile of naked people, Betsy is grossed out, she slams out of the theater, grabs a taxi, and asks the driver to get her away from here fast. Coming out onto the deuce, she asks rhetorically, "What am I doing here?" But we have seen her interact with the taxi driver, and we know why she's there: She is there because she is thrilled by his aura of danger.

Ths movie-within-a-movie, like Shakespeare's plays-within-plays, is one of *Taxi Driver*'s crucial points. It can give us some idea of what was right and what was wrong in Laura Mulvey's dystopian vision of "the male gaze." Mulvey, WAP, Dworkin-MacKinnon, a whole array of 1970s and 1980s feminists against pornography, all seemed to imagine men who were autonomous, in possession not only of women but of their own sexual feelings and of their overall sense of themselves, and women without autonomy, "bearers of the bleeding wound" who could feel excited or at home only when passive and victimized. Scorsese and Schrader suggest that the male embrace of pornography springs from the deepest sexual and existential confusion. When Shepherd rejects De Niro, he has no idea why: "Travis is so much a part of his own world," Schrader says, "he fails to comprehend another's world" (30). The problem with pornography is not that it is violent or dangerous, but that it isolates the self. If Travis wants to get close to Betsy, he has used a medium that guarantees he will fail. Rousseau, writing in the midst of the Enlightenment, pornography's first golden age, found a perfect image when he spoke of books written "to be read with one hand." He knew that getting close to another person takes both hands.[28] But Travis doesn't get it: Cluelessness is his most powerful quality. Schrader gives him one more strong impulse: He "wants to get that pure white girl into that dark pornographic theatre." But here, too, he is "completely unconscious"; he knows not what he does. Shepherd, the adult woman in the case, seems a lot closer to something like autonomy. She follows her impulses close to danger, but she pulls herself out of the "dark mill" and back onto the street.

When Shepherd walks out, we are meant to share her dread. But if Schrader's explanation of the dread is right—the dialectic of light and darkness, of innocence and its violation—doesn't this really implicate *all* cinema? And doesn't it place everybody, not just innocent girls, in danger in the dark? If this is so, then the danger comes not just from the deuce in its ruin, as it was in the 1970s and 1980s, but from the majestic "America's Movie Center" as it was in its prime of life. Scorsese and Schrader might well agree with this; indeed, they may have been leading us to this point all along. If so, it is a point they share with all sorts of people, not only with organizations like Women Against Pornography, which was founded in 1979, just after *Taxi Driver's* triumphant run, but with their own hero, who would surely see filmmakers like them as "scum and filth." One of the strangest things about this profoundly strange movie is that, in America's ongoing "culture wars," its makers enlist against themselves.

Soon after Bickle is rejected by Betsy, he embarks on a program of self-transformation. His aim is to turn himself into a lethal weapon—though it is not clear at first who his target is going to be. He buys an elaborate arsenal of guns and puts himself through a grueling series of calisthenics. "Total organization is necessary. Every muscle must be tight" (42–49). We see him both at a firing range and in front of his mirror, drilling himself to fire fast and fluently. Since the Italian Renaissance, when mirrors became cheap and widely available, the subject's encounter with his or her image in the mirror has been a powerful symbol of self-awareness and emotional growth.* In Scorsese's variation on this theme, the hero confronts himself in the mirror very dramatically—"You talkin' to me?"—and then, time after time, shoots his reflection dead. The gun, the mirror, the violent challenge, the idea that talking to the hero is a lethal offense, and the idea that he is committing it against himself—"You talkin' to me?"—have come together in one of American cinema's all-time classic images.

The trigger for Travis's metamorphosis is the child-woman Iris (Jodie Foster), a teenage prostitute whose radiant face appears in his mirror—and so, appears as an aspect of himself. She is his second "angel from the sewer." But Travis's rejection by the adult Betsy has brought him to a point where he finds all sexual feeling hateful. Or maybe we should say that all his sexual feeling is twisted into rage and hate. He judges all the predatory men who sustain Iris's sexual life—her pimp (Harvey Keitel), her customer, and an old man who works as a guard—and, in order to rescue her from the life, sentences them to death. The climax is a heavily rehearsed, intricately choreographed, horribly bloody shoot-out (blood in close-up), where he kills them all. These men can't believe he plans to kill them just like that, but once he starts shooting, they find guns and shoot back at him, so when the police arrive he is drenched in blood, both his and theirs. He smiles at the cops, makes a shooting gesture at his own bloody head, and passes out. The screenplay calls this scene "The Slaughter." Schrader says:

> The slaughter is the moment Travis has been heading for all his life, and where this screenplay has been heading for 85 pages. It is the release of all that cumulative pressure; it is a reality unto itself. It is the psychopath's Second Coming (86).

Iris goes back to her parents in Pittsburgh; Travis is written up as a hero. In the movie's finale (88ff.) he is still in New York, and still driving a taxi. But he, too, has, in Rechy language, "graduated from Times Square," and is

---

*In Goethe's *Faust*, Gretchen's awareness of herself in the mirror marks a crucial stage in her inner growth. See my *All That Is Solid Melts into Air*, 53–59. Scorsese presents himself in the rearview mirror as another one of the driver's selves, a murderous passenger with horribly vivid fantasies of how he will kill his wayward wife. Of course this is black humor, since it's the *character* who's one of the director's selves.

working a very grand locale, the Plaza, just across from Central Park. We see his scars, he looks ten years older, but his face is settled now. He banters with fellow drivers; they address him as "Killer"; he laughs it off. He isn't a walking grenade anymore; he seems mellow, easy to be with. Can it be that, thanks to murder, "the great rage is killed in him"?[29] In the movie's last minute, Betsy, representative of adult sexuality, steps into his cab. They have a Hollywood moment: We can feel the chemistry start up again. He says he sees her boss (his onetime passenger) has got the nomination. Who would have thought he would be so attuned to the world as to notice? She says she read about him in the papers; he says "the papers always blow these things up," but "I got over it." He won't take her money for the fare; she says they should see each other again. We know he won't take her to the deuce next time: He appears to have outgrown the pornographic world, to be ready for real love. When he says "I got over it," we want to believe that he really has overcome, that he will go on overcoming, that together they can "fly away / from that dirty boulevard." We root for him, we root for them, the way we always root for stars, maybe even more. It's only after his taxi glides away, and we are reading the credits against a dark ground, that we question some of the assumptions behind this romantic ending. Can real people, the men he killed, be simply dropped from life, the way a director can drop a character? Can an act of murder really overcome "the psychopath's Second Coming" and bring about inner liberation and growth? These questions don't have self-evident answers. We have to ask them because the movie forces us to identify with Cybill Shepherd, an adult woman who really wants to love this guy. *Taxi Driver* takes us on a trip, full of alluring moments but also of rough shocks; it doesn't give us the grace note of an ending, but leaves us worrying out on the street, unable to put that dirty boulevard behind us.

One of *Taxi Driver*'s ironies derives from the exploitation of children. The late-1970s media was full of stories of the "Minnesota strip," where teenage girls getting off the Greyhound from Minneapolis were supposedly hustled and drugged into becoming whores on the deuce. We are meant to feel that much of the wrong done against Foster has been to dangle her as a juicy morsel for adults. But, in a great Hollywood moment, Foster, Scorsese, Schrader, and their cinematographers came together and clicked. Together they turned Iris's image into a brilliant living billboard. Even in the midst of the misogyny and social disintegration of the dirty boulevard, the Times Square tradition of the magnification of woman found new life and triumphed again.[30]

This image had tremendous influence in fashion: a kid who may not even be a teenager, but whom a man can count on to be fluent in all imaginable grown-up sexual moves. It's both alluring and horrible, a blend of crude pornography with serious graphics and soulful cinematography. For years, millions of American girls experimented with this look. Many of them were my students. When it got warm, you could see them on every campus, in every mall. But you couldn't see many of them in Times Square. Girls knew it was dangerous to look this way in Times Square.

Times Square: *The New Degenerate Narrative as Pastoral*

Another girl who will solve her problems in Times Square by flying away is Patsy Pearl (Trini Alvarado), soulful heroine of Allan Moyle's 1980 feature film, *Times Square*. For Patsy, though, "home" is within walking distance; it's the liberal Jewish Upper West Side. Her mother is dead; her father is a real estate developer; they are emotionally closer than a teenager and her father should probably be. He displays a plastic model of "the new Times Square," which he hopes will obliterate "this X-rated street" where this whole movie takes place. Patsy loves the rebellious force of punk rock, then in its late-1970s heyday. (The movie's exciting soundtrack, featuring Lou Reed, Patti Smith, the Ramones, Talking Heads, *et al.*, is still selling, and will long survive the movie.) Punk rock draws her toward the Square, where she falls under the thumb of Nikki Marotta (Robin Johnson), who's nasty and vicious and (we are meant to feel) a *real* punk. Patsy writes a vicious song dedicated to her father. Thanks to a Murray the K / Wolfman Jack hip DJ, she actually gets to play it live on FM youth radio: "Spic / nigger / faggot / bum / Your daughter is one."

Patsy runs away from home and moves in with Nikki; they constitute themselves as "The Sleaze Sisters," and live together in an abandoned pier along the waterfront, an echo of the ruin that Jon Voight and Dustin Hoffman shared in *Midnight Cowboy*. The ruins are beautifully photographed, so that we can see the crumbling deuce as part of a whole orbit and a history of social disintegration. Patsy seems to be fulfilling Bruce Benderson's appeal,

Wannabee homeboys and homegirls, rebel! It's time to sacrifice yourselves to the dangers of the new degenerate narrative!

But life on the street, as shown here, isn't so scary. Her intimacy with Nikki doesn't seem to include sex; indeed, the whole of punk 42nd Street, as seen here, is as chaste as any Mickey Rooney / Judy Garland Hollywood small town in the years of the Code. Also wholly absent from this movie are drugs. Patsy's father puts her picture on a bus billboard, imploring her to come home. In a Times Square tradition as old as Hurstwood and Sister Carrie, the girls desecrate Patsy's sign. Neither girl has any source of income, but poverty is no problem for them. Stealing food, they get more than enough to eat. Somehow they stay clean. They dress smartly, seeming to wear new clothes in every scene, and every outfit looks fresh from the racks. They sample the deuce's small-time rackets, squeegee and three-card monte, and it is all a laugh. They get a loaded gun and sample mugging, but Patsy's laughter queers the job. They steal cars (the cars all start instantly), drive on the wrong side of the street, have several collisions but walk away from the wreckage and never stop laughing. Nikki starts stealing television sets and throwing them down from tenement roofs onto the street; miraculously, they never hit anybody, and people seem less worried than amused.

After the story ends, during the credit sequence, as the camera pans the street, a title announces: "Filmed entirely on location in New York City." This is supposed to reassure us of the movie's authenticity. Alas, this real street looks as contrived and phony as any studio back lot. To show that Patsy Pearl's father was wrong in calling the deuce an "X-rated street," the filmmakers reconstruct it as a "G-rated street." Not only does nobody get laid or drugged or robbed or beaten up, but our heroes can steal three meals a day (and snacks) on the stroll without worry. Not to mention that people drive on the wrong side and walk away laughing from the crash, and loaded guns don't go off. This pastoral vision portrays the deuce as a magic kingdom where adolescents are protected from all the pressures that haunt every American high school. It's the first 42nd Street theme park.

Jane Dickson: From Harvard Square to Times Square

Some dark and strong reflections on the Square have come from the painter
Jane Dickson, who has worked in the Square since the late 1970s and who
lived there with her husband, the filmmaker Charlie Ahearn, on the corner
of 43rd and Eighth from 1981 to 1993. Their two sons, high school students
today, were born there. Their family lives in Tribeca now, but Dickson still
has a studio on 39th and Eighth, right across from the bus terminal. Over
the years Dickson has made dozens of oil paintings and hundreds of drawings of this cityscape.[31] Some of her best paintings are street scenes from the
early and middle 1980s, when she and Ahearn had just moved to the
Square, and she was looking into the life teeming and boiling around her
and struggling to make a place for herself.[32]

Dickson describes herself as "a Harvard grad who moved from Har-

vard Square right to Times
Square."[33] Her 1980s street
paintings transmit very vividly
the shock, the sudden impact
of the place. They gave a
shock to me, though I'd been
going there all my life. She
seemed not to want to be
scared, as I didn't want to be,
but she also seemed to want
to say it from inside a place
she knew was scary. Dickson
is right to be proud of the
sense of immediacy in her
Times Square work. But she
is also right to suggest that it is
mediated by years in Harvard
Square. The contrast in
squares figures for her not just
in a sociological sense of
"high/low"—in fact, Harvard

Square in the 1970s, loaded with
drugged-out kids, could get pretty
low itself—but in an older, intellectual sense. I don't know what she
studied at Harvard, but her art shows
she learned plenty. Her work in
Times Square is striking, not only
for its openness to conflicting and
contradictory traditions in modern
art—Realism, Expressionism, Abstract Expressionism, Pop Art, *film
noir*—but for her drive to make her
art a street where they all can live.

The Realist painter most vividly
present in her work is Edward Hopper, who unfolded a classic vision of
the modern city nightscape as a
metaphor of cosmic aloneness, and
of its people (like the people in his
painting "Nighthawks") as monads
who were solitary even when they
were together. Dickson is at home in
Hopper's orbit: his low population
density, his focus on the vast empty
spaces between people, his figures
who lean forward yet turn away. But she has also assimilated the Abstract Ex-
pressionists, who cracked the patina of oil painting and piled up layers of
paint on canvas that made their work look as rough and grungy as the Square
itself. Dickson, working in their vein, drags oil sticks over abrasive sandpaper
to create a background of deep and rough blackness. Overlaid on her blackness, mixed up with it while pressing against it, is Times Square's world-
famous flood of neon light, canonized by a generation of Pop Art.[34]
Dickson's home turf is the Square's side chapels, where the spaces are
gloomier, the people and things are sleazier, but she knows the radiance
and loves it. In her world, the neon flares up even as the darkness closes in;
the dialectical energy in the conflict between them places her in second-

generation Pop Art's major league. Meanwhile, the twisted vertical planes that define her cityscapes derive from Expressionism, as it evolved in photography and cinema as well as in painting. Georg Grosz, William Klein, Alfred Hitchcock, all would have enjoyed her visually skewed, vertiginous compositions that at once invite us to take the plunge and pull us back. You could say that since Busby Berkeley's "Lullaby of Broadway," the plunge has been Times Square's default position. In that position, Dickson has made herself at home.

Two of Dickson's most striking Times Square paintings feature a young mother with a baby in a stroller. The mother/baby dyad, so central to Christian sentimentality for centuries, still central to the commercial sentimentality that fills Broadway's billboards, and unquestionably a force in plenty of contemporary artists' lives, has played a surprisingly small role in modern art. (Except for Picasso, who tries to make up for all the rest. And of course, that baby carriage hurtling down Eisenstein's Odessa steps.) In "Gem Liquors" (1983), Dickson puts the pair just out the window, a plunge below us. Perspective makes them quite small; the space around them is dark and empty, as if they were in the middle of a void; but the moves between them are complex and intense. Even if we can't quite tell what they are doing (is the mother giving the baby a bottle? Is the baby expressing discomfort, or just stretching its arms and legs to enjoy life?), this mother and child fill their void well.

In "Mother and Child" (1985), the pair dominate the canvas. Dickson's second mother looks a lot like her first: young, dark, slight, childlike—a size 2, a long way down from Dickson's own.[35] I can't tell if we are meant to think of this mother as the same woman, or merely the same type of woman. But here, weirdly, the mother is wearing a sundress, the baby a snowsuit: They seem to be dressed for two different worlds. It's as if the street emits dangerous rays, the mother has secured some sort of immunity by virtue of growing up, but the baby hasn't picked it up yet. All parents know what it is like to dress their babies with more protection than they give themselves; but here the spread between them seems planetary. Another weird thing in this painting is the perspective: Once more we are a plunge apart, only here they seem to be plunging down on us. To see them clearly, we would have to be stretched out on the ground like snakes, or peering up from underground like moles. The composition *might* make sense if we imagine the mother lowering her baby down subway stairs, while the observer is coming up those stairs but hasn't yet reached the street. If we look at this mother longer, she starts to look like a refugee, about to fly from the dirty boulevard. She is stalked by blinding strobe light, and by walls of neon and fluorescence that look like any minute they could crash down on her. If we look at the baby longer, we see the weirdest thing of all: It dwarfs its mother, and it looks cartoon-demonic. There's no way on earth a child this big could come out of a mother this small. Where it could come from, though, is the imagination: especially the feverish imagination of a pregnant woman who hasn't given birth yet, and so has no real child to test her fantasies, but who fears her child will overwhelm her, as in the painting it overwhelms us. (Or, as in Roman Polanski's *Rosemary's Baby*, it could be born from the imagination of a pregnant woman's husband.)[36] In fact, when Dickson painted this mother and child in the Square, she was living in its midst, pregnant with a child of her own.[37] It's as if her anxiety about her urban environment blended with anxiety about her inner environment to create some luminous art. In real life, Dickson and Ahearn and their children went on living in Times Square till the early 1990s, and she is still working there today. In art, her mother and child fled the Square, like Jodie Foster at the end of *Taxi Driver* and Pedro in Lou Reed's "Dirty Blvd.," and plunged into the underground just ahead of the exploding light and the collapsing signs: any way out of this world.

Alex Katz, "We're Still Here"

In the midst of its life as a *via dolorosa*, the deuce got its last great billboard vision of women. It was designed by the painter Alex Katz for the corner of Seventh Avenue and 42nd Street, directly at the Square's heart.[38] In 1977 he got this prime space with the help of the Public Art Fund; the space was there because, in the years of the city's fiscal crisis and "New York Drop Dead," American corporations had dropped Times Square. (In a couple of years, more resourceful Japanese corporations would pick it up. Sony, Fuji, Toshiba, Honda, Suntory, Canon, and many more created a whole new generation of fire signs, and gave the Square the most thoroughly global identity it had ever had. But not quite yet.)

It was an L-shaped frieze of women's faces, twenty feet high, running around the corner, just across from the "zipper" news sign. The women were young and middle-aged, mostly Caucasian but dark-skinned, neat and somber in style, reflective, tending toward melancholy in attitude. If we are at all familiar with Katz's work, we can recognize these women; they were variations on icons he has been painting for fifty years. But arrayed together and magnified to billboard size, their presence took on a new poignancy and grandeur. They became a kind of Greek chorus of citizens, and an echo of the group murals of the Popular Front. Katz, born in 1927, part of the first generation of Pop Art, was old enough to see its connection with the Popular Front. However, in the last part of the twentieth century, both the Popular Front and the whole idea of city citizenship had fallen on hard times. The women became a kind of Greek chorus of citizens, commenting by their presence, by their somber self-containment, on the human action going on below. On the bowtie side, facing Broadway, Katz's women offered a striking contrast with the other giant women around them, the figures on the Square's commercial signs. These women weren't smiling, they didn't look ingratiating or seductive, they weren't trying to sell anybody anything. Rather, they were like the millions of ordinary women who passed through the Square every day, and who were subject to its incessant barrage of salesmanship. But with gigantic proportions, surrounded by a sisterhood of their own size, they had the resources to survive the multimedia consumer capitalism that, in Times Square more than anywhere, inflames everyone—remember Dickson, "We're all running around constantly in heat"—and that feels overpowering to us all. The women on the deuce side, overlooking 42nd Street, were being there in a different way. They overlooked a masculinized street where only flattened, "unaccommodated" women like Ms. Complete could be at home—if there were any real women like her—and where all other women felt lucky if they were unseen and ignored. But Katz's women, from their perch in the sky, told the deuce: We're still human, and we're still here.

CHAPTER 6

The New Millennium: Living Inside the Deal

You have wished yourself a Scarsdale Galahad,
The breakfast-eating Brooks Brothers type . . .
—Sky Masterson to Sarah Brown, *Guys and Dolls*

A Decade of Deals

In my first piece on Times Square, written for the *Village Voice* a decade ago, I chose Ed Kleban's wonderful song "What I Did for Love," from *A Chorus Line*, as a metaphor for what I thought the city had to do:

> The city should fight like hell to get the best deals it can, but it should deal. And people like us should drop our pretense of purity and unsoiled virtue, and get our heads together to live with the deals, because if we love Times Square—which has to be in a very different way from the way we love Central Park—deals with bright lights are what we want. And if you don't believe in making deals, Times Square has no reason for being at all.[1]

It took years to put together the spectacular deals that have finally materialized in Times Square today. Joan Didion, writing about Hollywood years ago, said "the deal" was the real art form. This is equally true in the world of New York real estate—except that being a New Yorker means you have to live your whole life *inside* the deal.

Whatever else Times Square may be, it's always crowded, and the 1990s, that decade of deals, piled on a new traffic jam of ironies. One of the most striking ones was the torrents of invective emanating from City Hall against sex on the street, in tandem with the most blatant intercourse between our developers and our politicians. Their progeny was a great array of what the business press called "off-budget tax expenditures," overt and covert tax abatements, handouts, and subsidies, a swollen private treasury for which the public would have to pay. We knew billions of dollars were flowing through underground streams, but we also knew, because our press didn't press, we would never see more than the tip of this iceberg. The city acted like it was begging developers and corporations to come in just when they were pouring in, pouring in because by the early 1990s investment in Times Square had become a spectacular bonanza.[2]

Opponents of the plan could say plenty. Alas, much of what they did say was pretty silly, e.g., that it represented an "invasion" of the city by "outsiders" (Disney, Viacom, Bertelsmann, Reuters, Madame Tussaud's, etc.). I never figured out what weird magic could turn our town's super-cosmopolitans, always so eager to celebrate New York as "a world city," into a bunch of Babbitts proud of their provinciality, indignant that anybody from out of town should want to come here. It also seemed absentminded for critics not to notice all the local boys in the crowd, all the Tisches and Dursts and Rudins and Eichners and Kleins and Newhouses and Ratners and Milsteins pressing themselves forward to go into the Dark Mill with that other bunch of local boys, the Koches and Cuomos and Giulianis.

One group of people caught up in the decade's ironies were the smart, educated, dynamic middle-aged women who arrived in the top ranks of public and private management just then, and who did so much to drag the 42nd Street Development Authority plans forward. Tama Starr, president of the great sign company Artkraft Strauss, gives them special credit. "I can't help thinking," she said in 1998,

> that the sense of brightness and safety that now pervades the Square has a lot to do with its destiny being in the hands of women throughout the 1980s and 1990s. For the first time, women were stepping off the billboards and out of the movie screens into the action . . . women of power and ability were suddenly everywhere.[3]

Starr wants to say that Times Square has become a better place because women have gained power to shape and mold it. But she also posits an antithesis between the real women pressing the plan and the imaginary women starring in the movies and adorning the signs. Starr's image of women stepping down from signs and screens and "into the action" is intriguing and original. (I can imagine it filmed by Buñuel.) But why should women, in order to enter "the action," have to surrender the radiance and allure that have made them the stars of signs and movies for a hundred years? Does this sign maker really think it would make the Square bright and safe to pull women off the signs?

Starr's special favorites are a group of women whom reporters in the mid-1990s called "the Three Witches": Cora Cahan, of the New 42nd Street Foundation; Rebecca Robertson, head of the state 42nd Street Development Project; and Gretchen Dykstra, of the Times Square BID, or Business Improvement District. I can remember these three in hearings and press conferences; they worked well together, and sometimes finished one another's sentences. They all presented themselves with implacable hauteur, like graduates of the Christine Whitman political charm school. Here they are in 1996:[4]

These women deployed WAP-like righteous rage at the exploitation of women by the sex businesses of Times Square; but they also knew how to use body language to deploy themselves as classic Times Square babes. Look at them together, it could even remind you of the heroines of *Sex and the City*. Far from stepping down from the signs to enter the action, they strove to put up more and (they thought) better signs, even as they fought to tear signs down. Their patron saint was *Guys and Dolls'* Sarah Brown, a Broadway Baby who yearned to "take a pick-ax and rip up Broadway from end to end."

In the mid-1990s, Robertson, head of the 42nd Street Development corporation, hired designer Tibor Kalman, creator of the COLORS sign that we discussed in Chapter 1, and architect Robert Stern to create a series of bold, sexy visions of what the new Square could be. These drawings were actually ads for the "Interim Plan," developed in the late 1980s and ratified by the City Planning Commission in 1993. Kalman imagined something like the Virgin Records Store at the classic corner of 42nd Street and Broadway, a live MTV studio rising directly above, and enormous fire signs promoting both. Robertson's text, which went with Kalman's drawings, was entitled "The Street That Belongs to Everybody." It promoted the plan as an attempt to shape the Square as

> a Mecca for popular entertainment, a generator of urban mythology, a place where unfettered competition for audience and recognition would result in a vibrant, loud, unpredictable midway of modern attractions . . . [5]

Robertson in 1996 offered a slightly different version to the *Times*, one that evoked the classic motto of "eight million stories in the naked city."

> When we're done, we'll have 60 different stories on 42nd Street, arguing, fighting for product and advertising space. There are going to be conflicts. The idea is [to] make it a place of stories, which comes from all that crass commercialism. [6]

Lynne Sagalyn, in *Times Square Roulette*, describes this new plan as "a dramatic shift in values . . . from corporate business to popular culture." [7] Her dramatic language reflects the enthusiasm of the time: a widespread feeling that at last, "By George, they've got it!" I suspected the city would betray it or blow it, but I was thrilled that there was an "it" to betray or blow, that our city government had actually developed an appealing and complex vision of what the Square could be.

I worried: Could planners who were driven by a WAP-type rage against evil really create or sustain a "street that belongs to everybody"? Episodes that meant little in themselves could signal reasons to worry. For the holiday season in December 1997, an animal-rights group planned to deck the Square with a huge billboard that portrayed the blond actress Pamela Anderson Lee stark naked on a rug, testifying that she "would rather wear nothing at all than wear fur." This coy attack on fur had already run in *The New Yorker* and in the *Sunday Times Magazine*. Many readers rolled their eyes at its strategy, familiar in American advertising, of trying to mobilize our eroticism in the service of a new model of Puritanism. The ad was more silly than sexy; maybe the right word was "burlesque." But the UDC and the BID banned it, saying it was "too racy for Times Square."[8] It soon found a home on naughty, bawdy, gaudy, sporty 57th Street, close by such hot spots as the Art Students' League and Carnegie Hall. Now you could say this story was pure fluff. What is serious is that the curators of the new Times Square had just proclaimed an expansive and liberating vision for Times Square— "The street that belongs to everybody"—and it took them about two minutes to cave their vision in and pave it over with conformist paternalism. Or maybe we should say conformist *ma*ternalism, respecting Tama Starr's dictum that "women of power and ability were everywhere" and the Square's "destiny [was] in the hands of women" now."* If only the great Charles Ludlam (*d.* 1987) had survived the AIDS epidemic, this whole story could have been staged by the Theater of the Ridiculous, with Ludlam playing all the women's parts, and Everett Quinton as New York's Mayor Casanova doing a star turn as Savonarola. Then we could have laughed.

Signs and Wonders, 265. Full disclosure: I myself am in one of Robertson's "unfit" files. In the summer of 1999, I appeared on an MSNBC talk show with her and critic Paul Goldberger, to discuss Times Square's past and future. She said, Wasn't it wonderful to see 42nd Street as a place for families with their kids? I brought up my parents and said it was also nice for New York to have a place where adults could get away from their kids. As I mentioned my mother's red dress, I thought I saw her eyes narrowing. Later on, when I brought up the evolution of sex shops, she demanded to know if I had ever been in such places. I said Yes, I wouldn't talk about them if I hadn't, and she asked—I'm not sure who her question was addressed to— "Why is this man allowed on television?" At first I was flattered that she thought me important enough to be banned from TV; then I realized she must talk that way to all the guys.

The Three Witches have scattered today (Cahan alone has stayed close
to the Square), but their politics of demonology is alive and well. Before
everybody forgets, I want to anoint Robertson, Dykstra, and Cahan as authentic Times Girls, stretching their silken legs out over Broadway, working
through the night to destroy Times Square in order to save it. Their grand-
mother, the primal Times Girl, would have admired their energy and gravity and their real love for the Square. But wasn't grandma more open, more
willing to take a chance, to lean out too far?

As the 1990s advanced, there were bigger things to worry about. The city
had hoped to entice Wall Street law and investment banking firms to move
to the Square, but, despite alluring subsidy deals, met with indifferent success. In the early part of the decade, its vision refocused on world-class
media and entertainment conglomerates. Disney, Bertelsmann, Condé
Nast, Viacom/MTV, and Reuters were going to build in bulk directly on
42nd Street and Broadway, right at the Square's core. The city offered zoning variances that empowered builders to far exceed legal limits for height
and bulk. There was nothing inherently wrong with this form of deal. But
many details were secret, and the city often seemed to act as an agent for developers rather than an advocate for the public. For instance, the original
contract for the Reuters building had required two escalators, a minimal but
substantial amenity, to go with a huge subway entrance on the corner of
42nd Street and Broadway. But then, when the Rudin family asked if they
really, really had to build it, the MTA abruptly (and secretly) changed its
mind and said no, they didn't have to provide the amenity after all.* More
secret extra items kept leaking out, keeping the city's favorites free of risk,
forcing the public to take the flak. People's hearts sank: Would the new
Times Square be "the street that belongs to everybody," or the vestibule for
a gated community?

Late in the 1990s a kind of veil fell, and the whole neighborhood seemed
to become an enormous construction site. What would the new Times

---

*See *Times Square Roulette*, 398ff., 546. The Rudins' idea was, if they didn't have to build escalators
on the corner, then they could rent the corner site to a bank (astronomical extra profits, taxes written
off), move their subway entrance to a less accessible and less attractive point on their building's side,
and divert the crowds into other entrances for which they weren't responsible. It was the MTA's own
Inspector General who brought this story into the open, appalled that the agency had shortchanged
both the public and itself.

Square look like? There were several years when no one could say. In February 1997, I was the keynote speaker at a Columbia School of Architecture conference on the Square and its future. The overwhelming mood was gloomy nostalgia, though different people at the conference longed for different golden ages—the 1900s, "the Jazz Age," the 1930s, "the War," the *film noir* 1950s, the pre-AIDS gay 1970s, etc., etc. I said that "the discourse of nostalgia" was the Square's signature product: It had become a means of accrediting people as citizens, as *echt* New Yorkers, people who were really serious, who really cared, and not just hustlers or dilettantes passing through. I talked about how nostalgia was a way not to be here now; I had complicated fun with the cultural ironies of nostalgia, and I made people laugh.[9] It was only afterward that I realized that, as much as any apocalyptic pessimist in the house, I dreaded the worst. Juggling ideas frantically like a performer on New Year's Eve, I was struggling to find a way for us all to laugh through the dread we all shared.[10]

The Cleaned-Up Boulevard

Overall, it has turned out far less bad than we feared. The Square's new "built environment" is a combination of radically contradictory models and plans. The first model belongs to the horrible early 1980s "Rockefeller Center South." It features four bulky, gigantic skyscrapers right at the center, the Condé Nast, Reuters, Ernst & Young, and Times Square Tower buildings. The second, mixed up with it, is the Robertson-Kalman early-1990s "street that belongs to everybody." Alas, that vibrant street exists mainly at the fringes of the Square, rather than where it was meant to be, at its core. But the Square has lots of fringes.

There are some really good buildings in the new Times Square. The best buildings are the oldest, and they are live and lively theaters: the New Amsterdam, once home of the Ziegfeld Follies, now the Disney flaghip; the neo-Baroque New Victory, now a terrific avant-garde and cosmopolitan children's theater. They keep theater crowds flowing and overflowing at the Square's core. The best new buildings are small, like the New 42nd Street Rehearsal Studios, whose delicate lighting blurs the boundary between building and sign. The big new buildings are more overbearing than the ones they replaced, but none of them is anywhere near as bad as the really dreadful skyscrapers that blasted into the Square's heart a generation ago (One Astor Plaza, killer of the lovely Astor Hotel; the Marriott Marquis Hotel that killed the Automat and the Helen Hayes; the blocks of giant slabs on Upper Sixth), or the four giant Egyptian tombs designed by Philip Johnson for developer George Klein in the 1980s, part of an immense, abortive plan to turn Times Square into "Rockefeller Center South." (I called it "Albert Speer Plaza"; I still look back fondly on the hearings and demonstrations that kept it unbuilt.)[11] The worst of the new buildings are mediocre, not monstrous, and they are oriented toward the street system, rather than being, like the Astor and Marriott buildings, blown against it. When I think of the appalling level of big buildings erected in my lifetime, the mediocrity of the new Times Square looks like progress. Some of the new lines and planes are surprisingly graceful and delicate. The Condé Nast Building and the Westin Hotel were designed to look dynamic and original from the angles at which they are most often seen, but utterly pedestrian from everywhere else. In the daytime, the sunlight reflects in striking ways off the skyscrapers' glass, and the total ensemble looks a lot more exciting than we had any reason to expect.

On any given day, there are people in many differently colored uniforms—NYSD, UDC, BID, and more, plus people in assorted police uniforms, the NYPD, the DEA, the U.S. Military Police, the "Hercules Units," city cops with machine guns and light body armor, and a wide variety of street, building, and corporate security guards—working to guard the Square's cleanliness and order. I often feel sick of these uniforms, and flooded out and menaced by them. But I'm old enough to remember when you couldn't find any uniforms at all. One twilight evening on the deuce in April 1980, I saw a man crack another man's skull with a club that looked like a prop from *The Flintstones*. The man went out like a light and spurted blood all over the street, from which everyone instantly disappeared. I yelled "Help!" and found myself totally alone. I couldn't find a cop, no one in any nearby shop would let me call one, and the guy just kept bleeding. By and by the manager of one of the pornographic cinemas came out with his walkie-talkie (this was long before cell phones), and in a minute an ambulance came and took the man away. I don't think he ever stopped bleeding, but if they keep your head uncovered it means you're still alive, right? I'll take the uniforms, thanks, so long as they know how to keep people on the street alive.

Thanks to progress in computer graphics, the best of the new signs and the total ensemble of signs are more exciting than ever.[12] The sign that attracted most attention in the late 1990s was the electronic turret of the NASDAQ sign, on the north facade of the Condé Nast Building. At first that sign was a museum of kinetic art, with an amazing variety of forms, colors, textures, and patterns of motion. My Aunt Idie would have loved it: It could wash over you, you could get high. But once NASDAQ's book value plunged, its romantic graphics abruptly disappeared. As the Clinton boom became a memory, the sign decayed into a klunky, overgrown bulletin board, its adventurous graphics loved and mourned mainly by people who had little love for its market values.

Its eclipse drew attention to another capitalist beacon whose design made it less dependent on history's up and downs: the giant Morgan Stanley sign at the Square's northwest corner, enveloping the company's headquarters at 1585 Broadway. James Traub describes it as a spectacle of pure numbers in perpetual motion: "three bands of stock information," prices on the New York Stock Exchange, NASDAQ, and the Dow, "running across the facade at different speeds, [flanked by] forty-foot-high cylindrical maps, showing the time zones of Morgan Stanley offices across the world." Traub says it "makes essential statements about the company: that it traffics in information, not just in money; that it is a central switching device in the global economy; that it is in the moment; and that it is . . . a branding device both for Morgan Stanley and for Times Square." Tama Starr, whose company built it, points out its curved corners, "an optical illusion designed to give the feeling that the information was coming out of the building, going across the front, and then going back into the building to be reprocessed, as if it were a manufacturing process."[13] It will keep on flowing whether times are good or bad, a classic rather than romantic spectacle, immune to time's booms and busts. Ironically, its built-in optical illusions will enhance its capacity to tell us the truth—but also its capacity to mislead us. Traub savors the irony that so many of Morgan Stanley's executives apparently did not want to be in New York in the first place, did not want to locate in a prominent part of the city, and did not want to have a spectacular sign. The company triumphed in spite of itself.

The most romantic new sign in the Square is the half-scale model of the Concorde, the British-French supersonic jetliner, installed on top of the Times Square Brewery, right at the Square's core, in 1996.[14] The Concorde had always presented technical and environmental problems, and its outrageous fares seemed designed to make everyone feel like part of an excluded underclass. Yet it was one of the most glorious forms ever created by modern design, looking at it was always a thrill, and in the Square it was a perfect fit. The plane's three-dimensionality made it look "real" in a way that other signs in the Square were not. It never had much space, and its awkward placement created ironies: If you approached it from the east, walking across 42nd Street, there was a video screen with an image of the plane that blocked out the plane itself. It was mounted on top of one the Square's few surviving low buildings, and we knew it was only a matter of time before the model was evicted for some new skyscraper. What no one imagined was that the world tourist industry was even more volatile than the New York real estate industry, and that even before Boston Properties had a chance to pull the model from the roof, a close-to-bankrupt British Airways would pull the thing itself, the Concorde, from the sky. Living in New York has always given people a chance to see in close-up how capitalism destroys the most marvelous things it creates.

One more striking case of this process is the fate of the electronic "zipper" that transmits breaking news. The Square's original zipper flashed fresh news across the triangular structure of the old Times Tower: It made breaking news part of the building. The zipper immediately became an integral part of the experience of being here: You would stop, read, and reflect. ("Meanwhile . . .") It was a terrific ad for the *Times*, telling us that even in the midst of the Square's carnival phantasmagoria, we could trust the paper to keep us in touch with what was going on in the real world. Its electronic power suggested not that newspapers were being superseded by "new media," but that this paper was resourceful enough to do whatever it takes to keep the public in touch. That zipper was one of the highlights of the "paper America," the America that existed to be written about, that Jack Kerouac celebrated in *On the Road*.[15] The *Times*'s abandonment of its primal zipper is a parable of its betrayal of the Square as a human space. It still zips, its century-old technology classically cheap and adequate. But the program, now sponsored by Dow Jones, consists mainly of stock quotations and ball scores. This sign works wonderfully as a travesty of what it was. For people old enough to remember, it is a lightning rod for rage.

In the light of the void the *Times* left a generation ago, electronic media have finally begun to stake claims. ABC now produces *Good Morning America* live in the office tower at 1500 Broadway, between 43rd and 44th Streets. Late in the 1990s, it created a news zipper of its own, running along the building's marquee. The most striking thing about the marquee is that, against a background of angular forms and voids, it is daringly, romantically curved. People with point-and-shoot cameras love to be shot, and to shoot each other, against the background of this curve. Its shape suggests a roller coaster stood on its side; it evokes and strengthens the Square's perennial claim to be carnivalesque. There is a giant video screen just above the curved marquee, designed to illustrate the news events the zipper describes. ABC's texts and images alike run to the shallow and the horrific: debris after bombs, blood saturating streets in neon red. The roller-coaster structure of its sign suggests a world that is full of startling leaps and plunges, but that can finally be contained, so that everything can come back to where it started, and a life full of dread can still be a carnival.

One of the first groups of people to fit itself comfortably into the new Times Square has been teenage kids. They are all over the place, but their biggest crowds are on the sidewalk in front of (really underneath) the MTV production studio, on the west side of Broadway between 44th and 45th. The biggest continuing draw is a program called *TRL*, "Total Request Live," broadcast weekdays at 5 P.M. The format is that "scouts" come down from above, survey the crowd on the street, and choose a couple to "go upstairs," where they can become a small part of the day's action; if they look great or sound great, somebody somewhere, besides their parents and friends, will know. MTV's production values fuse sexual display, salesmanship (or rather sales*person*ship), and spectacle in a way that harmonizes with some of the Square's oldest traditions. Those kids could be auditioning for the primeval *42nd Street* or *A Chorus Line*. Any one of them could be the Times Girl or the Jazz Singer of tomorrow. Many adults are scornful and would like to throw it all out. But they will need a pretty big garbage bag, marked "popular culture" or "American dreams" or "city life." Some adults are sure they can live without all that jazz. Others will have second thoughts, which is what adults are supposed to have.

Hardly any of those kids will get on the air, except as part of the crowd, which seems to mean a lot to quite a few. Some of them, if they hang out long enough, may make it as extras into one of the Condé Nast mags produced here, *Vogue, Vanity Fair, GQ, Self, Allure.* Since these publications were centralized in the Square, they have all been drawn to exploit what ad people call "the backyard." You can't keep MTV on for long without seeing a dramatic perspective of "the outside," and MTV's outside is Times Square. The planners who imagined the new Square as a center for media production, not just for consumption and display, were onto something real. The reality of production in the Square generates not only many new jobs, but a distinctive vitality and allure. This has been so ever since the coming of *The New York Times* a century ago.

One of the virtues of today's spectacle is its capacity not only to contain but to nourish protests against it. In 2001 *The New York Times* ran a story by Neil Strauss about a one-man protest against MTV, in the name of Tupac Shakur, a rapper who had died young:

> Adam Gassman, a 14-year-old from Queens, stood amid a gaggle of teenybopper girls outside MTV's Times Square studios, as he does almost every day after school. While the schoolgirls begged producers to let them into the studios for the day's taping of "Total Request Live," Adam looked on dour-faced. In his hand was a large white sign with two words sloppily scrawled in thin black marker: TUPAC LIVES.[16]

This story is more complex than it looks. Adam Gassman sounds like a great kid: the capacity of a fourteen-year-old to create a one-man demonstration intelligible to the *Times* four years ago is impressive; what is he creating today? But it may be premature for the *Times* to embrace his picture of reality, a reality divided into "a gaggle of teenybopper girls" who crowd the pavement, wave to the people in the studio upstairs, and are dying to be invited in to expose themselves, versus a solitary, honest avant-garde guy who stands alone, scrawls sloppily, and wouldn't go inside if MTV paid him to. The *Times* is snide about those girls; but isn't it a little early to write off kids who often haven't even reached high school? And isn't that bright boy part of their generation? Doesn't he, like every avant-garde in history, share their desire for exposure and publicity? Maybe, too, considering the line of fire where he has placed himself, he even wants to meet girls! For boys and girls together, looking for publicity or for each other, the new Times Square looks like the place to be.

As for Tupac, his early death was tragic. His murder in 1998 is still unsolved. But are we supposed to think of him as more heroic, or more authentic, *because* he's dead? That was how people talked about James Dean and about Charlie Parker (they scrawled BIRD LIVES in the subway) when I was fourteen. Pac's rapping was intense and powerful, so was his movie acting (see *Juice*), but he was flamboyantly theatrical, expert in creating spectacle, and heavily dependent on MTV, which has kept him in heavy rotation long after his death and put him in platinum from beyond the grave. Actually, Neil Strauss might have learned this from that "gaggle of teenybopper girls" if he had bothered to talk to them. If he had, it could have helped him confirm his story's idea: *Don't mourn the new Times Square*; its blend of toys, electronics, T-shirts, groupies, demonstrators, spectators, and reporters is developing into a fruitful place, a place where "the kids are all right."

A fair number of grown-ups are all right here, too. Harvey Pekar is a writer in his late sixties who has lived his life in Cleveland. He grew up poor, surrounded by poor Jews, he got a scholarship to Wayne State but dropped out, he slacked around for a while, then at last found a civil-service job as a clerk in the local VA hospital. For the next thirty years he clung to that job for dear life. Since 1976 he has used his small savings to publish *American Splendor*, a *samizdat* "adult comic book" based on his everyday life in Cleveland. He has worked with a number of illustrators; the best known are Robert Crumb and Joe Sacco. It was clear right away that he was brilliant, and that he could write, in ways that evoke George Gissing, Sherwood Anderson, James Farrell, early Hemingway, early Malamud, Doris Lessing. Much of his best writing is in the Russian "underground" tradition, intensely, angrily, and sometimes paranoiacally subjective, but also strongly visual and—his many illustrators show this vividly—embedded in concrete urban environments.[17] Since the early 1980s, fans have called his work cinematic, and people in the movie industry have tried to raise money to film it, but nobody ever could raise it; options were taken but ran out. In the 1990s, the comic-book industry caved in, and Pekar went through not one but two episodes of cancer. Year by year, *American Splendor* unrolled the multiple forms of anguish, dread, and rage that both drove and crushed his life. Meanwhile, though, he had somehow learned something, and he held onto people in his middle age in a way he hadn't done in his youth; his wife and his teenaged daughter helped him overcome. And just when he was sick of thinking about it, his movie luck changed. Not only did Good Machine produce and Miramax distribute the *American Splendor* movie, not only did it turn out to be a terrific movie, with fine performances by Paul Giamatti and Hope Davis, but it and he were recognized by the world: a prize at Sundance, another at Cannes, and a special Oscar, and all of a sudden there were people all over the world who were dying to hear what Harvey had to say.

This is the context, in his latest book, *Our Movie Year*,[18] where we see

Harvey with his wife, Joyce, and their daughter Danielle, walking east on the deuce, with the huge MADAME TUSSAUD'S sign at their backs. Gary Dumm, one of Harvey's longtime illustrators, makes him look very clean, as he always has (Robert Crumb's Harvey is a lot dirtier). There may also be a suggestion that he is a Historic Figure now, like the wax figures at Madame Tussaud's. Dumm's Pekar family all smile sweetly and openly, just like a couple from "Meadowville" on the town. The parents' smiles are exhausted (I know those smiles), the child's smile pure radiance. Harvey asks his daughter which statue she liked best; she says Frida Kahlo. "Why?" "Because she's an artist . . . and besides, Joyce told me to like her." Their family can sample art, play with history, check out the scene. They can be happy to be here. The new Times Square is the pot of gold at the end of their abyss. Look! They have come through.

People who have lived their lives close to the edge may be glad at last to be clean. But what's gone around has come around, and New York today is full of people, mostly very respectable people, complaining that the new Times Square is *too* clean: not vulgar, not sleazy, not dirty, as in the good old days. I'm pretty suspicious of the discourse of nostalgia, including my own. And I find today's Square's exploding lights and multicultural crowds as hot and sexy as any I've ever known, if people would only stretch themselves to look and feel. So how come there are so many people out there who don't? It's a bad sign, but a sign of what? Attention must be paid, but how? Not by tearing down the place we are in. We've been down that road before, "The Road to Nowhere," as the Talking Heads sang.[19] There is plenty of nowhere in Times Square right now. But maybe, if we can get people to feel good and dirty again, they will see what a terrific somewhere they're in.

One of the people who has done most to *schmeer* Times Square is Dave Chappelle, a young black standup comedian with a half-hour weekly show on Comedy Central. Last year, he presented a routine that made elaborate use of the Square as both a container and a condenser. He exploited its people, its crowds, its cityscape, and its raw power to generate vulgar comedy.[20] After seeing Chappelle work Times Square, it gets harder to complain that the place has grown too genteel.

The routine begins with Chappelle addressing a studio audience and informing them that he spends a lot of his life in lonely hotel rooms masturbating. A couple of people giggle, but the audience is quiet, unsure of how to take this. Then he says he excites himself by thinking of women's bodies, and especially "their breasts, their boobs." Women's breasts are beautiful, aren't they? So why shouldn't he think about them? It is clear that he is revving himself up by saying this at last in public. He loves the summer, because women "take them out on parade" (in the fall they have to "pack them away"). He would love to express his love for women's breasts more openly and directly, but he realizes that the things he'd like to say are likely to gross them out. At this point the studio audience seems to relax, and (as the camera shows it) the women start laughing as hard as the men. We're meant to infer that these women appreciate being recognized as human beings, and that they would be happy to hear sexual compliments if only they didn't make them feel like pieces of meat. If men in public space can express desire in ways that treat women with respect, plenty of women will be glad to play. We feel all this is too reasonable, we're being set up, but it's hard to see for what. It makes sense in the context of an encounter group or an adult education course on men and women in "public space," or in "civil society"; but we can't imagine what on earth is going to be the joke.

The camera now cuts to public space, to Times Square on a balmy summer day. Chappelle says, in a solemn voice-over, that the solution "we" have devised is to give prizes for the best "New York boobs." The award is a big blue ribbon, a circle with a tail, reminiscent of state fairs or of the Good Housekeeping Seal of Approval, but inscribed NEW YORK BOOBS. The prize-giver is "Lyle," a television announcer carrying a mike, wearing a fedora that clashes with his Hawaiian sport shirt. Lyle belongs to the new Times Square, the TV production center with studios right upstairs. He is played by Chappelle, but sounds like he has about half the IQ of the man who was just talking to us. He ambles around the Square, endlessly repeating his mantra, "New York Boobs," and comes across the way television people often do, as an ingratiating idiot. He approaches a great range of women, none of them at all glamorous, but all displaying their breasts in the way that women in ordinary summer clothes do. They are young and old, black, white, and yellow; most sound American, but some speak with European or Asian accents. A few of the winners look startled and uncomprehending, a couple turn and run away, but most are genial and accept their awards with a smile. An old Eastern European woman with bad teeth looks downward, asks, "These?" But she smiles, amused that these Americans seem to enjoy them. A girl in her early twenties shrieks, "Do you know this man's my father?" Lyle, showing for the first time that he has a mind, remarks to him chivalrously, "Well, sir, you have spectacular genetics."

Gradually it dawns on us that this stuff is serious. Lyle's seemingly random ambling has been unfolding an idea. "New York Boobs": The women spreading their life and energy around Times Square are *living for the city.* We can enjoy women's bodies without disrespect if we anoint them as supercitizens of New York. Now we realize we are in the midst of a living mural of a new Popular Front. Women, badly underrepresented in original Popular Front art, are finally getting the adoration they deserve. As they are glorified here—"side by side, they're glorified"—they are also getting respect on the street. And the street, too, is getting respect: the new Times Square is the microcosm of a world far more diverse and multicultural than the old Popular Front could conceive. The lubricious Chappelle won't let us forget the dirty possibilities: He wants to grab and squeeze and fuck this whole world of women. But he makes us see it *is* a whole world. As his hero moves from hotel rooms to TV studios to "live" Times Square, he grows from jerking off to embracing real people, and he goes through a metamorphosis, from being a horny adolescent to being a world citizen. Chappelle, in the Whitman tradition, conceives New York as a world city, and sex as metaphysics as well as biology, a way for a modern man to transcend his isolation and merge with this world.

If the Square's two great elements are people and light, both look great today. The crowds of people there today are bigger and more vibrant than ever. They come in more different colors and languages. It's hard to find a time when, for blocks and blocks around, the whole neighborhood isn't mobbed. But why not? Why else have cities in the first place? My biggest problem is trying to sort them out, to figure out who they are. When I was twelve or so, my father and I had a Times Square game: We would take a bunch of people and guess where they were going—theater? The movies? A jazz club? A hotel—which one? A restaurant—what kind? A game arcade? Then we would follow them, not too closely, five blocks was our limit. I was amazed how often we could guess right. ("See, sonny," he said the first time I did, "you know the street!") My father also told me before he died that "sportswear will conquer the world"; the fact that it has makes it harder to play our game today. Of course, that can make the game more exciting, as

Dave Chappelle understands so well. That game is just a spinoff of the
primeval urban art of hanging around, and Times Square is as delicious a
place as ever for doing that. The force that Rem Koolhaas, a quarter century
ago, called "Manhattanism, or The Culture of Congestion,"[21] is alive and
well here. Whoever these people are, in their sportswear, with their breasts,
they are fulfilling Motown's 1960s vision of urban democracy: *It doesn't
matter what you wear/Just as long as you are there.*

One hot afternoon in June 2004, as my book approached its homestretch, I
decided to take one last swing through the Square, to check it out. It was
thrilling on the ground. The women in the streets—costume designers,
travel agents, camerawomen, dancers, tourists, students or models with port-
folios, ladies who lunched—were letting it all hang out. They were arrayed
in purple designer suits, black dresses with slanted hems and swooping
necklines, artfully slashed jeans, multilayered undershirts, red combat boots
(in June? *Oy!* I thought in my mother's voice), five-inch heels, mauve flip-
flops, five hundred different shades of skin and nails and hair; they looked
artful, imaginative, highly individualized, terrific. Like the Parisian women
described in Montesquieu's *Persian Letters*, they were a grand spectacle in
themselves. On the other hand, the women on the signs above, advertising
sportswear and makeup and perfume, and promoting plays and films, were
massively pallid. They looked like attempts to reinvent the giant camp pinups of the 1950s. Is any evidence that any of the other billboard owners had
a wider horizon? These women all seemed to have the same light pink skin
and blond hair and frontal pose and empty smiles. Dreiser in 1900 spoke of
the "fire signs" in Times Square; in today's signs, the fire has been put out.
These women's images were matronly even when they were young, "white-
bread" even when they were black; their project seemed to be selling something by expressing nothing. These billboards suggest women's wear in
Brezhnev's Red Square, and they make it clear why the Berlin Wall had to
come down. Even when a woman on a sign was naked, like the black model
advertising Rocawear on West 47th and Broadway, she managed to look im-
peccably and impermeably dressed. Ironically, the flowing, curving numbers on the Morgan Stanley sign are more like live women than are the
death masks that pass for women on those fire-extinguished signs on Broadway.

The aura was so weird! I could feel the openness and verve in the real women on the ground, along with a mysterious imaginative shrinkage and devitalization in the signs of the women in the air. This contrast between the ground and the air, between the Square's streets and its signs, seems like an apt symbol of what has become of America in our new millennium. American feminism has had real success in enabling millions of women to direct their lives and fight to control their future on the ground. Yet after thirty years of feminism, our collective moral life is in the hands of the old men of the Christian right, working overtime to put women's inner light out and propel them back into the past. The Clear Channel Company of Dallas, one of America's biggest media conglomerates, and one of the most prominent sponsors of the Christian right, is said to own more billboard space than anyone else in Times Square today. Do they want to make the Square square?* If they do, it's not working. The overflowing life on the ground testifies that the squares so powerful in our mass media haven't yet found a way to kill the street.

That day in June, my last field day, there were only two human images above the ground that gave off real life. One was a very large billboard, visible from a long way off, on Times Girl's old building, One Times Square. The sign promoted a boxing match between one Vitali Klitschenko and one Corrie Sanders, for the "World Heavyweight Championship," to be telecast on HBO. They brought me back to the years when there had been a third-floor gym on 42nd Street between Sixth and Seventh, right above Tad's Steak House. The gym kept the windows open in the heat, and I could see (and hear) the guys pound the bags as I headed home from my CUNY seminars, or stood on the street in front of my Dad's old office (the Busch Terminal Building, 130 West 42nd Street) and talked about Plato and Marx. That gym was a vestige of the world of the old Garden, on 49th and Eighth, the Garden of *Killer's Kiss* and *Body and Soul*. The boxing world is much more fragmented now than it was then, so that any championship claim will be recognized by some and denied by others. What's most striking about the sign is the out-and-out sleaziness of these contenders, their five o'clock shadows, their aggressively nasty glances. These guys could be headliners in the

*Soon after I wrote this I met an employee of Clear Channel, who acknowledged what I called the Brezhnev Look, but blamed it on the unending intrusive censorship of the BID, and insisted that her company was "struggling to stretch the envelope." Well, we shall see.

old *Police Gazette*; or they could be time travelers from the deuce of a decade or two ago. You don't have to be interested in boxing (I am not) to welcome a couple of faces that seem glad to look "bad," in an environment full of giant images of people looking aggressively "good." And the sign makes a welcome claim on their behalf: LET THE NEXT ERA BEGIN. The manifest content of this sign is probably, "Let our boxing association—and our cable network—be recognized above all the rest." But its latent content, legible to anybody who loves the Square, is something like this: *Let badness be recognized along with goodness as part of Times Square's essential life, so that the Square can be once more what we know it always has been, a chupah for the marriage of heaven and hell.*

The second sign was an image of a young woman with a mysterious but radiant smile. Is it really a smile? Maybe a sort of down payment on a smile, a suggestion that "I would smile at you if I could." Beside her image is the caption "HAVE WE 'MET'?" In fact, she is a girl from the 1660s or early 1670s, painted by the Dutch artist Johannes Vermeer. Her portrait, "Study of a Young Woman," is visible on the walls of the Metropolitan Museum of Art, the Met, for which her sign is an ad.[22] The Met placed her there for a year, from June 2003 to June 2004, as a kind of intern or visiting student. She's one of several mysterious Vermeer girls whom nobody knows anything about. Painted against a background of pure black, with a faint emanation of light behind her head, she evokes Catholic devotional paintings of Mary and the saints. In fact Vermeer grew up Protestant but converted to Catholicism, and lived most of his life as a Catholic outsider in Protestant Delft. Many people who love his work (including me) believe he creates an aura of supreme holiness in completely anonymous ordinary people, especially in women engaged in humble everyday domestic tasks. That is the theme of Tracy Chevalier's wonderful 1999 novel, *Girl with a Pearl Earring*.[23] Chevalier imagines the "Girl" as Griet, a kitchen maid who color-codes vegetables as she cuts them, to Vermeer's delight. The name that Chevalier gives her connects her with Gretchen, heroine of Goethe's *Faust*, modern archetype of a lower-class girl with a desire and capacity for spiritual growth.[24] The dignity and depth of these ordinary girls, and of many more of his figures, make Vermeer an authentic hero of feminism, and also, it needs to be said, of democracy. And a hero of Times Square as well: Times Girl is one of his daughters.

That "Girl" painting was reproduced as the main advertisement for the movie, released in 2003,[25] in which she is beautifully played by Scarlett Johanssen. The subjects of "Girl" and of "Study" have different features, their heads and necks are differently shaped, and they are differently dressed, but it is easy to confuse them—as I did at first, and as many visitors to Times Square have done—because of an aura they share: a youthful eagerness for life combined with a youthful embarrassment and vulnerability, a strength of feeling alongside an uncertainty as to what she feels, an assurance that she is unforgettable plus a vagueness about who she really is.[26]

I have used the word "aura" about this girl. I first heard that word in beginners' Art History, where it was used to explain how Giotto, in his crowd scenes, made a few of the people in the crowd matter infinitely more than the rest. The idea was conceptualized by Walter Benjamin in his 1936 essay, "The Work of Art in the Age of Mechanical Reproduction."[27] Most of the time, Benjamin used it to describe something he believed all modern people were losing or had lost. An artwork's "aura," he said, was bound up with its uniqueness. But modern art was moving more and more toward works, like photographs and movies, that were infinitely reproducible. When a culture "substitutes a plurality of copies for a unique existence," he said, art's aura is lost. But is this really so? Look at this picture of the Vermeer girl on West 42nd Street: On a street saturated with images all designed to make sales pitches that are simple and shallow and abrasively loud, this girl looks like a visitor from another planet, a planet where people are subdued, complex, ambivalent, profound. She may be selling something—in Times Square, who isn't?—but it isn't obvious what. In a context where new products and images and new sales pitches are thrown in people's faces like every season's crop of Broadway shows and pop songs, we can see her as a figure with a history—even if we don't know what her history is. She is a reproduction, yet unique *in the context of Times Square*. This should tell us that an aura is not created by a uniqueness of canvas or stone, but by a uniqueness of space and place. Doesn't this "young girl" get her aura from being *geworfen* into Times Square? Benjamin would trace her aura to "the cult of remembrance of loved ones, absent or dead." To me, in her full spatial and social context, she looks so *alive*. She looks like Times Girl's newest incarnation, like proof that in spite of everything, they haven't been able to kill the goddess of the street. True, the goddess seems to be urging us to take her away from all this, to fly-fly-fly-fly from this cleaned-up boulevard. And the Met's an easy subway ride away. But still, wherever she takes us, the Square will always be the place where we got together. As Humphrey Bogart in *Casablanca* told Ingrid Bergman they would always have Paris, so we and the Vermeer girl will always have Times Square.

The one real danger to the Vermeer young girl was a danger also experienced by many live New Yorkers: Her space wasn't controlled or stabilized, and she could lose her lease. On the afternoon of June 24, 2004, when I went to look for her, I was startled to find she was gone.[28] In her place was a huge billboard advertising the current revival of *42nd Street*. The figures on the sign were a sort of chorus line of smiling faces, all girls in their twenties, remarkable in their cleanliness and their emptiness. In fact, they looked like cleaned-up incarnations of "Ms. Complete." Wherever did they find such inexpressive faces? Human beings need to work on themselves—or else need "to have work done," as they say in show biz about cosmetic surgery— to get a look like this. I imagined the audition for this poster, a travesty of the auditions that animate the show: girls up onstage straining to look blank, while cigar-smoking men in the seats shout, "Empty those faces! Blank! Relaxed and empty!" I pictured the tearful faces of all the girls rejected because their faces showed something. It made me mad. I asked myself, do these guys really think they can sell something by expressing nothing? Do they think people will pay big money and schlep through the 42nd Street crowds to see a play that will leave them blank? Is this the latest meaning of "show business": a business that shows nothing? It seemed like a joke worthy of *The Producers*. Then I realized that even if there was some truth in this riff, I was doing something I have criticized many other people for doing with Times Square: using nostalgia to suck life out of the present. Even if, let's say I'm right, and current mass cultural productions are "nothing," yet the people who see them and hear them will do just what I've done all my life, just what my parents did on the subway going back to the Bronx, just what my kids are doing when they remember songs and movie lines in their own funny ways. They will put their something into that nothing, and then, out of the fusion of something and nothing, they will create something new.

EPILOGUE

Reuters and Me

My reverie about something and nothing was going on in front of Three Times Square, the Reuters Building, the enormous new office building at the corner of Broadway and 42nd. My spot was rich in Times Square history. The Times Square Theater and the Playland Arcade were just about where I stood. Alex Katz's Women's Mural was just above me, John and Yoko's peace billboard ("WAR IS OVER, If You Want It") was just to my north. The Times Square "Interim Plan," adopted by the City Council in the late 1980s and operating through the mid-1990s, provided for crowd-pleasing commercial occupancies all along the ground; hence a branch of Ferrara's Italian Coffee Shop anchored the south corner, and Ellen's Star-dust Diner anchored the north. But the Clinton boom of the late 1990s put the private real estate market in a position to blow the popular Interim Plan away. Where shops and signs used to be, immense office buildings loom today. Their owners were given discretion over what stores to have on the ground, and they have mostly chosen to have none at all. Reuters rented its curved south corner to the J. P. Morgan Bank, which has provided a sculpted steel globe. The city's development deals gave global developers huge tax incentives to build these buildings. Reuters America Holdings got the biggest break of all, $26 million, for building this one.[1]

Anyway, I was standing and doing something I've done often through the past couple of years: sketching and taking notes on the people and the signs. As I was noting the details of the LET THE NEW AGE BEGIN sign, I was rudely disturbed by a man wearing a plastic vest marked SECURITY, a black man around forty years old, who told me I was not allowed to stand in front of the building. I was taken aback: *What?* I noted there were three men standing in front of the building, all large middle-aged men in brown suits talking on cell phones. I asked, were they, too, forbidden to stand in front of the building? The guard shrugged and looked at me sadly: Why was I making his job hard? I said I was writing a book on Times Square, and taking notes on what was there; where was I supposed to do it if not here, at the Square's core? He clearly wasn't prepared for encounters like this. First, he suggested "in the street." As we observed the midday traffic rushing by, he seemed to abandon that idea. He pointed to what looked like a pillar used by construction men, and said I could stand against or behind it; I replied that there I wouldn't be able to see the things whose presence I was trying to record. Again he shrugged and looked sad. Look, he had his orders; if I didn't leave, I would be "forcibly removed."

Now I was really mad. *Did Reuters think it owned the street?* It sounded like it did. Was I making too big a deal of this? Maybe it was just a slow day, and the guard, a lower-level employee, felt that in order to keep his job, he had to convince his superiors he could handle strangers like me—an old fat man with a beard, in a T-shirt and shorts, with a red notebook. Maybe it was the "Alice's Restaurant" syndrome in action, where lots of crime-fighting capability meets little crime, and cops get itchy? Or maybe Michael Moore has changed the ball game, so that wherever security forces meet, fat men are dangerous? In any case, this guard wasn't on routine patrol: He had come out of the building specifically to accost me; he had a cell phone attached to his belt, and he had clearly been talking to somebody. This situation oozes irony. On one hand, Reuters, the British news service, is probably the freest in the world, offering a picture of reality that is probably more incisive and generally accurate than those of any of its American competitors. (It carried an excellent series on the anti-GOP mass demonstration that took place just a few blocks away from this building on August 29, 2004.)[2] On the other hand, here it was acting just like the many despotic regimes it covers so well around the world, regimes to which the British feel so superior, regimes that deny their people are a public and deny their city streets are public space. New York City had offered immense tax breaks to Disney, to Virgin, to MTV, and at last to Reuters, in the context of what Lynne Sagalyn calls "a dramatic shift in values, from corporate business to popular culture." But so much of our popular culture today is organized by media conglomerates, which are just as suspicious and hostile to people as steel conglomerates, liquor conglomerates, cereal conglomerates, auto conglomerates! Some of their products are thrilling and humanly liberating. The fact that they depend on our fantasies and dreams for their money has not done much to bring them and us humanly closer.

I felt terrible, and I still feel terrible, that I just let it be. What kind of citizen was I? I should have stayed on the spot in protest, forced a confrontation, got arrested—I wonder what would it have been for, for loitering? For disorderly conduct? For disturbing the peace by being there? I might have had an unpleasant night, but I would have spoken up in court for the freedom of the city; my wife would have called people we knew in the press, and some of them would have seen something alarming enough to print. But it was my son Danny's tenth birthday. In fact, I was in the Square that day to buy him gifts: an Eminem CD, an MTV Times Square T-shirt. His long-planned party was going to start in an hour uptown. There was no way on earth I could explain not being there to him: not yet. I moved on—the guard said "Thanks"—and I got on the subway and headed back home. If I were a serious citizen, as I liked to think I am, I would protest another day. The Reuters Building has a castle-like bulk and heft, so I could be sure there would be plenty of days.

What has made Times Square special for a century is that, to a remarkable extent, it really did belong to *everybody*. It enveloped the whole world in its spectacle of bright lights, it gave everybody a thrill, it was a trip where the whole world could cruise. The old spectacles are gone, but the people on the street look like they have the life and energy to create new ones—including big or small demonstrations ("Tupac Lives") that things are wrong. But the people look great, the lights look great, so I let it be, until the day one of these global corporations touched me, and told me I wasn't allowed to stand on the street on 42nd Street and Broadway.

Where did these guys get the idea that they own the street? How many more of the Square's new corporate giants share this belief? And how did they get it? When Disney arrived on the deuce in the middle of the 1990s, some people said it was turning Times Square into one of its private theme parks. I and many other people said this was silly, because on the sidewalks of New York, unlike inside Disneyland (and all other theme parks), *they didn't control the space.* But maybe somebody in city government gave the big boys a signal, or at least a hint, not to worry. Could it have been Mayor Giuliani, who was so proud to be photographed signing the documents that brought them in? No, this sounds too conspiratorial. More likely it was a misunderstanding. World-class conglomerates simply take it for granted that their plus-size bottom lines entitle them to control the space around them.* When they signed in, nobody wanted to complicate the party by explaining that New York's everyday life depends on the simple but complex practice of sharing space. Will our city government explain it now? Will it be posted on the zipper, or on the Morgan Stanley sign? I'd hate to wait for that post. Most likely, people who care about our streets and our spaces and our city will have to make signs and make noise and find ways to post it ourselves.

As we close, there are two big ideas we need to sign. The first big idea, which goes back to the start of the Enlightenment, is that *the right to the city is a basic human right.* The second big idea, flowing from the first, is *the right to be part of the city spectacle.* This spectacle is as old, and as modern,

---

*The corporate sense of entitlement extends to *imaginative* space as well. When the makers of the movie *Spider-Man* created digital images of Times Square that diverged from current reality, some billboard and building owners sued them for "depicting Times Square in a mixture of a fictionally and an actually depicted Times Square." They claimed that "altering the billboards in the movies violated trademarks and amounted to trespassing," and that "their prime Times Square space becomes less valuable if they can't guarantee customers exclusive rights both on and offscreen." Luckily, Federal Judge Richard Owen threw the case out of court, saying that "digital alterations [in a movie] are protected free speech" with "First Amendment protection." Against the companies' objection to laser beams and digital filming of the Square, the judge remarked, "Light beams bounce off plaintiff's three buildings day and night in the city that never sleeps." CNET News.com, "SPIDER-MAN" CAN ALTER TIMES SQUARE, story by Lisa Bowman, August 5, 2002. This case, which could be called "Landlords *v.* Light Beams," suggests an underlying desire for a "capitalist realism," a sort of travesty of the "Socialist realism" that strangled Soviet culture for most of the life of the USSR. (Remember Marx, in *The Eighteenth Brumaire of Louis Bonaparte:* "The first time as tragedy, the second as farce.")

We may get some surprise help from *The New York Times.* On September 23, 2004, it ran a prominent, highly critical story by senior writer David Dunlap on the concrete barricades in front of the new Morgan Stanley corporate headquarters at 1585 Broadway. Dunlap calls it "a forbidding penlike enclosure . . . one of the more aggressive occupations of public space in the name of private security." His story includes a large photograph that features a private security guard, quite like the one I encountered at Reuters (both are black men in their forties), in the act of waving the photographer away. In a surprisingly surreal perspective, the guard's forbidding hand appears gigantic. The *Times* seems to be having second thoughts on the new Times Square. It's never too late!

as the city itself. Most forms of city spectacle are designed at once to give their spectators a thrill and to reduce them to docility. This was true for the Roman circuses lamented by the poet Juvenal in the first century, and for the Nuremburg Rallies that typified the horrors of the twentieth. Must it happen here? Times Square, all through its "one hundred years of spectacle," has always been a place that wakes people up and makes them feel alive, more alive than they are supposed to be. It presents the modern city at its most expansive and intense. It gives people ideas, new ideas about how to look and how to move, ideas about being free and being oneself and being with one another. I have been telling stories about how the Square has enticed and inspired all sorts of men and women to step out of line, to engage actively with the city, merge their subjectivity into it, and change the place as they change themselves. Sometimes this has crushed the self ("I'll quit this"), but sometimes it has brought joy and creative triumph ("my name in electric lights"). There are other stories I could have told, and still others I can't tell; there are whole generations of stories waiting to be lived. If people want a chance to live them, they must get a foothold on the street. They must realize they have more power today than the crumbling Hurstwood had a century ago. If they want to be here now, they can't be made to move on. The squarest and soberest people who love Times Square today may have to do, in all seriousness, what those Marx Brothers of Rap, the Beastie Boys, told their MTV audience they would have to do in 1986: *"You gotta fight for your right to party."*[3] Whatever this fight consists of, it may be the only way we can translate the Enlightenment idea of "the right to the city" into twenty-first-century Times Square.

Acknowledgments

This book has been germinating for a long time. When did it really start? One version of the beginning is set on a bright fall Saturday in the early 1950s, when my father and I got our own personal tour of the Times Building from my father's friend Meyer Berger, the great local reporter of *The New York Times*. He showed us the newsrooms, the conference rooms, the assignment books, the world maps, the wire, the morgue. We saw editors who were busy editing; I recognized a couple of their names; they waved, and gave me some discarded proofs. Berger and my father talked to each other in raucous Yiddish, a mile a minute, but he shifted into a precise and courtly English to explain things to me. Our tour ended in the basement, where we saw the amazing giant printing presses in action and the Sunday papers being loaded on the trucks. It was like being inside the castle in a fairy tale. It was one of my life's great thrills. My dad must have told Berger that I wrote editorials for my school paper (JHS 117, Bronx), because when I asked how I could ever repay him, he said, *"Keep writing, don't stop."* He added, "Don't forget *them*," and he and my father shared a Yiddish curse and a bitter laugh. Later I asked my father who were *them*, and he said something like this—this was how he talked: "Meyer writes about the people *on* the street, but he can't write about the people who *own* the street."

This story sounds like such a grand beginning, not just for this book, but for my whole life as a writer. Yet for the next fifty years I forgot it; I didn't remember it again until this book was done. Did it really happen? Did I imagine it? The only two people who might know are long dead. Yet I know my very detailed knowledge of the Times Building's insides comes from somewhere; and I know that at my father's funeral, just a couple of years later, Meyer Berger was there.

Here is another beginning, and for this one the witnesses are alive: Cut to forty years later, a hot Sunday night close to midnight, June 1995. My wife, Shellie, and I were in bed, almost asleep, when the phone rang. It was our friend Bob Christgau, then executive editor of *The Village Voice*. The city was about to sign a series of billion-dollar contracts with an array of world media behemoths and leviathans—Disney, Bertelsmann, Condé Nast, Reuters, Viacom/HBO—for an array of giant office buildings that would radically change the nature of 42nd Street and Times Square. The *Voice* was doing a special section on the Square, on the world that was passing away; it already had several large pieces almost ready to go to press. The only thing they didn't have, Bob said, was an historical introduction to the Square, explaining what it has meant to New Yorkers and to the world in the past, and how it matters now. Could I write this in three weeks? I wasn't very awake. My first thought was all the other things I had promised to write but couldn't seem to deliver. "Thanks but no thanks," I said. My wife nudged me: "What was that?" I said Bob wanted something about Times Square; she shouldn't worry, I told him no. I drifted closer to sleep, but she sprang awake. "Did you say Times Square? *Idiot!* This is your big chance! Now you can *put things together*—sex and real estate and the movies and your parents and the subway and the signs and the street—all the stuff you always say you want to do. And you're going to sleep through it?" Now I woke up: I thought "slept through my big chance" was such a perfect line. "Come on, you've got to call him back this minute!" It was after midnight, but I called back. Bob laughed: he said he had figured I would call him back, it was such a perfect fit. Did these folks know more about me than I knew myself? Why not? Three weeks later my first Times Square piece came out—"Signs Square," *Village Voice*, July 21, 1995—and I was on my way. I don't understand why it was such a long way from there to here. You could say I made lots of local stops; I could have made more. But I'm here now.

I've had lots of company and lots of help getting here. If I tried to sort out all the ways in which people have taught me, often unintentionally, it could eat up this book. (It could be another book; maybe it will be someday.) Instead, here is one big not-quite-alphabetical list. Most of the people on it will know at once why they are there, and I hope they will be glad. A few people will be surprised; I hope their surprise is pleasant. A few are dead, like Meyer Berger himself. (A few are left off thanks to my absentmindedness, which grows with age; I hope they will forgive me.) Then there are Charlie Ahearn, Arnie Birenbaum, Georges Borchardt, Ric Burns, Bob Christgau, Emily Coates, Jerry Cohen, Thomas Cripps, Jane Dickson, Morris Dickstein, Jason Epstein, Susan Fainstein, Vojiaslava Filipoevic, Madeleine Lee Gilford, Todd Gitlin, Beryl Goldberg, Richard Goldstein, Jim Hoberman, Anne Hollander, Irving Howe (d.), Allan Jacobs, Jonathan Jao, Irene Javors, Deborah Jowitt, Tibor Kalman (d.), Jeremy Kalmanovsky, Elizabeth Kendall, Stuart Klawans, Bill Kornblum, John Leonard, Lorraine Mortimer, Victor Navasky, Joan Ockman, Max Page, Charles Perrier, Simone Plastrik (d.), Trude Pollock, Shelley Rice, Mel Rosenthal, Andrea Simon, Ilene Smith, Mike Sorkin, Judith Stein, Taylor Stoehr, Gary Stone, Manny Tobier (d.), Camilo Vergara, Mike Wallace, Michael Walzer, and Sharon Zukin. My family, small but close, the dead and the living, gets a list of its own: my parents, Murray and Betty Berman; my aunt Ida Gordon; my sister Diane Berman and her husband, John Gerson; my cousin Marilyn Gordon; my sons, Elijah Tax-Berman and Danny Berman; and my in-laws, Marvin and Debbie Sclan.

Another group that deserves a list is institutions that have mediated my life. Most of them are schools: The City College of New York (CCNY), where I have taught since the Johnson administration, and the City University Graduate Center (CUNY), where I have been teaching since the Nixon administration; the Harvard Graduate School of Design and the New School University, where I taught in the reign of Bush I, and the CCNY School of Architecture, where I have taught through the reign of Bush II; Columbia, Princeton, NYU, Rutgers, and Berkeley, where I presented early versions of much of this book; the Professional Children's School, where my wife teaches literature, and where I talked with young dancers, actors, and musicians about my work on Jerome Robbins; PS 75, Manhattan, "The Emily Dickinson School," from which my son Danny has just graduated, and where he and we spent six radiant years. One is a library, the Lincoln Center Library for the Performing Arts, especially its Dance Division and its immense Robbins Archive. One is a museum, the Museum of the City of New York. One is a magazine, the democratic socialist magazine *Dissent*, where I have worked as an editor for more than twenty years, and where much of this book appeared. One is a city, New York, where the subway runs all night, and where a man can call up an enormous range of people, including total strangers, ask them the most complex questions about art and life, and get immediate, serious responses. (Many of those calls are recorded in this book in footnotes and endnotes.) All these institutions are full of smart, imaginative, soulful people who have helped me more than they can know.

I've saved the best for last: my "fast-talking dame," my dear wife, Shellie. Her love, friendship, enthusiasm, intellectual power, skill as a critic, knowledge of the performing arts and of "show biz" have done so much to help me, as she said on that fateful night, *put things together*: put together culture and politics, put together New York's past and its present, put together my life as a man with my life as a child, put together my intellectual quest for deep truths with my primitive love for bright lights. When I could write, she's been my ideal reader; when I couldn't, she's been my partner in dialogue, helping me see where I wanted to go, so I could start again. I dedicate this book to her. Let Times Square symbolize our years together: a bath of light.

New York
July 2005

Notes

Author's Note: *New Girl in Town*

1. I found what looked like an original edition in the museum archives in 1999. I couldn't find it when I looked again in the summer of 2004. But it is reproduced in the *Columbia Historical Portrait of New York*, edited by John Kouwenhoven (1953; Harper/Icon Editions, 1972), 409.

2. "Gabey's Comin'," by Betty Comden and Adolph Green, from the 1944 stage version of *On the Town*. Text in *The New York Musicals of Comden and Green* (Applause, 1997), 13ff. "I'm Still Here," words and music by Stephen Sondheim for *Follies*, opened on Broadway in 1971. See Merle Secrest, *Stephen Sondheim: A Life* (Knopf, 1998), 294ff.

Preface: *One Hundred Years of Spectacle*

1. Rem Koolhaas, *Delirious New York: A Retroactive Manifesto for Manhattan* (Oxford University Press, 1978), 7.

2. Montesquieu, *The Persian Letters* (1721), Letters 58, 63, 88. I wrote about this marvelous, unappreciated work more than thirty years ago, in my first book, *The Politics of Authenticity* (Atheneum, 1970, 1972), Chapter I, and, more recently, explicitly linked to Times Square, in an article, "The Marriage of Heaven and Hell," *Harvard Design Magazine*, Winter/Spring 1998, 23–25.

3. William Blake, "The Marriage of Heaven and Hell," in Alfred Kazin, editor, *The Portable Blake* (Viking, 1946, 1968), 252–55.

4. Charles Baudelaire, "Crowds," #12 in *The Parisian Prowler*, translation of *Le Spleen de Paris, petites poèmes en prose* by Edward Kaplan (University of Georgia Press, 1989), 21–22. Baudelaire and the modern crowd are discussed in my book, *All That Is Solid Melts into Air: The Experience of Modernity* (1982; Penguin, 1988), Chapter 3, "Modernism in the Streets."

5. The most recent translation is by Harvey Mansfield and Delba Winthrop (University of Chicago, 2001). "Individualism" is in Part II, Chapter 2, 482–88. Although I disparage Tocqueville's insensitivity to democratic public spaces, my vision of Times Square's mass media owes a lot to his reading of the American press: See "Freedom of the Press," I, 3, 172–80, and "The Relationship Between Associations and Newspapers," II, 6, 493–95.

6. *A Chorus Line*, a show with no stars, opened in 1975 and played more than six thousand performances.

7. Frankie Lymon and the Teenagers, "I Want You to Be My Girl," by Herman Santiago, Gee Records, 1956.

8. *Sister Carrie*, Introduction by Alfred Kazin (Penguin, 1994), Chapter 49, 476–78; 50, 493–94. It is well known that the 1900 version of *Sister Carrie* was censored by many hands, including Dreiser's own. This 1994 Penguin is based on the 1981 University of Pennsylvania scholarly edition, which is the closest thing to an unbowdlerized text we will ever see.

9. *42nd Street*, screenplay, edited with an Introduction by Rocco Fumento (University of Wisconsin Press, 1980), 182.

10. "42nd Street," song, by Al Dubin and Harry Warren, 1932.

11. Jim Hoberman's British Film Institute monograph, *42nd Street* (BFI Film Classics, 1995), highlights the movie's New Deal insight and sensitivity. Alas, these qualities are totally absent in the early-2000s *42nd Street* stage revival.

12. Reproduced in William Klein's *New York, 1954–55* (1955; Dewi Lewis, 1995), 212–13. This marvelous volume has at least two other titles: its original title, *New York Is Good & Good For You in New York*, and *William Klein's Trance Witness Revels*.

13. "Dancing in the Street," by Ivy Jo Hunter, William Stevenson, and Marvin Gaye, Motown Records, 1963.

14. Edward Dimdenberg, *Film Noir and the Spaces of Modernity* (Harvard University Press, 2004), 138ff., sees that Times Square is one of the stars of this film, and offers a brilliant reading of its cityscape.

15. See, above all, Kenneth Jackson, *Crabgrass Frontier: The Suburbanization of the United States* (Oxford University Press, 1985), and Bruce Springsteen, "My Hometown," on *Born in the USA* (Columbia Records, 1984).

16. Colson Whitehead, *The Colossus of New York: A City in Thirteen Parts* (Double-day, 2003), 9.

17. See Stevie Wonder, "Living for the City," on *Innervisions*, Tamla/Motown, 1973.

18. I owe this formulation to the existential Marxist Henri Lefebvre (1901–91). His 1967 essay, *Le Droit à la ville*, is translated by Christian Hulbert and reprinted in Joan Ockman and Edward Eigen, editors, *Architecture Culture 1943–1968* (Columbia/Rizzoli, 1993), 427–36.

19. Beastie Boys, "Fight For Your Right," on *Licensed to Ill*, Columbia Records, 1986.

Chapter 1: *Home Fires Burning*

1. See David Nye, *Electrifying America: Social Meanings of a New Technology* (MIT, 1992), Chapter 2, "The Great White Way," 29ff., and Tama Starr and Edward Hayman, *Signs and Wonders: The Spectacular Marketing of America* (Doubleday/Currency, 1998), "America's Great White Ways," 50ff. Starr is heiress and CEO of Artkraft Strauss, the biggest maker of Times Square signs.

2. See Starr and Hayman, *Signs and Wonders*, 63–64; and Guy Gilmartin, "Times Square," in his *Shaping the City: New York and the Municipal Art Society* (Clarkson-Potter, 1995), 443–44.

3. *Signs and Wonders*, Chapter 5, "War and Peace," presents good background detail on both signs.

4. The identity of the uniform fluctuated with the years. At different points in the war, he was a soldier, a sailor, an airman, a marine. *Signs and Wonders*, 141ff.

5. Cf. Jonas Barrish, *The Anti-Theatrical Prejudice* (University of California, 1976).

6. *Signs and Wonders*, 164.

7. Isaac Bashevis Singer, "The Third One," in *A Crown of Feathers* (1973; Crown, 1974), 210. Translated by the author and Laurie Colwin.

8. These difficulties and others are suggested by various contributors to *TIBOR: Tibor Kalman, Perverse Optimist*, edited by Peter Hall and Michael Bierut (Princeton Architectural Press, 1998). The 1992–93 COLORS sign is reproduced at 240ff. This volume also contains about fifteen pages of Kalman's work on Times Square, 228ff., and about eighty pages excerpted from COLORS, 240–320.

9. Frank Rich, longtime drama critic of the *Times*, as quoted by Hal Prince in Kantor and Maslon, *Broadway: The American Musical*, 368ff. For core image from *A Chorus Line*, see 340ff.

Chapter 2: *Broadway, Love, and Theft*

1. In Constance Rourke's classic study *American Humor: A Study of National Character* (1931; NYRB Classics, 2002), blackface minstrelsy is central to Amer-

ican humor and character. It is a subject that has generated many fascinating books. See, for instance, Robert Toll, *Blacking Up: The Minstrel Show in Nineteenth-Century America* (Oxford University Press, 1974); Eric Lott, *Love and Theft: Black Minstrelsy and the American Working Class* (Oxford University Press, 1993); Wesley Brown, *Darktown Strutters* (Cane Hill, 1994). More fine work continues to appear; note Margo Jefferson in note 3 below.

2. Jim Hoberman, "The Show Biz Messiah," in *Vulgar Modernism: Writing on Movies and Other Media* (Temple University Press, 1991), 64–68. Hoberman has another fine piece, "On the Jazz Singer," in *Entertaining America: Jews, Movies, and Broadcasting* (Princeton University Press, 2003). This volume, the catalogue for a show that opened at New York's Jewish Museum in 2003, features a provocative and visually strong section on *The Jazz Singer*. It includes a splendid essay by Mark Slobin, "Putting Blackface in Its Place," and an elaborate chronology of Jolson's and *The Jazz Singer's* many incarnations up to 1998. Hoberman occludes another strong candidate for "the world's first superstar": Charles Chaplin.

3. From an essay on humor that Williams wrote in 1918 for *American* magazine. Cited in Margo Jefferson, "Blackface Master Echoes in Hip-Hop," *The New York Times*, October 12, 2004. Italics mine.

4. *The Jazz Singer*, screenplay by Alfred Cohn, edited with many appendices by Robert Carringer (University of Wisconsin Film Center, 1979).

5. Erikson, one of Freud's most creative followers who developed the concept of ego-identity, had identity problems of his own. In 1975, in the *New York Times Book Review*, I reproached him for his cover-up of his Jewishness. In the language of 1970s culture, this was translated as *"outing* Erikson as a Jew." This episode is discussed skillfully by Lawrence Friedman in *Identity's Architect: A Biography of Erik H. Erikson* (Harvard University Press, 1999).

6. Michael Alexander, *Jazz Age Jews* (Princeton University Press, 2001), 1. My italics.

7. *Jazz Age Jews*, 164. Alexander calls this "a theology of exile" growing out of the basic contradiction in Jewish life, "a communal covenant with God and a communal exile" (180ff.).

8. William Blake, "For the Sexes: The Gates of Paradise" (1793, 1818), in *The Portable Blake*, edited by Alfred Kazin (Viking, 1946, 1968), 268.

9. But he would never have tolerated charges like those made by my late, dear friend Mike Rogin in his book *Blackface, White Noise: Jewish Immigrants in the Hollywood Melting Pot* (University of California Press, 1996), that not only *The Jazz Singer* but virtually all popular culture created by Jews is a giant rip-off of blacks. Rogin was one of the best minds of my generation, but this late work is over the top.

10. Story included as appendix to screenplay, *The Jazz Singer*, 167.

11. Oscar Handlin, *The Uprooted: The Epic Story of the Great Migrations That Made the American People* (Grosset & Dunlap, 1951). For more complex reflections on this theme, see John Higham, *Strangers in the Land: Patterns of American Nativism, 1860–1925* (1955; Atheneum, 1963). For more recent treatments, see Nancy Foner, *From Ellis Island to JFK: New York's Two Great Waves of Immigration* (Russell Sage / Yale University Press, 2000), and Gary Gerstle, *American Crucible: Race and Nation in the Twentieth Century* (Princeton University Press, 2002).

12. "Trans-National America" is reproduced in Randolph Bourne, *War and the Intellectuals: Collected Essays, 1915–1919*, edited by Carl Resek (Harper Torchbooks, 1964), 107–23.

13. *Jazz Age Jews*, 161, and Chapter 17, "The Jews on Tin Pan Alley."

14. *Chronicles, Volume One* (Simon & Schuster, 2004). Disclosure: An early form of this essay appeared in *Dissent*, Summer 2002, entitled "Love and Theft: From Jack Robin to Bob Dylan."

Chapter 3: *A Human Eye*

1. Jorgensen's photo is also available in enlarged jigsaw-puzzle format from The History Channel.

2. A reduced version of this article is available on the Internet, under "Alfred Eisenstaedt." I found a full copy, along with outtakes, in the "Eisenstaedt" file of the ICP, the International Center of Photography.

3. Professor Mike Wallace (History, CUNY; Gotham Center for New York City Studies) has helped me block this out.

4. On the 1970s, see William Kornblum *et al.*, *West 42nd Street Study*, "The Bright Lights Zone" (CUNY, 1978), 22–25, "The street is largely male territory." On the 1930s, see *The WPA Guide to New York City* (1939; Pantheon, 1982), 167–81, on the neighborhood's overall dilapidation and nastiness.

5. George Chauncey, *Gay New York: Gender, Urban Culture, and the Making of the Gay Male World, 1890–1940* (Basic Books, 1994), 191ff., 421ff.

6. On "urban blight" as a general American problem, especially after World War Two, see Robert Beauregard, *Voices of Decline: The Postwar Fate of American Cities* (Blackwell, 1993).

7. In Lynne Sagalyn, *Times Square Roulette* (MIT, 2001), 46.

8. In Jane Livingston, *The New York School of Photographs, 1936–1963* (Stewart, Tabori, and Chang, 1992), 142, 268.

9. William Klein, *New York, 1954–55* (Dewi Lewis, 1995), 162–63. This book was published first in Paris in 1956, under the (English) title of *Life Is Good & Good for You in New York!*

10. *The New York Times*, 1957, photo by Neal Boenzi. Illustration in article by Richard Shepherd, "It Was the Pits. It'll Be Missed," *Times*, April 14, 1996, one of the best things ever written about 42nd Street.

11. In Geoffrey O'Brien, *The Times Square Story* (Norton, 1998).

12. Mark Eliot, in *Down 42nd Street: Sex, Money, Culture and Politics at the Crossroads of the World* (Warner Books, 2001), 98–102, 296, offers a much more generous assessment of the 42nd Street cinematheque than mine. We don't really disagree about what was going on on the deuce, but he seems to have an ability, which I lack, to draw nourishment from all-male environments.

13. On the history and phenomenology of the fairy, see Chauncey, *Gay New York*, especially chapters 2 and 4, and John Loughery, *The Other Side of Silence: Men's Lives and Gay Identities, a 20th Century History* (Holt, 1998). The "fairy" style and the "queer/trade" style were sharply different on the street, but plenty of gay men at different times have embraced both.

Tennessee Williams, for much of his life, seems to have been a model of the queer in rough encounters. His writing is startling in its candor. In his 1975 *Memoirs*, he "recalled cruising Times Square with Donald Windham in the early 1940s, where he made 'very abrupt and blunt overtures [to groups of sailors or GIs], phrased so bluntly that it's a wonder they didn't slaughter me on the spot. . . . They would stare at me in astonishment, burst into laughter, huddle for a brief conference, and then as often as not would accept the solicitation. . . .'" In October 1940 he wrote Windham from Missouri, where he was visiting his family: "Have to play jam [straight] here, and I'm getting horny as a jack-rabbit, so line up some of that Forty-Second Street trade for me for when I get back." Quoted in *Gay New York*, 421.

14. Shepherd, in "It Was the Pits," on 42nd Street during the war: "The street was buzzing with soldiers, marines and sailors who had not yet found girlfriends to row around Central Park Lake." Eliot, in *Down 42nd Street*, highlights GIs (plus veterans) as prime customers in 42nd Street's edgiest sexual markets.

15. Old Oligarch, "The Constitution of Athens," translated by Henry Dalkyns, in Donald Kagan, ed., *Sources in Greek Political Thought* (Free Press, 1965), 99–110. When I quote this pamphlet, I sometimes change Dalkyns's syntax for clarity's sake.

16. I am using Robert Fagles's translation (Viking, 1990).

17. Beth Genné's formula for the American version of this archetype is "the boy next door." See her brilliant article, " 'Freedom Incarnate': Jerome Robbins, Gene Kelly, and the Dancing Sailor as an Icon of American Values in World War Two," *Dance Chonicle* #24.1 (2001), 94.

18. The Simone de Beauvoir passage, from her memoir *The Prime of Life* (translated by Peter Green; London, Penguin, 1962), is excavated by Genné as her epigraph to "Freedom Incarnate," 83. It is worth noting that de Beauvoir's "carefree

young Americans" were almost certainly soldiers from General Patton's Third Army. Genné seems to blend soldiers into sailors, and I have followed her strategy here, though much old and new literature about soldiers and sailors posits a polar opposition between them.

19. "Where There Is Authority There Is No Freedom," anonymous pamphlet, 1921, in support of the sailors' rising. In Paul Avrich, ed., *The Anarchists in the Russian Revolution* (Cornell, 1973), 162.

20. "Sailors," in Goodman's *Collected Stories*, Volume 3, *The Facts of Life: Stories, 1940–1949*, edited by Taylor Stoehr (Black Sparrow, 1979), 65–73.

21. Richard Meyer, "Profile: Paul Cadmus," in *Art Journal*, Fall 1998. The scandal story is also told well by Jonathan Weinberg, "Cruising with Paul Cadmus," *Art in America*, November 1992.

22. "The Work of Art in the Age of Mechanical Reproduction," 1936, translated by Harry Zohn, in the Benjamin anthology *Illuminations*, edited by Hannah Arendt (Schocken, 1969), 217–51.

23. "Sailors," in *The Facts of Life*, 65–73. After Goodman's death in 1972, his literary executor, Taylor Stoehr, discovered "Sailors" among his effects and incorporated it into his edition of Goodman's *Collected Stories*.

24. Montesquieu's *Persian Letters* (1721) is the first great book about the modern street. I have discussed it in *The Politics of Authenticity*. On Baudelaire, Dostoevsky, and Jacobs, see my *All That Is Solid Melts into Air*.

25. Tobi Tobias, "Bringing Back Robbins' 'Fancy,' " *Dance Magazine*, January 1980, 76. Tobias's evocative and searching piece was written to coincide with a revival by the New York City Ballet.

26. Quoted in Greg Lawrence, *Dance with Demons* (Putnam's, 2001), 68.

27. *Democracy in America*, Volume I.2, 11, "In What Spirit Americans Cultivate the Arts."

28. "Fancy Free" scenario in *Balanchine's Complete Stories of the Great Ballets* (1954), 139. Numbers in parentheses over the next few pages are drawn from this collection.

29. Robbins to Tobias, 71. His casting principle, which he says led him to Johnny Kriza and Harold Lang, to Muriel Bentley and Janet Reed, was to choose "my best friends" and "my home team."

30. *Dance with Demons*, 58.

31. Gilford and Kate Mostel's memoir, *170 Years of Show Business* (Random House, 1978), gives a vivid portrait of life under the blacklist and how their and other blacklisted families survived.

32. Phone conversation, August 23, 2003. Osato quoted in *Dance with Demons*, 76. Madeline Lee Gilford says Osato was widely considered "the most beautiful woman in New York."

33. This was the verdict of Charles Perrier and the archivists on the Dance Desk at

the Lincoln Center Library for the Performing Arts, where the immense Robbins archives are deposited. However, in the summer of 2003, the library was still in the midst of processing its Robbins material, and librarians allowed that all sorts of things might still turn up.

34. The book also includes scripts of *Wonderful Town* and *Bells Are Ringing*. I will refer to it below as "Comden & Green." The Times Square Ballet can be found there, I.11, 56–58. See also the dance highlight of Act Two, the "Dream Coney Island Ballet," II.2, 76–83.

35. Comden & Green, I.3, 14.

36. Comden & Green, I.11, 56–58. Note also the dance highlight of Act Two, the "Dream Coney Island Ballet," II.2, 76–83.

37. From her 1980 memoir *Distant Dances*; quoted in *Dance with Demons*, 76.

38. Comden & Green, I.4, 18.

39. Comden & Green, I.8, 41–43.

40. Molly Haskell, in *From Reverence to Rape: The Treatment of Women in the Movies* (1973; 2nd edition, 1992), writes brilliantly about this genre, whose ambiguities have inspired much feminist criticism.

41. Comden & Green, I.11, 55.

42. *On the Town*, I.4, 21. Brunhilde's role in *The Ring* was explained to me by Mitchell Cohen on the telephone (November 8, 2003).

43. Kelly and Sinatra had played dancing sailors together in *Anchors Aweigh* (MGM, 1944, same year as the stage version of *On the Town*). I don't think Munshin had worked with either one, but he worked with both in Busby Berkeley's *Take Me Out to the Ball Game*, also in 1949.

44. James Sanders, in *Celluloid Skyline: New York and the Movies* (Knopf, 2001, 2003), Part 3, especially 332, describes the fierce internal conflicts faced by the Hollywood studios before they would allow the outdoor "location shooting" that distinguished *On the Town*. J. J. Cohn, production manager at MGM, was said to have sent a telegram: "A TREE IS A TREE. A ROCK IS A ROCK. SHOOT THE PICTURE IN [Los Angeles's] GRIFFITH PARK." Several other postwar movies shot in New York, including *The Lost Weekend*, *The House on 92nd Street*, and *Naked City*, shared *On the Town*'s tremendous success, and this, Sanders argues, reestablished New York as a permanent force in Hollywood cinema.

45. Nietzsche, *Thus Spoke Zarathustra*, translated by Walter Kaufmann, in *The Portable Nietzsche* (1954; Penguin, 1989), IV.10, 387–90.

46. Ironically, Jules Dassin, director of the greatest postwar police movie, *Naked City* (1948), would become another victim of the blacklist, for politics very similar to Kelly's. But Dassin was able to build a new career in France.

47. See especially Paul Fussell, *The Great War and Modern Memory* (Oxford, 1975, 2000).

48. "Bart the General," directed by David Silverman, written by John Swartzwelder,

first shown February 4, 1990. Included in DVD, *The Simpsons: The Complete First Season*, Twentieth Century–Fox Home Entertainment, 2001.

49. The only people who could plausibly affirm the nihilistic horror at the core of even our "Good War" were people who were really *there*. This is why Joseph Heller's 1961 novel, *Catch-22*, is so compelling, and why Heller's comedy entraps us so effectively into tragedy. Morris Dickstein explains this well in *Gates of Eden: American Culture in the Sixties* (1977; Penguin, 1989), Chapter 4, "Black Humor and History."

50. This is a chorus from "The Cure at Troy," Heaney's version of Sophocles' tragedy *Philoctetes*. It was reproduced in late 1989, just after the Wall was torn down, on the Op-Ed page of *The New York Times*.

51. *Liz Phair* (Capitol, 2003). My son Danny, looking through the photos, asked, "Does this girl dance in a bar?" (I said, "No, but she'd like you to think she does.")

52. *Sex and the City* has several elaborate websites. They contain plot summaries (of a not very high quality, I should say) and photos from every program since the show's start, along with chat rooms that focus both on every action and on every character, and a questionnaire (intimate if not deep), "Which woman do you match?" The action I discuss comes from "Episode 67: Anchors Away," directed by Charles McDougall, written by Michael Patrick King.

53. This is from an 1844 essay, "Private Property and Communism," written on his honeymoon in Paris but not published until the 1920s. Translated by Martin Milligan, in Robert Tucker, ed., *Marx-Engels Reader* (Norton, 1978), 87.

Chapter 4: *Times Girl and Her Daughters*

1. Pierre Loti, "Electri-City, New York in the Golden Age of Signage," in *CASA-BELLA (Milan)* 673/674, 1999/2000, issue in English on "Architecture USA: Forms of Spectacle," edited by Nicholas Adams and Joan Ockman, 50.

2. *On Liberty* (1859), Chapter 3, "Of Individuality as One of the Elements of Well-Being," in *Mill: Texts and Commentaries*, edited by Alan Ryan (Norton, 1997), 83. In the twentieth century this came to be said as "experiments *in* living."

3. Aline Bernstein, *An Actor's Daughter* (Knopf, 1941), 126–27.

4. Susan Glenn, *Female Spectacle*, note to illustration 26. Armond Fields and Mark Fields, *From the Bowery to Broadway: Lew Fields and the Roots of American Popular Theater*, Introduction by Helen Hayes (Oxford University Press, 1993); and Lewis Erenberg, *Steppin' Out: New York Nightlife and the Transformation of American Culture, 1870–1930* (University of Chicago Press, 1981), especially Chapter 3, feature the gradual unfolding of this female archetype.

5. See Brooks Atkinson, *Broadway* (Macmillan, 1970), chapters 1–9; Erenberg's essay, "Impresarios of Broadway Nightlife," in *Inventing Times Square: Com-*

merce and Culture at the Crossroads of the World, edited by William Taylor (Russell Sage Foundation, 1991), 158–77; David Nye, *Electrifying America: Social Meanings of a New Technology, 1880–1940,* especially Chapter 2, "The Great White Way" (MIT Press, 1990); David Nasaw, "Cities of Light, Landscapes of Pleasure," in *The Landscape of Modernity: New York City, 1900–1940,* edited by David Ward and Oliver Zunz (Johns Hopkins, 1992), 273–86; Clifton Hood, *722 Miles: The Building of the Subways and How They Transformed New York* (Simon & Schuster, 1993), especially 102–8; on the Square's signs, Tama Starr and Edward Hayman, *Signs and Wonders* (Doubleday/Currency, 1998).

6. Richard Harding Davis, "Broadway," in *The Great Streets of the World* (1892). Quoted in David Nasaw, "Cities of Light, Landscapes of Pleasure," in *The Landscape of Modernity,* 275.

7. See Erenberg, *Steppin' Out,* 62–64, for this dualism.

8. Gilfoyle, *City of Eros,* 248. Lawrence Senelick, in his essay "Private Parts in Public Places," gives a cogent account of the Raines Law and its unintended consequences. *Inventing Times Square,* 331.

9. Quoted in Erenberg, 77.

10. Erenberg, "Impresarios of Broadway Nightlife," in *Inventing Times Square,* 158; cf. Gilfoyle, *City of Eros,* chapters 10–11.

11. *Philosophy of Right,* edited and translated by T. M. Knox, note to paragraph 273 (Oxford University Press, 1940), 286.

12. Carrie's first glimpse of Broadway, in *Sister Carrie,* Chapter 34, page 323.

13. This theme is developed in David Nasaw's article "Cities of Light, Landscapes of Pleasure," cited in note 5, and in his book *Going Out: The Rise and Fall of Public Amusements* (Basic Books, 1993). Nasaw calls this neighborhood "a new kind of public space."

14. *Sister Carrie,* published by Doubleday in 1900, went through censorship by many hands, including Dreiser's own. The closest thing to an unbowdlerized text, based on Dreiser's handwritten copy of the manuscript, was published only recently, by the University of Pennsylvania Press in 1981, as part of a complete scholarly edition of Dreiser. It has been reprinted by Penguin (1994), with a fine Introduction by Alfred Kazin. This is the edition I will cite here: numbers in parentheses designate chapter and page. The Norton Critical Edition (2nd edition, 1991) acknowledges the Pennsylvania project and presents interesting historical background and critical commentary. However—perversely, it seems to me—it retains the heavily censored 1900 text. (It does include eleven pages of the censored material in an appendix.)

15. *Newspaper Days: An Autobiography,* edited with notes and historical commentary by T. D. Nostwich (Black Sparrow, 2000), 578. This book was first published in a censored version by Boni & Liveright in 1922, entitled *A Book About*

Myself. The edition I have used follows the 1981 University of Pennsylvania version, which, as with *Carrie,* is the closest thing to a complete text we will ever see.

16. Atkinson, *Broadway,* 11, 101–4.

17. Gustave Flaubert, *Madame Bovary,* Chapter 8, translated by Francis Steegmuller (Modern Library, 1957), 58. It is worth noting that *Madame Bovary's* first English translator was Eleanor Marx Aveling, Karl Marx's daughter.

18. Gabriel García Márquez, *One Hundred Years of Solitude,* 1967, translated by Gregory Rabassa (1970; Avon, 1973), 51.

19. W. A. Swanberg, *Dreiser* (Scribner, 1965), 88–89. Dresser's name was on the song, and he raked in the money, but Dreiser was the source of the line. This story is told in depth in Richard Lingeman's biography of the youthful Dreiser, *At the Gates of the City: Theodore Dreiser, 1871–1907* (Putnam, 1986), 178–83. It could be argued that America's flourishing tradition of country music, more than a century old and still flourishing today, starts with this line.

20. Guy Debord, *Society of the Spectacle* (1967), translated with spectacular graphics by Freddy Perlman (Detroit: Black & Red, 1970).

21. This is a central theme in many contributions to William Taylor's wonderful collection in *Inventing Times Square: Commerce and Culture at the Crossroads of the World* (Russell Sage Foundation, 1991). See especially Taylor's own essay, "Broadway: The Place That Words Built."

22. Morand's *New York, New York* was published by Henry Holt in 1930, but clearly written before the 1929 Crash. Selections are reproduced in Philip Lopate's delightful collection *Writing New York: A Literary Anthology* (Washington Square / Pocket Books, 1998), 515–17.

23. Corbusier's title was *"Vers une architecture."* But his ideal architecture became "new" in the 1927 English translation, *Toward a New Architecture,* by Frederich Etchells (Praeger, 1959).

24. *Gypsy* (new edition, Frog, Ltd., 1999), 254–55.

25. For Atkinson's numbers, see *Broadway,* 287. Slightly different but similar figures are offered in the "Entertainment and Commerce" section of *Inventing Times Square.*

26. Margaret Knapp, in *Inventing Times Square,* 128.

27. Edna Ferber and George S. Kaufman, *Stage Door,* in *Twenty Best Plays of the Modern American Theater,* edited by John Gassner (Crown, n.d.), 819–68.

28. See Leslie Cabarga, *The Fleischer Story* (Nostalgia Press, 1976), especially Chapter 3; Amelia Holberg, "Betty Boop, Yiddish Film Star," in *American Jewish History* 87.4 (December 1999), 292–312. New York's Jewish Museum included a small but delightful Boop display in its 2003 show, *Entertaining America: Jews, Movies, and Broadcasting.* Its catalogue, cited in Chapter 2, note

2, contains an abbreviated version of Holberg's article (164ff.), with delicious illustrations. See also Paul Buhle's recent book, *From the Lower East Side to Hollywood: Jews in American Popular Culture* (Verso, 2004), 76ff.

29. This point is made explicitly a number of times in the film. The theme of work, the need for work, the fear of being out of work, is stressed very powerfully by J. Hoberman in his British Film Institute monograph, *42nd Street* (London, BFI Publishing, 1993).

30. Morris Dickstein found this for me in the British *Film Encyclopedia* (1982). Other books don't list her at all.

31. This is rectified in the 1955 Pocket Books edition of *Guys and Dolls*.

32. *Great American Love Stories*, edited and introduced by Lucy Rosenthal (Little, Brown, 1992).

33. People have often alluded to the Pentagon, OSS, and CIA agents active on post-war Broadway, but I don't think anyone has explored this overlap in any depth. One alluring item: Richard Bissell, author of *The Pajama Game*, played a lead-ing "Quiet American" role in Vietnam. See Robert Scheer, *How the United States Got Involved in Vietnam* (Santa Barbara, Center for the Study of Demo-cratic Institutions, 1965).

34 *Guys and Dolls*, in *The Modern Theatre*, edited by Eric Bentley (Anchor, 1956), Volume 4, *From the American Drama*, 1.2, 304.

35. *42nd Street* and many others are lovingly described and lavishly illustrated in James Sanders's *Celluloid Skyline: New York and the Movies* (Knopf, 2003).

36. This movie, introduced to me by Shellie Sclan, was written by Tess Slesinger and her husband Frank Davis, adapted from a story by Vicky Baum, and released in 1940 by RKO. It is available in video.

37. Shown at the exhibit "Crossroads of Desire: A Times Square Centennial," cu-rated by Max Page, exhibited in December 2004 at the AXA Gallery in the Equitable Building, sponsored by the Times Square Alliance. This show was scheduled by the New-York Historical Society but dropped early in 2004, when the Society abruptly metamorphosed into a right-wing theme park.

38. When the existence of burlesque was threatened in the late 1930s, one way the industry fought for its life was to emphasize the amount of honest work involved in its production, and the social costs of throwing hundreds of wage earners out of work. Andrea Friedman, *Prurient Interests: Gender, Democracy, and Obscen-ity in New York City, 1909–1945* (Columbia, 2000), 86–89, 222. See also Judith Mayne, *Directed by Dorothy Arzner* (Indiana University Press, 1994). Mayne insists on the continuity of the "work" theme throughout Arzner's career.

39. Quoted in Mayne, *Arzner*, 75.

40. Mayne, *Arzner*, 145.

41. This is one of Mayne's central themes. It is said to have been introduced into feminist discourse by the British film theorist Laura Mulvey in a 1974 article,

"Visual Pleasure and Narrative Cinema." It is reprinted in Mulvey's collection *Visual and Other Pleasures* (Indiana, 1989), 14–26. I will discuss Mulvey later in the context of the 1970s.

Chapter 5: *The Street Splits and Twists*

1. See Chapter 3 for *On the Town*'s highly diverse incarnations.
2. On the Port Authority, Eric Darton, *Divided We Stand: A Biography of the World Trade Center* (Basic Books, 1999), especially chapters 2–3.
3. Good photographs of the lost buildings can be seen in Nathan Silver, *Lost New York* (1967; Schocken, 1971). For the Times Tower, 170ff.; for the Astor, 225. Read it and weep.
4. *Annie Get Your Gun* opened on Broadway in May 1946 and ran for more than three years. It was a Rodgers and Hammerstein production, but all songs were by Irving Berlin. Annie's competitor and lover, Frank Butler, who finally becomes both her husband and her manager, was played by Ray Middleton, producer Buffalo Bill by Frank Morgan. See Gerald Boardman, *American Musical Theatre: A Chronicle* (1978; 2nd edition, Oxford, 1992), 552–53, 649.
5. For instance, James Traub gives an enthusiastic account of the play in his recent book on Times Square, *The Devil's Playground* (Random House, 2004), 106ff., but no trace of feminism can be found.
6. Susan Glenn, in *Female Spectacle*, Chapter 1, delineates "The Bernhardt Effect" as a central feature of turn-of-the-century American culture. On the association of Bernhardt with Barnum, 25ff.
7. *Gypsy: Memoirs of America's Most Celebrated Stripper,* by Gypsy Rose Lee (1957), with an afterword by her son Erik Lee Preminger (Frog, 1999).
8. *Gypsy* opened on Broadway in May 1959 and played for not quite two years. Arthur Laurents wrote the book, and Stephen Sondheim the lyrics; Robbins choreographed—the *West Side Story* team, minus Leonard Bernstein; Karen Moore played the young Gypsy, Jack Klugman the boyfriend/manager. David Merrick and Leland Hayward coproduced. Boardman, *American Musical Theatre*, 611–13. The movie, with Rosalind Russell, Natalie Wood, and Karl Malden, appeared in 1962.
9. Ethan Morden, in *Coming Up Roses: The Broadway Musical in the 1950s* (Oxford, 1992), argues that, in *Gypsy* as in *West Side Story*, "the musical finally gives up its membership in the popular arts" and learns "to *confront* its audience." He explains: "Pop affirms us, art questions us," and *Gypsy* is authentic art. Morden, who has seen hundreds of musicals, considers Merman's performance in *Gypsy* the greatest in musical history (248–51).
10. William Goldman, in his brilliant book *The Season: A Candid Look at Broadway* (1969; Limelight, 1984), Chapter 1, gives a vivid description of a Garland

Palace performance sometime in "the season" of 1967–68. He cites "jokes about how the phrase JUDY TAKES OVERDOSE is set in permanent headline type at the *Daily News*" (7). Garland died of one of those overdoses in 1969, the year Goldman's book came out.

11. Thomas Hess, "Pinup and Icon," in Hess and Linda Nochlin, eds., *Woman as Sex Object* (Newsweek, 1972), 222–37.

12. "Pinup and Icon," 230.

13. This is argued by George Chauncey in *Gay New York*, and elaborated in Chapter 3.

14. The classic study is Barry Bluestone and Bennett Harrison, *The Deindustrialization of America: Plant Closings, Community Abandonment, and the Dismantling of Basic Industry* (Basic Books, 1974).

15. *Times Square Red, Times Square Blue* (New York University Press, 1999), 9. Delany's book is part of an abundant gay male literature that focuses on Times Square. Among its highlights are Rechy's 1963 *City of Night*; James Leo Herlihy's novel *Midnight Cowboy*, 1965, which inspired John Schlesinger's movie, 1969; Benjamin Schaefer, ed., *The Herbert Huncke Reader*, foreword by William Burroughs (Morrow, 1997); John Fergus Ryan, *Watching* (Rosset/Morgan, 1997); Bruce Benderson, *User* (Plume, 1995) and "Toward the New Degenerate Narrative," 2004. The most notorious book in this tradition may be Paul Rogers's novel *Saul's Book* (1983; Penguin, 1984), which must be read along with Guy Trebay's coda, "Dead Man's Bluff: Writer Slain by His 'Son,' " *The Village Voice*, January 22, 1985.

16. This story is told in *Red/Blue*, 25–31.

17. "Toward the New Degenerate Narrative," pamphlet, March 2004.

18. *King Lear*, Act III, Scene 4, 108ff.

19. Act IV, Scene 1, 28: "the worst is not / So long as we can say, 'This is the worst.' "

20. On the immediate experience, see *The Last Picture Show*, novel by Larry McMurtry, 1968, movie by Peter Bogdanovich, 1971, and "My Hometown," song by Bruce Springsteen, 1980. On the long waves and overall dynamics, see above all Kenneth Jackson, *Crabgrass Frontier: The Suburbanization of the United States* (Oxford, 1985). On the linkage between changes in mass culture and changes in city life as a whole, the best book is David Nasaw, *Going Out: The Rise and Fall of Urban Public Entertainment* (Basic Books, 1993). Ironically, New York, more than any other American city, retained its classical downtown and its texture as a "walking city." It was, and still is, ultramodern in the sky but relatively conservative on the ground.

21. "Visual Pleasure and Narrative Cinema" first appeared in London in 1975, in the British *Screen*. It is readily available today, with some elaboration, in Mulvey's collection *Visual and Other Pleasures* (University of Indiana Press, 1989).

22. Todd Gitlin's *The Sixties: Years of Hope, Days of Rage* (Bantam, 1987) is still

the best book on the metamorphosis from hope to rage. Gitlin, president of the SDS in its early, hopeful years, lived through the nightmare and came out the other end. See his Chapter 17, "The Implosion," especially its last sections, "We Have to Create Chaos" and "Death Culture."

23. Many feminist critical studies, like Molly Haskell's classic *From Reverence to Rape* (1973; Penguin, 1978), Wendy Lesser's *His Other Half: Men Looking at Women Through Art* (Harvard, 1991), Jeanine Basinger's *A Woman's View: How Hollywood Spoke to Women, 1930–1960* (Wesleyan, 1993), and Maria DiBattista's *Fast Talking Dames* (Yale, 2001), offer visions of movies where women are subjected but not annihilated, and where they keep the capacity to look and talk back. See also Jessica Benjamin's "The Fantasy of Erotic Domination," and more like it appear in *Powers of Desire: The Politics of Sexuality*, edited by Ann Snitow, Christine Stansell, and Sharon Thompson (Monthly Review Press, 1983). See also the pamphlet *Caught Looking: Feminism, Pornography & Censorship* (FACT Book Committee, 1986), with essays by Snitow, Ellen Willis, Carole Vance, Paula Webster, Kate Ellis, Pat Califia, *et al.*, and pages of spectacular pornography.

24. These laws were passed in Minneapolis and Indianapolis, but found unconstitutional on First Amendment grounds by federal district and appellate courts and finally by the Supreme Court: see *American Booksellers' Association v. Hudnut* (1984). The best discussion of the laws and the case is Nadine Strossen's intelligent polemic *Defending Pornography: Free Speech, Sex, and the Fight for Women's Rights* (Anchor, 1996), 73–82. See also Martha Nussbaum's 1995 essay "Objectification," reprinted in her collection *Sex and Social Justice* (Oxford, 1999), 223–39.

25. *Art in America*, December 1999, contains a great deal of material on this depressing episode, including a short piece of mine, "From Tombs to Agoras: Museums in the Age of Giuliani."

26. *Taxi Driver*, screenplay by Paul Schrader (Faber & Faber, 1990), 7.

27. Translated by Eugen Weber, reprinted in Irving Howe, editor, *Literary Modernism* (Fawcett Premier, 1967), 169–70.

28. This phrase occurs on the first page of Rousseau's *Confessions*, where he says that his book, though it contains intimate scenes, is *not* a book to be read with one hand. Most readers will agree, but some won't.

29. *King Lear*, Act IV, Scene 7, 78ff. DOCTOR: "Be comforted, good madam: the great rage / Is killed in him."

30. It should be noted that the "Iris" scenes of *Taxi Driver* are actually shot on the Lower East Side. But the hero does not make subtle distinctions. His city is torn between "bad" neighborhoods, of which the deuce establishes the archetype, and "good" neighborhoods like Fifth Avenue, near the Plaza, where the movie ends.

31. On Dickson in Times Square, see catalogues: "Life Under Neon," Moore College of Art and Design, Philadelphia, 1989; "Peep Land," Illinois State University, 1994; "Paradise Alley," Whitney Museum of American Art at Philip Morris, 1996.

32. Ahearn's late-1980s film *Doin' Time in Times Square* deserves recognition here. He is seeing pretty much the same world Dickson sees—indeed, from the same window—but with an entirely different sensibility.

33. Letter to me, November 16, 1997. Moved by Dickson's 1996 show at the Whitney, I looked her up in the Manhattan phone book and called to ask about her story. She turned out to be married to Ahearn, whom I had met years before in the South Bronx. She obligingly sent me copies of the material cited here. After so many years, I am glad I have found a way to talk about it.

34. One of the first generation of Pop artists, James Rosenquist, began his career as a painter of billboards in Times Square. Dickson's trajectory updates his tradition: In the early 1980s, she worked on the "Spectacolor board," a computerized billboard at the north end of the old Times Tower. For several years it had public funding and artist administrators, and it generated many exciting designs.

35. A portrait of Dickson by Ahearn appears in *Peepland*, 39.

36. *Rosemary's Baby* (1968), written and directed by Polanski, adapted from a novel by Ira Levin.

37. Phone conversation with Ahearn, February 6, 2004.

38. See Thomas Hess in *New York* magazine, October 6, 1977. There is plenty of literature on Katz (Sandler, et al.), but I haven't been able to find anything else on this now-destroyed mural, which always seemed to me one of the most impressive of his works. I can't even find out precisely when it was torn down.

Chapter 6: *The New Millennium*

1. "Signs Square," *The Village Voice*, July 18, 1995.

2. Ada Louise Huxtable, in her fine essay "Re-Inventing Times Square: 1990," conceptualized the rip-offs and situated them amid the long waves of the Square's commercial history. In William Taylor's collection *Inventing Times Square: Commerce and Culture at the Crossroads of the World* (Russell Sage Foundation, 1990), 356ff. This collection is probably still the best single book on the Square.

3. *Signs and Wonders*, 265.

4. *The New York Times*, June 21, 1996.

5. Kalman's drawings and Robertson's text are reproduced in *TIBOR*, 228–33.

6. *Times*, June 21, 1996.

7. *Times Square Roulette: Reinventing the City Icon* (MIT, 2001), 243. Cf. Alexan-

der Reichl, *Reconstructing Times Square: Politics & Culture in Urban Development* (University Press of Kansas, 1999), which tells a similar story from a much more skeptical and cynical perspective.

8. *Times*, January 7, 1998.

9. Parts of my talk are reprinted in *Dissent*, Fall 1997, as "Signs of the Times," other parts in *Harvard Design Magazine*, Winter/Spring 1998, as "The Marriage of Heaven and Hell." This *HDM* also includes excellent Conference papers by Michael Sorkin and Andreas Huyssen, and dynamite 1970s photos by Michael Ackerman. Sagalyn quotes my paper, 457.

10. Richard Sandler's delightful film *The Gods of Times Square* interviews apocalyptic preachers from various religions, often uncertain, while the work of wrecking is going on, so that real buildings disappear in the time lapse between one prophecy of destruction and another.

11. These monstrous towers are discussed in Sagalyn, *Roulette*, Part II, Chapter 6, "Troubled Execution." Models are portrayed in plates 9–10.

12. See *Signs and Wonders*, chapters 8 and 10, on the new sign technologies.

13. *The Devil's Playground*, 259–62; *Signs and Wonders*, 288ff. Starr writes in her enthusiastic prose that "it is not a sign. It is a manifestation of pure intelligence." Sagalyn in *Roulette*, 212, reminds us that the model for the Morgan sign was the Durst family's much smaller computer-driven "National Debt Clock," whose numbers, an overall total and an average per family, changed every nanosecond.

14. *Signs and Wonders*, 292–301, contains a moving narrative, with images between 144 and 145.

15. *On the Road* (1957; Penguin, 1976), 106ff. "This is where paper America is born." See the first epigraph to this book, page xiii.

16. *Times*, April 11, 2001.

17. I wrote an enthusiastic appraisal of his work many years ago: "Harvey Pekar, Underground Man," *Village Voice*, August 1982.

18. *American Splendor: Our Movie Year* (Ballantine, 2004), 97. Picture by Gary Dumm. This title plays off his book *American Splendor: Our Cancer Year* (Four Walls Eight Windows, 1994). It's his way of saying "I'm still here."

19. Talking Heads, "Road to Nowhere," on *Little Creatures*, Sire Records, 1985.

20. *Chappelle's Uncensored Show*, Season One (Paramount DVD, 2004), Episode 4. Special thanks to my son Elijah Tax-Berman, who introduced me to Chappelle and his world.

21. This is the central theme of his classic book *Delirious New York: A Retroactive Manifesto for Manhattan* (1978).

22. She can be found on the second floor, in the Department of European Paintings. She is in the Museum's Official Guide (2nd edition, 1994; Abrams, 2002), European Paintings, #90, and on its website. See also catalogue for the National

Gallery's great 1996 show *Johannes Vermeer* (National Gallery of Art, Washington / Royal Cabinet of Paintings, The Hague, 1996), 75, which offers interesting discussion of the scant data on Vermeer's life.

23. *Girl with a Pearl Earring*, Plume Books, 2001.

24. My book *All That Is Solid Melts into Air* starts with a reading of *Faust*, "The Tragedy of Development," and highlights Gretchen's self-development. This theme, absent in virtually all literary readings of Goethe, is central in Berlioz's and Gounod's *Faust* operas.

25. Released 2003, directed by Anand Tucker and Peter Webber.

26. The museum's Guide highlights the similarity of the two paintings, and says scholars believe both were made in the late 1660s (215).

27. Reproduced in Walter Benjamin, *Illuminations* (Schocken, 1969), translated by Harry Zohn, introduced by Hannah Arendt, 217–51. "Aura" is mainly on 220–26.

28. Actually, the Met had lost it: It ran from June 2003 to (but evidently not through) June 2004.

Epilogue: *Reuters and Me*

1. For numbers, see Sagalyn, *Roulette*, 436–37. Whatever the numbers, these packages are put together in a way that there is always much—much public cost, much private benefit—that we won't see.

2. "Huge Anti-Bush March Hits NY on Eve of Convention," by Grant McCool *et al*. This story was widely circulated on the Internet, on the *moderator@portside.org* service. (Disclosure: my family was there.)

3. Beastie Boys, "Fight For Your Right," on *Licensed to Ill*, Columbia Records, 1986.

Index

About the Author

MARSHALL BERMAN is Distinguished Professor of Political Science at City College New York and CUNY Graduate Center, where he teaches political theory and urban studies. He writes frequently for *The Village Voice, The Nation,* and *Dissent,* on whose editorial board he serves. He is the author of *Politics of Authenticity: Radical Individualism and the Emergence of Modern Society, Adventures in Marxism,* and the seminal book *All That Is Solid Melts into Air,* which charted the progress of the twentieth-century modernist experience. He has received degrees at Columbia, Oxford, and Harvard universities.

About the Type

This book was set in Electra, a typeface designed for Linotype by W. A. Dwiggins, the renowned type designer (1880–1956). Electra is a fluid typeface, avoiding the contrasts of thick and thin strokes that are prevalent in most modern typefaces.